Foundations of Physical Science Education:
Integrating Psychology, Curriculum, and Instruction

Foundations of Physical Science Education:
Integrating Psychology, Curriculum, and Instruction

Dr Ismail Thamarasseri

Anie Kuriyan

GenNext Publication

Published by

GenNext Publication
5, Ansari Road
Daryaganj, New Delhi-110002
Phone: 011-47034999, 9811692060
E-mail: gennextpublication@hotmail.com

Distribution Network
gyanbooks.com
India, USA, Canada, UK, Australia, France

ISBN: 978-93-5663-244-8 (PB)

First Published, 2024

Printed at: Gyan Press, Delhi.

Foundations of Physical Science Education: Integrating Psychology, Curriculum, and Instruction

Author: Dr Ismail Thamarasseri & Anie Kuriyan

Contents

Preface

> "The fundamental concepts of physical science, it is now understood, are abstractions, framed by our mind, so as to bring order to an apparent chaos of phenomena." – William Cecil Dampier

In the evolving landscape of education, the integration of psychological perspectives and curriculum development in physical science teaching emerges as an important venture. This book, "Foundations of Physical Science Education: Integrating Psychology, Curriculum and Instructions," serves as an inclusive guide to navigating the complex interplay between theory and practice, offering insights and strategies to enhance teaching effectiveness and optimize student learning outcomes.

The psychological dimensions that intersect with physical science education stand at the forefront of our exploration. We investigate behaviourism, multiple intelligences theory, constructivism, and critical pedagogy, by examining their implications in instructional design, classroom management, and student engagement. By incorporating these psychological principles, educators can create dynamic and inclusive learning environments that avail the diverse needs and abilities of students. The process of instructional planning, infused with meaning, importance, and purpose, is central to effective teaching practice. We are exploring the significance of lesson planning, unpacking its various components, and elucidating different types of plans, from year plans to unit plans and lesson plans. Adopting diverse approaches to lesson planning, including Herbartian and constructivist methodologies, can assist educators in crafting engaging and rigorous learning experiences that foster deep conceptual understanding and critical thinking skills.

Examining the realm of evaluation in physical science teaching and learning, this book offers practical guidance on developing achievement tests, diagnostic assessments, and resources for self-evaluation by teachers and students in the realm of physical science teaching and learning. By involving a comprehensive assessment approach, educators can adeptly track student progress, identify improvement areas, and tailor instruction to meet individual learning needs. Moving forward, we explore techno-pedagogic content knowledge, examining ways to leverage technology to enhance pedagogical content knowledge and enrich the teaching-learning process. From online learning resources to instructional support such as textbooks, workbooks, and virtual classrooms, educators are equipped with innovative tools and methodologies to engage students and facilitate meaningful learning experiences.

Thereafter, we turn our attention to curriculum development in physical science education, inquiring into the foundational principles of curriculum construction, different approaches to curriculum organization, and various types of curricula tailored to meet the diverse needs of learners. Educators can ensure coherence, relevance, and rigour in the physical science curriculum by aligning curriculum design with national frameworks like the National Curriculum Framework (NCF) and the Knowledge, Curriculum, and Pedagogy (KCF). As we embark on this exploration and discovery journey, let's wholeheartedly embrace the transformative power inherent in psychological perspectives and curriculum development within physical science education. By seamlessly connecting theory with practical application, we have the opportunity to craft learning environments that not only ignite curiosity but also nurture critical inquiry, ultimately empowering students to evolve into lifelong learners and responsible stewards of scientific knowledge.

The authors express their sincere gratitude to all faculty members and administrative staff of School of Pedagogical Sciences, Mahatma Gandhi University for their valuable support and facilities given during the course of the study. The authors are grateful to their friends and colleagues for their emotional support and valuable ideas, which greatly helped in the completion of the study. In preparation of this book the authors had to refer to the works of other authors and information sources. The authors extremely indebted to various authors, editors, educationists and scholars whose views and opinions are integrated in this book. The authors shall ever remain obliged to their parents, teachers, friends, and family members for their kind guidance and assistance. Above all, the authors humbly solicit the God Almighty's blessings and is always thankful for the strength and presence of mind showered up on them for completing the work successfully. To them all, the authors offer their grateful thanks to **M/s. Gyan Books Private Limited New Delhi** who came forward willingly undertakes the publishing of this book.

March 2024 **DR ISMAIL THAMARASSERI**
Kottayam, Kerala **ANIE KURIYAN**

Abbreviations Used

AR	Augmented Reality
AT	Achievement Test
CCE	Continuous and Comprehensive Evaluation
CK	Content Knowledge
GAFE	Google Apps for Education
ICT	Information and communication Technology
KCF	Kerala Curriculum Framework
MI	Multiple Intelligence
MKO	The More Knowledgeable Other
NCERT	National council for Educational Research and Training
NCF	National Curriculum Framework
NEP	National Educational Policy
NPTEL	National Programme on Technology Enhanced Learning
NRC	National Research Council
OER	Open Educational Resources
PCK	Pedagogical Content Knowledge
PK	Pedagogical Knowledge
TCK	Technological Content Knowledge
TK	Technological Knowledge
TPACK	Techno Pedagogic Content Knowledge
TPK	Technological Pedagogical Knowledge
UNESCO	United Nations Educational, Scientific and Cultural Organization
VL	Virtual Laboratory
ZPD	The Zone of Proximal Development

Chapter - 1

Psychological Dimensions of Physical Science Teaching

INTRODUCTION

In the realm of physical science teaching, understanding the psychological dimensions is paramount for effective pedagogy. This chapter delves into various psychological theories and their implications on teaching practices. Beginning with behaviourism, which emphasizes observable behaviours and conditioning, we explore how it influences instructional methods. Moving on to Howard Gardner's theory of multiple intelligences, we examine its impact on recognizing and catering to diverse student strengths. Additionally, cognitive and social constructivism are explored, highlighting their significance in fostering active learning and social interaction within the classroom. Lastly, critical pedagogy is introduced as a framework for promoting critical thinking and societal awareness in science education. By delving into these psychological dimensions, educators can gain insights into crafting engaging and impactful learning experiences for their students.

BEHAVIOURISM - IMPLICATIONS

Behaviourism is an approach to psychology that focuses on an individual's behaviour. Behaviourism is primarily associated with Ivan Pavlov (classical conditioning theory) Thorndike, Watson and particularly B.F. Skinner (Theory of operant conditioning). According to B.F. Skinner, behaviourism is the philosophy behind the science of behaviour. According to behavioural perspective learning can be defined as an observable change in behaviour. Since all behaviours are outcomes of learning, modification of behaviour is possible. Behaviourist techniques have long been employed in education to promote behaviour that is desirable and discourage that which is not.

From the behaviouristic point of view, all behaviour ranging from simple to complex is primarily learnt in the same manner. Hence it is modifiable. Simple *contracts* can be effective in helping children focus on behaviour change. The relevant behaviour should be identified, and the child and teacher should decide the terms of the contract. Behavioural contracts can be used in school as well as at home. It is helpful if teachers and parents work together with the student to ensure that the contract is being fulfilled. E.g. If a student is not completing homework assignments. The teacher and the student design a contract providing that the student will stay for extra help, ask parents for help, and complete assigned work on time. Teacher will be available after school, and during free periods for additional assistance.

Behaviourism is primarily concerned with observable behaviour, as opposed to internal events like thinking and emotion. Observable (i.e. external) behaviour can be objectively and scientifically measured. Behaviourists emphasize the importance of environment in the development of human personality. The behaviour of a person develops in constant interaction with the environment. A person's environment determines their behaviour and not his hereditary endowments.

There is little difference between the learning that takes place in humans and that in other animals. Therefore, research can be carried out on animals to learn more about human behaviour. Behaviour is the result of stimulus – response association. In assuming that human behaviour is learned, behaviourists also hold that all behaviours can also be unlearned, and replaced by new behaviours; that is, when a behaviour becomes unacceptable, it can be replaced by an acceptable one. A key element to this theory of learning is the rewarded response. The desired response must be rewarded in order for learning to take place (Parkay & Hass, 2000).

In education, advocates of behaviourism have effectively adopted the system of rewards and punishments in their classrooms by rewarding desired behaviours and punishing inappropriate ones. Rewards vary, but must be important to the learner in some way. For example, if a teacher wishes to teach the behaviour of remaining seated during the class period, the successful student's reward might be helping the teacher in class work, or being allowed to go to the library to do homework at the end of the Class period. As with all teaching methods, success depends on each student's stimulus and response, and on associations made by each learner.

Learners' response to stimuli can be reinforced using positive or negative feedback. Reinforcement is defined as anything which increases the probability of a response or particular behaviour. Positive reinforcement occurs when something rewarding happens after the behaviour, while negative reinforcement occurs if something unpleasant is removed after the behaviour. Positive reinforcement is presentation of a stimulus that increases the probability of a response. This type of reinforcement occurs frequently in the classroom. Teachers may provide positive reinforcement by: smiling at students after a correct response; praising students' ability to parents; selecting them for a special project etc.

Negative reinforcement increases the probability of a response that removes or prevents an adverse condition. Many classroom teachers mistakenly believe that negative reinforcement is punishment administered to suppress behaviour; however, negative reinforcement increases the likelihood of a behaviour, as doe's positive reinforcement. Negative implies removing a consequence that a student finds unpleasant. E.g. obtaining a score of 80% or higher makes the final exam optional; perfect attendance is rewarded with a "homework pass." etc.

Punishment is defined as anything which decreases the probability of a particular behaviour, either by the production of something unpleasant or the removal of something rewarding after the behaviour. Punishment involves presenting a strong stimulus that decreases the frequency of a particular response. Punishment is effective in quickly eliminating undesirable behaviours. Examples of punishment include: Students who fight are immediately referred to the principal; late assignments are given a grade of "0".

BF Skinner highlighted the importance of generalised reinforces such as praise, stars and points. He also said that an effective way to reduce the occurrence of a behaviour is to ensure that it is not reinforced; this is known as *extinction*. Punishment should be avoided; extinction i.e. ignoring is the way to remove inappropriate behaviour. Punishment is less effective because it only suppresses behaviour temporarily; eventual removal of punishment allows the behaviour to reappear.

Learning for behaviourists is incremental i.e. it happens in small steps and not huge leaps. Behaviourism highlighted the role of motivation and the definition of the aims and purposes in learning and shaping of behaviour. Behaviourism gave rise to new ideas and innovations in the field of learning and instruction like programmed instruction and other individualized self-instructional programmes. In educational settings, behaviourism implies the dominance of the teacher. The challenge is for a teacher to work out what constitutes reinforcement and punishment for each child and then very specifically to target desirable and undesirable behaviour.

Behaviourism mostly focuses on teacher-centred instruction. Behaviourism is seen when teachers use the following methods (a) more individual work than group learning, (b) using positive and negative reinforcement, (c) provides constant feedback to students, and (d) utilizing various technologies in the classroom.

THEORY OF MULTIPLE INTELLIGENCES- IMPLICATIONS

Howard Gardner propounded a unique theory of intelligence called the theory of multiple intelligence. Gardner questioned the idea of general intelligence and the validity of intelligence tests and its capacity to measure human abilities, talents and skills. Gardner proposed the theory of multiple intelligence in 1983 through his book *Frames of Mind: The Theory of Multiple Intelligences*. He suggested that human intelligence is a set of multiple abilities, talents and mental skills related to a multiple number of domains of knowledge in a particular cultural setting and initially postulated 7 types of intelligences. Later he added two more intelligences and the nine types of intelligences as postulated by Gardner are:

1. Linguistic intelligence
2. Logical mathematical intelligence
3. Musical intelligence
4. Spatial intelligence
5. Bodily kinaesthetic intelligence
6. Intrapersonal intelligence
7. Interpersonal intelligence
8. Naturalistic intelligence
9. Existential intelligence

According to Gardner "we are all able to know the world through language, logical-mathematical analysis, spatial representation, musical thinking, and the use of the body to solve problems or to make things, an understanding of other individuals, and an understanding of ourselves. Where individuals differ is in the strength of these intelligences - the so-called profile of intelligences -and in the ways in which such intelligences are invoked and combined to carry out different tasks, solve diverse problems, and progress in various domains."

Gardner says that these differences "challenge an educational system that assumes that everyone can learn the same materials in the same way and that a uniform, universal measure suffices to test student learning. Indeed, as currently constituted, our educational system is heavily biased toward linguistic modes of instruction and assessment and, to a somewhat lesser degree, toward logical-quantitative modes as well." Gardner argues that "a contrasting set of assumptions is more likely to be educationally effective. Students learn in ways that are identifiably distinctive. The broad spectrum of students - and perhaps the society as a whole - would be better served if disciplines could be presented in a number of ways and learning could be assessed through a variety of means."

(i) Verbal or Linguistic Intelligence: People with high linguistic intelligence display competency with words and languages. They are typically good at reading, writing, telling stories and memorizing words along with dates. These learners have highly developed auditory skills and often think in words. They like reading, playing word games, making up poetry or stories. They can be taught by encouraging them to say and see words, read books together. This type of intelligence is most visible in lawyers, lecturers, writers, lyricists etc.

(ii) Musical Intelligence: People with a high musical intelligence show sensitivity to rhythm and sound and normally have good pitch, are able to sing, play musical instruments, and compose music. They love music, but they are also sensitive to sounds in their environments. They may study better with music in the background. They can be taught by turning lessons into lyrics, speaking rhythmically, and tapping out time. It is visible in musicians and composers.

(iii) Visual or Spatial Intelligence: People with high spatial intelligence show the ability to visualize with the mind's eye. They think in terms of physical space, as do architects and sailors and are very aware of their environments. They like to draw, do jigsaw puzzles, read maps, and daydream. They can be taught through drawings, verbal and physical imagery. It is visible in architects, land surveyors, engineers, mechanics, navigators, sculptors, chess players etc.

(iv) Logical–mathematical Intelligence: This type of intelligence is related to mathematics and reasoning. This area has to do with logic, abstractions, reasoning, numbers, calculating, critical thinking and are able to see and explore patterns and relationships. They like to experiment, solve puzzles, and ask questions. They can be taught through logic games, investigations, and mysteries. It is most visible in mathematicians, philosophers, physicists etc.

(v) Bodily–kinaesthetic Intelligence: The core elements of the bodily-kinaesthetic intelligence are control of one's bodily motions and the capacity to handle objects skilfully. People with high bodily-kinaesthetic intelligence use their body effectively and have a keen sense of body awareness. They like movements, making things and touching. They communicate well through body language and can be taught through physical activity, hands-on learning, acting out and role playing. Tools include equipment and real objects. People who have high bodily-kinaesthetic intelligence should be generally good at physical activities such as sports, dance, acting, and making things.

(vi) Intrapersonal Intelligence: This area has to do with introspective and self-reflective capacities. This refers to having a deep understanding of the self; what one's strengths/ weaknesses are, what makes one unique, being able to predict one's own reactions/emotions and understanding one's own interests and goals. These learners tend to shy away from others. They're in tune with their inner feelings; they have wisdom, intuition and motivation, as well as a strong will, confidence and opinions. They can be taught through independent study and introspection. Tools include books, creative materials, diaries, privacy and time. They are the most independent of the learners.

(vii) Interpersonal Intelligence: This area has to do with interaction with others. Individuals who have high interpersonal intelligence are characterized by their sensitivity to others' moods, feelings, temperaments and motivations, and their ability to cooperate in order to work as part of a group. Those with high interpersonal intelligence communicate effectively and empathize easily with others, and may be either leaders or followers. They often enjoy discussion and debate, understanding and interacting with others. These students learn through interaction. They have many friends and empathy for others. They can be taught through group activities, seminars and dialogues.

(viii) Naturalistic Intelligence: This area has to do with nurturing and relating information to one's natural surroundings. Students with high naturalistic Intelligence demonstrate an empathy with nature, like to make collections of materials and like to classify natural forms such as animal and plant species and rocks and mountain types. This sort of ecological receptiveness is deeply rooted in a "sensitive, ethical, and holistic understanding" of the world and its complexities–including the role of humanity within the greater ecosphere.

(ix) Existential Intelligence: It is a concern with ultimate issues i.e. the ability to be sensitive to or have the capacity for tackling questions about human existence. Individuals who exhibit the tendency to pose and ponder questions about life, death, and ultimate realities possess this intelligence.

The Figure 1.1 indicates the skills and career preferences according to the above-said nine types of intelligences:

Figure 1.1 The skills and career preferences according to the multiple intelligence theory

The 9 Intelligences of MI Theory

Intelligence		Skills and Career Preferences
1.	**Verbal-Linguistic Intelligence** Well-developed verbal skills and sensitivity to the sounds meanings and rhythms of words	**Skills** - Listening, speaking, writing, reaching **Careers** - Poet journalist writer, teacher, lawyer, politician translator
2.	**Mathematical-Logical Intelligence** Ability to think conceptually and abstractly, and capacity to discern logical or numerical patterns	**Skills** - Problem solving (logical & math), performing experiments **Careers** - Scientists, engineers, accountants, mathematicians
3.	**Musical Intelligence** Ability to produce and appreciate rhythm, pitch and timber	**Skills** - Singing, playing instruments, composing music **Careers** - Musician, disc jockey, singer, composer
4.	**Visual-Sparial Intelligence** Capacity to think in images and pictures, to visualize accurately and abstractly	**Skills** - puzzle building, painting, constructing, fixing, designing objects **Careers** - Sculptor, artist, inventor, architect, mechanic, engineer
5.	**Bodily-Kinesthetic Intelligence** Ability to control one's body movements and to handle objects skillfully	**Skills** - Dancing, sports, hands on experiments acting **Careers** - Athlete, PE teacher, dancer, actor, firefighter
6.	**Interpersonal Intelligence** Capacity to detect and respond appropriately to the moods, motivations and desires of others	**Skills** - Seeing from other perspectives, empathy, counseling, co-operating **Careers** - Counselor, salesperson, politician, business person, minister
7.	**Intrapersonal Intelligence** Capacity to be self-aware and in tune with inner feelings values, beliefs and thinking processes	**Skills** - Recognize ones S/W. reflective, aware of inner feelings **Careers** - Researchers, theorists, philosophers
8.	**Naturalist Intelligence** Ability to recognize and categorize plants, animals and other objects in nature	**Skills** - Recognize ones connection to nature, apply science theory to life **Careers** - Scientist, naturalist, landscape architect
9.	**Existential Intelligence** Sensitivity and capacity to tackle deep questions, about human existence, such as the meaning of life, why do we die, and how did we get here	**Skills** - Reflective and deep thinking, design abstract theories **Careers** - Scientist, philosopher, theologian

Implications of Multiple Intelligence theory

According to this theory teaching/ learning should focus on the particular intelligences of each person. It suggests that teachers should be trained to present their lesson in a wide variety of ways using music, cooperative learning, role play, multimedia, field trips, experimentation, and inner reflection and so on. Assessment of abilities should measure all forms of intelligence, not just linguistic and logical-mathematical. It provides a conceptual framework for organizing curriculum, assessment and pedagogical practices. The verbal-linguistic and logical-mathematical intelligences are the ones most frequently used in traditional school curricula. A more balanced curriculum that incorporates the arts, self-awareness, communication, and physical education may be useful in order to leverage the intelligences that some students may have Students may exhibit competencies in certain intelligence areas, and thus an observable means for assessing student strengths and weaknesses is needed.

COGNITIVE AND SOCIAL CONSTRUCTIVISM - IMPLICATIONS

In recent years the concept of constructivism has captured considerable attention among science education researchers. Constructivism focuses on knowledge construction. Learning is active reconstruction and reinterpretation of experiences. Constructivism is a view of the nature of knowledge and its development, based on certain epistemology (i.e., a theory of knowledge). Constructivist epistemology is based on three assertions:

1. Knowledge is a way of making sense of experience
2. Knowledge is always an interpretation
3. All interpretations are based on prior knowledge.

In constructivist approach, the leaner is not seen as a passive receiver, but as an active constructor of knowledge. Learners construct their own knowledge by testing ideas and approaches based on their prior knowledge and experience. Learners may perceive the world differently, based on their own unique experiences. The learners may then share their knowledge with teachers which make the teacher and the taught active participants in the learning process. Learning is determined by the interplay among learners existing knowledge, the social context and the problem that is to be solved.

The major theories upon which constructivism is based include Genetic Epistemology by Jean Piaget, Bruner's Discovery learning, Vygotsky's Social constructivism and Multiple intelligence theory by

Howard Gardner. Bruner defines constructivism as a learning theory in which learning is seen as an active process in which learners construct new ideas or concepts based on their current and past knowledge. Even though there are numerous interpretations of constructivism, some central ideas are common to all constructivist theories. Cunningham and Duffy identified two major similarities that are the foundation of all constructivist theories. They are (1) Learning is an active process of constructing rather than acquiring knowledge, and (2) Instruction is a process of supporting knowledge construction rather than communicating knowledge.

The two major streams of constructivism are *social constructivism* and *cognitive constructivism.* These two streams share the following characteristics:

- Learning is an active process
- All knowledge is constructed through a process of reflective abstraction rather than innate, or passively absorbed
- All learners' cognitive structures facilitate the learning process
- An individual's cognitive structure is constantly developing
- Learning is essentially a process of making sense of the world
- Effective learning requires meaningful, open-ended, challenging problems for the learner to solve
- Constructivist learning requires constructivist learning methods and pedagogy.

Piaget's Theory (Cognitive Constructivism)

Over a period of six decades, Jean Piaget conducted a programme of naturalistic research that has profoundly affected the understanding of child development. Piaget called his general theoretical framework *"genetic epistemology"* because he was primarily interested in how knowledge developed in human organisms. The term "genetic" has been restricted to the mechanisms of heredity and the term can be coined to mean "development". The term "epistemology" refers to the study of knowledge. In contemporary terms "genetic epistemology" would mean "developmental theory of knowledge" It explains how humans develop cognitively from birth throughout life. Genetic epistemology, which includes Piaget's theory of cognitive development, describes human knowledge acquisition and the stages cognitive development that determine thought processes and function. Through these specific knowledge processes and stages, humans are able to grow intellectually and learn. Piaget had a background in both Biology and Philosophy and concepts from both these disciplines influences his theories and research of child development. His main focus for all of his theories is how humans acquire knowledge and focused specifically on children and their development. Three Basic Components of Piaget's Cognitive Theory are Cognitive Structure, Cognitive Functioning and Stages of Cognitive Development. Let's discuss one by one:

Cognitive Structure

According to Piaget, human beings interact with the environmental stimuli, process the various items of information that draw their attention, internalize these, integrate the related ones and thus build up a cognitive structure. By cognitive structure Piaget meant a totality of integrated whole containing all items of knowledge internalized by a person. Piaget considered '*Schema*' as the basic unit with which the cognitive structure is built up. In more simple terms Piaget called the schema the basic building block of intelligent behaviour – a way of organizing knowledge. Indeed, it is useful to think of schemas as *units of knowledge*, each relating to one aspect of the world, including objects, actions and abstract (i.e. theoretical) concepts.

Wadsworth (2004) suggests that schemata (the plural of schema) be thought of as 'index cards' filed in the brain, each one telling an individual how to react to incoming stimuli or information. It may be conceived as the mental image of an experience that has been received by an organism. It may the as simple as a physical schema like shutting the eyes to a complex schema like writing. Piaget believed that new born babies have a small number of innate schemas - even before they have had much opportunity to experience the world. For example, babies have a sucking reflex, which is triggered by something touching the baby's lips. A baby will suck a nipple, or a person's finger. Piaget therefore assumed that the baby has a 'sucking schema'.

Similarly, the grasping reflex which is elicited when something touches the palm of a baby's hand, or the rooting reflex, in which a baby will turn its head towards something which touches its cheek, are innate schemas. Shaking a rattle would be the combination of two schemas, grasping and shaking. As the individual draws more and more experiences, the number and complexity of the schemas also increase. When a chain of schemas is involved in a particular task, it may be said to be a scheme. For example, a person might have a schema about buying a meal in a restaurant. The schema is a stored form of the pattern of behaviour which includes looking at a menu, ordering food, eating it and paying the bill. Whenever they are in a restaurant, they retrieve this schema from memory and apply it to the situation. The efficiency of the cognitive development of an individual is determined by the number, variety and quality of the schemas (schemata) and also the way in which these are systematically arranged to form a structure.

Cognitive Functioning

According to Piaget, biologically every living organism would like to remain in the existing state of equilibrium without being disturbed. This is because loss of equilibrium brings out changes in the energy level which in turn create anxiety and threatens its safety. But at the same time, the organism cannot remain static because it has to face constantly internal and external stimuli. The disequilibrium thus experienced is so distressing that the organism is motivated to take steps to bring back the disturbed energy level to a state of equilibrium. When equilibration is made possible, the organism gets relieved because it has adapted with the situation biologically.

The same type of cyclic action can be seen in the case of cognitive development also. While facing a problematic situation that challenges intellectual competence, the individual finds himself in a state of intellectual disequilibrium. This distressing state has to be set right by equilibration. In order to achieve this, the individual has to act and reach the solution. While doing so, the individual will have to process new information required for solving the problem. This results in the formation of a number of new schemas. If these are internalized and systematically integrated, the cognitive structure becomes richer.

According to Piaget *equilibration* is possible when the individual operates. Operation is a mental action intended to establish new links of schemes with a view to arrive at solution for an unfamiliar problematic situation. Operation results in equilibrium through two process *assimilation and accommodation.* Assimilation has been conceived by Piaget as the process by which an unfamiliar schema is made familiar by linking it with familiar schemas already existing in the cognitive structure. For this purpose, schemas are to the shuttled forward and backward using the ability for reversibility. When once assimilation takes place, the unfamiliar schemas become ready to enter the cognitive structure. Equilibrium occurs when a child's schemas can deal with most new information through assimilation. However, an unpleasant state of disequilibrium occurs when new information cannot be fitted into existing schemas (assimilation). Equilibration is the force which drives the learning process as we do not like to be frustrated and will seek to restore balance by mastering the new challenge.

Accommodation occurs when a child is confronted with a new experience or stimulus which does not fit into any existing schemata. The child can do any one of the two things. (a) Create a new schema into which he can place the stimulus. (b) Modify an existing schema so that the stimulus fits into it. Thus, accommodation is a process of modifying existing cognitive structures based upon new information.

Example 1: A two-year-old child sees a man who is bald on top of his head and has long frizzy hair on the sides. And shouts "Clown, clown" (Assimilation). In the "clown" incident, the boy's father explained to his son that the man was not a clown and that even though his hair was like a clown's, he wasn't wearing a funny costume and wasn't doing silly things to make people laugh. With this new knowledge, the boy was able to change his schema of "clown" and make this idea fit better to a standard concept of "clown" (Accommodation).

Example 2: Riding bus for the first time, Anna recognizes the things she needed to do. She receives a ticket, she pays, then she calls the attention of the driver to stop the bus and go down. Learning this, she rides the bus again confidently as she knows what to do. (Assimilation). The next day, Anna rode a different bus. This time, the passengers don't call the driver's attention but rather press the button beside the window. She starts to worry. (Disequilibrium) Anna, seeing her stop is near, presses the button. The driver stopped the bus and she went down. She was able to go down at the right stop (Equilibration). Anna realizes that there are different ways to call the attention of the driver for the bus to stop and that different bus has different styles. The next time she rides a bus, she knows that she can either call the driver or press the button (Accommodation). Equilibrium is attained when a person was able to seek balance in a certain situation. A person will be able to reach equilibrium if he was able to accommodate information and fit this into his schema. He feels comfortable with the new challenge. Disequilibrium could contribute to learning as it motivates a person to seek for equilibration and allows him to accommodate information.

Piaget's Stages of Cognitive Development

According to Piaget, cognitive development is the result of continuous interaction between the organism and the environment. Piaget has divided cognitive development into four well defined stages. They are sensory-motor stage, pre-operational stage, concrete operational stage and formal operational stage. Each stage is marked by the emergence of new intellectual activities. All children pass through these developmental stages. Although no stage can be missed out there are individual differences in the rate at which children progress through stages, and some individuals may never attain the later stages. Piaget did not claim that a particular stage was reached at a certain age - although descriptions of the stages often include an indication of the age at which the average child would reach each stage.

- **Sensory Motor Stage** (Birth to two years). This stage is preverbal and is marked by physical and motor activities. Motor experiences of the child during this period have a great bearing on the development of his/her later intellectual abilities. In the world of the child an object exists when it is physically present. Hidden objects are located through random physical searching. The main achievement during this stage is object permanence - knowing that an object still exists, even if it is hidden. It requires the ability to form a mental representation (i.e. a schema) of the object. Practical basic knowledge is developed which forms the structure of later knowledge.
- **Pre-Operational Stage:** This stage is divided into two:
  - **Pre-Conceptual Stage** (2-4 years): This stage marks the beginning of organized language and symbolic function and as a result thought and representation develop. During this stage, objects gradually take on symbolic meaning. For example, a bottle is considered a source of milk. The child acquires familiarity with language and begins to engage in symbolic play. His tricycle may be used as a racing car, a stick may be used as a gun and soon. He can now think about objects that are not immediately present. The child now becomes ego-centric, i.e. primarily concerned about oneself.
  - **Intuitive Stage** (4-7 years): During this period cognitive behaviour of the child is still controlled by perception. The thinking of the child is not logical, but is based mostly on intuition. Intuitive thought is primarily concerned with static conditions, but the child is able to use concept as stable generalization of his past and present experiences. However, he cannot adequately link a whole set of successive conditions into an integrated totality. The child can grasp only one relationship at a time because he has not developed the ability for reversibility in thinking. That is in the thinking process, the child is unable to return to his starting point. The child has difficulty in realizing that an object has several properties and lacks the ability to coordinate variables.

- **Concrete Operational Stage** (7-12 years): Piaget considered the concrete stage a major turning point in the child's cognitive development, because it marks the beginning of logical or operational thought. This means the child can work things out internally in their head. But it has to be remembered that during this stage, operation is possible only when concrete objects or experiences are available. Hence purely abstract thinking is not possible. That is why this stage is named as the concrete operational stage. During this stage, the concept of reversibility is possible for the child. A child belonging to this age group can learn the four fundamental mathematical operations using concrete objects, which he is able to group together or classify in terms of one or more attributes. Piaget uses the term 'grouping' to describe a set of such operations that involve competencies like formation of classes and sub classes, seriation (arranging in same order according to given attributes like number, size, shape, weight etc.). The concepts of conservation develop in children. Conservation is the understanding that something stays the same in quantity even though its appearance changes. The child has the ability to reverse experience and he proceeds from step to step in thinking.
- **Formal Operational Stage** (12 Years – Adulthood): This stage reflects the most advanced period in the functioning of the cognitive system. In the final stage of formal operations, thinking involves abstractions. The thought process becomes quite systematic and reasonably well integrated. The individual no longer requires concrete objects or experiences to engage in thinking, because he has acquired a capacity for abstract thinking and he can reason using hypotheses. He is capable of reasoning with propositions free of concrete objects or experience. He develops an experimental spirit and solves problems more systematically and the basis of action and not by trial and error. The youngsters at this stage organize information, reason scientifically, build hypotheses based on understanding and test these hypotheses. In the concrete operational stage, the child could classify objects or arrange in series only in their presence, but a child in the stage of formal operations can 'operate with operations! That is, he can engage in an operation by means of symbolic mental manipulations only.

Example: The following activity illustrates how responses differ greatly from one stage of development to another. Take two identical containers, such as drinking glasses and fill them the same level with coloured water. Adjust the level until the child agrees that they are the same in both containers. Then pour water containers into the two containers which have different heights one by one. Then ask the child which container has more liquid or have the same amount. Younger children would say that the amount of water has changed when it is poured into containers of different heights/shapes. Some may say that there is less water in the wide container, because it is low while others may say that it is spread out and so there is more. An intermediate stage may also be observed where the child may solve part of the problem, but become confused and uncertain. Older children however realize that the amount of water remains constant in all the containers and may give reasons such as: it is the same water; water is not taken away or added more to it.

Educational Implications of Piaget's Theory on Physical Science Teaching

- Cognitive development should be facilitated by providing activities or situations that engage learners and require assimilation, accommodation and equilibration.
- With children in the sensory motor stage and preoperational stage, teachers should try to provide a rich and stimulating environment with ample objects to play with. On the other hand, with children in the concrete operation stage, learning activities should involve problems of classification, ordering, location and conservation using concrete objects.
- A science teacher should use activity methods at the primary level and at the middle school level an extensive use of teaching aids would help in the formation of correct concepts. Lecture method should be used only at the higher secondary level.
- Use teaching methods that actively involve students and pose challenges.
- Because Piaget's theory is based upon biological maturation and stages, the notion of 'readiness' is important. Readiness concerns when certain information or concepts should be taught. According to Piaget's theory children should not be taught certain concepts until they have reached the appropriate stage of cognitive development.
- The science teacher should arrange classroom activities so that it foster discovery learning and experiential learning.
- Students should be encouraged to work on projects. A teacher may divide the class into groups with children in different stages of

cognitive development in each group and allot projects to each group. This will not only faster the collaborative learning, but will also help each child build his new schema gradually.

- Identifying the stage of a child's cognitive growth will help the teacher to plan activities that help in building schema in a logical way. Unless the foundation is strong, future learning is likely to be hampered.
- Framing the science curriculum in keeping with the developmental level of the class is necessary.
- Within the classroom learning should be student centred an accomplished through active discovery learning. The role of the teacher is to facilitate learning, rather than direct tuition. Therefore, teachers should encourage the following within the classroom: (a) Focus on the process of learning, rather than the end product of it, (b) Using active methods that require rediscovering or reconstructing "truths", (c) Using collaborative, as well as individual activities (so children can learn from each other), (d) Devising situations that present useful problems, and create disequilibrium in the child, (e) Evaluate the level of the child's development, so suitable tasks can be set.

Lev Vygotsky's Social Cognition Theory (Social constructivism)

Social constructivism is a theory developed by the psychologist Lev Semyonovich Vygotsky. Vygotsky's theory is very similar to Piaget's assumptions about how children learn, but he places more emphasis on the social context of learning. Vygotsky has developed a socio-cultural approach to cognitive development. Social constructivism is a variety of cognitive constructivism that emphasizes the collaborative nature of learning. Social constructivism agrees that students can grasp concepts and ideas that they cannot understand, with the help from adults or children who are more advanced. In Vygotsky's theory, the teacher plays a very important role. Unlike cognitive constructivism teachers in social constructivism do not just stand by and watch children explore and discover. The teacher may guide students as they approach problems, encourage them to work in groups, ask questions to think about issues, and support them with encouragement and advice.

According to Vygotsky, language and culture play essential roles both in human intellectual development and in how humans perceive the world. Vygotsky highlighted the role that the environment and culture played in learning and development. Humans' linguistic abilities enable them to overcome the natural limitations of their perceptual field by imposing culturally defined sense and meaning on the world. Language and culture are the frameworks through which humans experience, communicate, and understand reality. Social constructivism views each learner as a unique individual with unique needs and backgrounds.

The learner is also seen as complex and multidimensional. Social constructivism encourages, utilizes and rewards the uniqueness and complexity of the learner as an integral part of the learning process (Wertsch, 1997). Social constructivism encourages the learner to arrive at his/her own version of the truth, influenced by his/her back ground and culture. For Vygotsky, the environment in which children grow up will influence how they think and what they think about. Language, logic and mathematical systems are inherited by the learner as a member of a particular culture and these are learned throughout the learner's life.

Vygotsky and Language

Vygotsky believed that language develops from social interactions, for communication purposes. Vygotsky viewed language as man's greatest tool, a means for communicating with the outside world. According to Vygotsky (1962) language plays two critical roles in cognitive development; viz. (a) It is the main means by which adults transmit information to children, (b) Language itself becomes a very powerful tool of intellectual adaptation. According to Vygotsky, cognitive development results from an internalization of language. Cognitive development results when a child learns through problem-solving experiences shared usually with a parent or teacher or a sibling or a peer. As learning develops, the child's own language comes to serve as the primary intellectual tool which eventually directs behaviour.

Major Themes of Vygotsky's Theory

Vygotsky's theory is one of the foundations of constructivism. It asserts three major themes regarding social interaction, the more knowledgeable other, and the zone of proximal development. The central themes of the Vygotsky's theory are discussed as under:

Social interaction

Social interaction plays a fundamental role in the process of cognitive development. In contrast to Jean Piaget's understanding of child development (in which development necessarily precedes learning), Vygotsky felt social learning precedes development. He states: "Every function in the child's cultural development appears twice: first, on the social level, and later, on the individual level; first, between people (inter psychological) and then inside the child (intra psychological)".

The More Knowledgeable Other (MKO)

The MKO refers to anyone who has a better understanding or a higher ability level than the learner, with respect to a particular task, process, or concept. The MKO is normally thought of as being a teacher, coach, or older adult, but the MKO could also be peers, a younger person, or even computers.

The Zone of Proximal Development (ZPD)

Vygotsky suggested that children learn not so much in terms of what they can do on their own, but rather, in terms of what they can achieve when they are given help. In this context, Vygotsky coined a term 'Zone of Proximal Development' (ZPD). The ZPD is the distance between a student's ability to perform a task under adult guidance and/ or with peer collaboration and the student's ability in solving the problem independently. According to Vygotsky, learning occurs in this zone. Zone of principal development is the difference between what children can do in their own and what they can do with the help of adults or peers. 'Vygotsky clarified the ZPD as 'the distance between the actual development level as determined by problem solving and the level of potential development as determined through problem solving under the guidance or in collaboration with more capable peers.

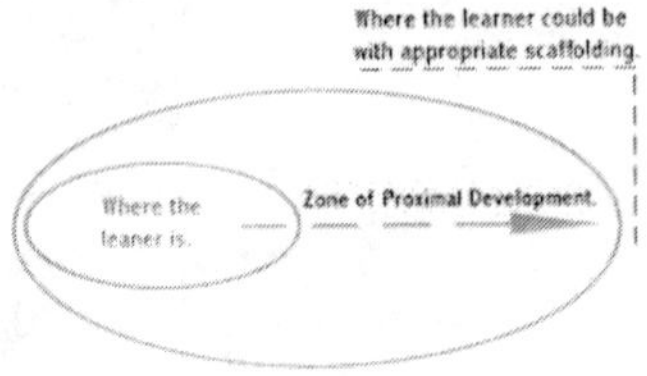

Figure 1.2 Zone of Proximal Development (ZPD)

Scaffolding

In this context, the term 'scaffolding' has been used to describe the role of the teachers. During 'scaffolding' the teacher does not adjust the task, but offers support and guidance in such a way that the learners are able to extend their intellectual range. Scaffolding can be done by a teacher, peer or an adult. Scaffolding can take different forms such as, (1) highlight important features of the task, (2) make the task meaningful in terms of what the pupils already know, (3) establish a familiar context for the task, (4) Split a task into a series of manageable stages or reduce the mathematical or linguistic complex. Further a task can be made emotionally and socially appealing by reducing stress and anxiety. This help to create a classroom environment that is supportive of learning. As the competence of the child increases, the teacher needs to gradually remove the support (or scaffold) and the timing of this is both sensitive and crucial.

According to Vygotsky, students' problem-solving skills fall into three categories, viz. (a) Skills that the student cannot perform, (b) Skills that the students may be able to perform, (c) Skills that the students can perform with the help of scaffolding. Allow students to perform tasks that are normally slightly beyond that ability with the assistance and guidance from the teacher. Shaffer (1996) gives the example of a young girl who is given her first jigsaw. Alone, she performs poorly in attempting to solve the puzzle. The father then sits with her and describes or demonstrates some basic strategies, such as finding all the corner/edge pieces and provides a couple of pieces for the child to put together herself and offers encouragement when she does so. As the child becomes more competent, the father allows the child to work more independently. According to Vygotsky, this type of social interaction involving cooperative or collaborative dialogue promotes cognitive development. Thus scaffolding, is giving the learner the right amount of assistance at the right time. If the learner can perform a task with some assistance, then he or she is closer to mastering it. This theory is relevant to healthy adolescent development because if students work in pairs, they are interacting with people and therefore can learn different academic ideas from one another. This theory shows that students learn from each other; they can assist one another and co-construct knowledge.

Internalization

According to Vygotsky, humans use tools that develop from a culture, such as speech and writing, to mediate their social environments. Initially children develop these tools to serve solely as social functions, ways to communicate needs. Vygotsky believed that the internalization of these tools led to higher thinking skills. It refers to the process of internalizing a rich body of knowledge and tools of thought that first exist outside the child.

The effect of Vygotsky's Theory on learning

Vygotsky's concept of the zone of proximal development is based on the idea that development is defined both by what a child can do independently and by what the child can do when assisted by an adult or more competent peer (Daniels, 1995; Wertsch, 1991). Knowing both levels of Vygotsky's zone is useful for teachers, for these levels indicate where the child is at a given moment as well as where the child is going. The zone of proximal development has several implications for teaching in the classroom. According to Vygotsky, for the curriculum to be developmentally appropriate, the teacher must plan activities that encompass not only what children are capable of doing on their own but what they can learn with the help of others (Karpov & Haywood, 1998).

- **Curriculum:** Since children learn through interaction with teachers, peers and society, curriculum should be designed to emphasize interaction between learners and learning tasks.
- **Instruction:** With appropriate adult help, children can often perform tasks that they are incapable of completing on their own. With this in mind, scaffolding – where the adult continually adjusts the level of his or her help in response to the child's level of performance – is an effective form of teaching. It is due to the effect of scaffolding that second and third generation learners are able to reach higher levels of academic achievements than first generation learners. Parents and the support system at home help students in their quest of reaching higher academic heights. The child will only memorize what the adult says about an idea. To make it his/her property, the child must link the idea to his prior conceptions and use the concept. Scaffolding not only produces immediate results, but also instils the skills necessary for independent problem solving in the future.
- **Assessment:** Assessment method must take into account what children can do on their own. This is their level of actual development. What they can do with help is their level of potential development. Two children may have the same level of actual development, but given appropriate help from an adult, one may be able to solve more problems than the other. Assessment methods must target both the level of actual development and the level of potential development.

Implications of Constructivism on Science learning

In constructivism, the focus is on the students, their interests, their learning skills and their needs in a broad sense. Science instruction should aim at providing students with science knowledge in such a way that they understand the science concepts and principles rather than learning derivations and formulae by heart. The focus of such a science instruction is not merely the significance of certain content areas in science but is also for the individual and society in general. Constructivism in science education is towards 'science for all' so as to make scientific knowledge more meaningful. The aim of constructivism is to develop a reflective learner who is aware of the strengths and limitations of his/her thinking. The characteristics of a constructivist classroom are:

- Shared knowledge between teachers and students
- Shared responsibility among students and teachers
- Small heterogeneous classrooms
- Learners construct knowledge through individual and social activities.
- Emphasis of learning rather than instruction
- The environment is democratic and support collaborative learning
- The teacher as a guide and facilitator in instruction, depending on the knowledge level of students.

In a constructivist model it is very important to know what the students already know. Students use prior (previous) knowledge to construct the new knowledge. Brooks and Brooks (1993) as well as Yager (1991) summarized the characteristics of a constructivist teacher. Thus, a constructivist teacher should:

- Become one of the many resources that the student may learn from and not the primary source of information.
- Engage students in the experiences that challenge previous conceptions of their existing knowledge
- Seek student ideas before presenting teacher ideas
- Encourage students to challenge each other's conceptualizations and ideas.
- Encourage the spirit of questioning by asking thoughtful, open-minded questions.
- Encourage thoughtful discussions among students
- Insist on clear expression from students
- Promote student leadership, elaboration, location of information and taking actions
- Extend learning beyond the class period, classroom and the school
- Use, cognitive terminology such as 'classify' 'analyses' and 'create' while framing tasks.

Behaviourism vs. Constructivism

Behaviourism and constructivism are two prominent theories in psychology and education that offer different perspectives on how people learn and develop. The below table 1.1 distinguishes between the Behaviourism and Constructivism.

Table 1.1: Behaviourism vs. Constructivism

Behaviourism	Constructivism
B.F. Skinner, popularized the behaviourist theory of learning	Jean Piaget, popularized the constructivist theory of learning
Based on Behavioural Changes	Based on learning that is actively constructed and built from reflective thinking by each individual learner
This learning theory suggests that students are passive learners. They propose that the amount of learning that takes place can be measured by observing overt behaviour.	Views students as active learners who process information and reflect on prior experiences based on their individual perceptions. Learning is considered as a social, collaborative endeavour.
Teacher centred Education	Learner centred Education
Learning as a mechanical process	Learning as a natural process
Learner viewed as empty vessels	Learner having unique abilities
Importance on product of learning	Importance on process of learning
Behaviourists believe that behaviour can be modified by positive/ negative reinforcement and rewards/punishments.	Constructivists believe that the learning process is different for each learner, and based upon their individual perspective and experience.
Teacher as dispenser of information	Teacher as coach, mentor, and facilitator
Emphasis on "covering" the material Strict adherence to fixed curriculum	Emphasis on discovering and constructing knowledge
Emphasis on short-term memorization	Emphasis on application and understanding
Learning is stimulus-response relationship	Learning is active mental process
Assessment primarily through testing	Assessment interwoven with teaching

In summary, behaviourism emphasizes external stimuli and observable behaviours, with learning viewed as a process of conditioning. Constructivism, on the other hand, focuses on learners' active engagement, prior knowledge, and social interactions in constructing their understanding of the world. Both theories have influenced educational practices and continue to shape discussions about effective teaching and learning strategies.

CRITICAL PEDAGOGY

Critical pedagogy is an educational approach proposed by Paulo Freire for developing critical consciousness or critical awareness in the learner. Critical consciousness is the ability to critically perceive the causes of social, political and economic oppression and to take action against the oppressive elements of the society. It is a teaching approach that attempts to help students question and challenge domination and the beliefs and practices that dominate. In other words, it is a theory and practice of helping students achieve critical consciousness.

Critical Pedagogy is child-centred pedagogy. It facilitates collective decision-making through open- mindedness and by encouraging and recognising multiple views of the learners. It emphasises to move beyond authoritative role of the teacher by promoting sharing of power with the learners by encouraging critical thinking and commitment to democratic form of interaction. It is a pedagogy that takes into accounts the experiences and perception of learners and helps them to learn in a fear free and independent form.

Critical pedagogy was heavily influenced by the work of Paulo Freire, the most celebrated critical educator. Paulo Freire, Professor of history and philosophy of education at the University of Recife in Brazil, experienced and learned from the plight of poverty and hunger during the Great Depression of 1929. This experience imbued in him a deep concern for the poor, which influenced his views on education. He is best known for his book "Pedagogy of the Oppressed" in which he described how people have been untaught or have never learned to think critically about their situation. Most people accept their situation as inevitable and as belonging to life itself. Only when they become aware of their situation and are able to assign meaning to it (collectively called a process of "conscientization"), a step can be made toward changing the situation. Freire heavily endorses student's ability to think critically about their educational situations. This way of thinking allows them to 'recognize connections between their individual problems and experiences and the social contexts in which they are embedded. Critical Pedagogy gives voice to the voiceless; gives power to the powerless.

Critical pedagogy is particularly concerned with reconfiguring the traditional student/ teacher relationship, where the teacher is the active agent, the one who knows and the students are the passive recipients of the teacher's knowledge. Instead, the classroom is envisioned as a site where new knowledge, grounded in the experiences of students and teachers is produced through meaningful dialogue. The critical consciousness of the individuals leads to critical consciousness of the society and this would force a collective political struggle to challenge and transform oppressive social conditions and to create a more egalitarian society.

Joe L. Kincheloe lists the basic concerns of critical pedagogy as given below:

- All education is inherently political and all pedagogy must be aware of this condition
- A social and educational justice and equality should ground all education
- Issues of race, class, gender, religion and physical ability are all important dimensions of oppression.
- The alleviation of oppression and human suffering is a key dimension of educational purpose.
- Schools must not hurt students
- All positions including critical pedagogy itself must be problematized and questioned.
- Professionalism of teachers must be respected and part of the role of any educator involves becoming a scholar and a researcher.
- Education must both promote emancipatory change and the cultivation of the intellect – these goals should never be in conflict; they should be synergistic.
- Education often reflects the interests and needs of new modes of colonialism and empire. Such dynamics must be exposed, understood and acted upon.

Basic Principles

- Education can never be neutral; it is either an instrument of liberation or an instrument of domestication.
- The basic tenet of critical pedagogy is that there is an unequal social stratification in our society based upon class, race and gender. Critical pedagogy aims at teaching and learning practices that are designed to raise learner's critical consciousness regarding oppressive social conditions.

Critical Pedagogy opposes the Banking Concept of Education

The banking concept of education positions students as empty vessels to be filled by the teachers. According to the oppressed education is traditionally formed as "an act of depositing in which students are the depositories and the teacher is the depositor. Freire explains that banking education is generally characterized by several oppressive attitudes and practices. Freire criticized the traditional education method of simply depositing knowledge, or what he called the "banking concept of education"; which only strengthens the established order. Instead of communicating with the students, the teacher gives deposits which the students have to patiently receive. They are not considered as able to do more than to organize and accumulate the deposits. This "banking" concept is the reflection of the dichotomous oppressive society we live in: the teacher knows everything and the students know nothing, the teacher thinks and the students are being thought, the teacher talks and the students listen obediently. The features of banking concept of education given as under:

- The teacher teaches and the students are taught
- The teacher knows everything and the students know nothing
- The teacher thinks and the students are thought about
- The teacher talks and the students listen meekly
- The teacher disciplines and the students are disciples.
- The teacher chooses and enforces his choice and the students comply
- The teacher acts and the students have the illusion of acting through the action of the teacher
- The teacher chooses the programme content and the students adapt to it.
- The teacher confuses the authority of knowledge with his own professional authority, which he sets in opposition to the freedom of students.
- The teacher is the subject of the learning process while the pupils are mere objects.

Problem Posing Education

Problem posing education is an alternative method of education suggested by Paulo Freire instead of the existing authoritarian and oppressing banking education. It rejects banking education or education as the process of transferring information and embraces a view of education as consisting of acts of cognition that take place through dialogue. It is based on the principle that a student learns better when he creates knowledge and when knowledge is created for him. In problem posing education learning always begins from a problem thrown up in the classroom. Students and teachers become critical co-investigators in dialogue with each other. According to Freire with problem posing education, "no one teaches' another, nor is any one self-taught. Men teach each other, mediated by the world, by the cognizable objects which in banking education are 'owned' by the teacher".

Problem posing education encourages students to become active in thinking about and acting upon the world. It involves co- creation of knowledge in which students and teacher learn together. The teacher just acts as a mediator and organizer and encourages the students to think critically.

Steps in Critical pedagogy

Critical pedagogy has the following steps. There are of course dealing with the different elements involved in critical pedagogy.

- **Context:** Students come from different context or background. The educators must know the family, social, political, economic or religions context or background of each student.
- **Vocabulary:** Educators observe students in order to 'tune in' to the universe of their vocabulary. Even within one state or country people use different vocabulary.
- **Codification:** There is codification of culture or context in vocabulary or words. Teachers should know the culture or context of students codified in their vocabulary. For example, some words used in Kottayam may not be used in Trivandrum or may have different meanings.
- **De-codification:** Words and themes are generated by a 'culture cycle'. By listening to the vocabulary used by a person, we can say whether he/she belongs to a particular place or not, whether the person is Hindu, Muslim or Christian, whether the person is educated or not etc.
- **Dialogue**: The dialogical approach to learning abandons the lecture format and the banking approach to education. According to Paulo Freire, in this method all teach and all learn. The dialogical approach contrasts with the anti-dialogical method, which positions the teacher as the transmitter of knowledge. Dialogical method is based on the dialogue between persons. In the dialogical relations, no one teaches another, not is any one self-taught. People teach each other. In dialogical relations,

agreements based on authority are no longer valid. Authority is on the 'side' of freedom, not 'against' it.

- **Praxis (Action):** The dialogue leads to action. Praxis means an ongoing reflective approach of taking an action in order to transform the world. Those who were formerly illiterate or not conscious of their condition now begin to oppose exploitation, oppression, injustice and bring justice and social transformation. Praxis is a complete activity involving a cycle- theory, application, evolution, reflection and then back to theory. Social transformation is the product of process at the collective level.

Critical pedagogy advocates dialogical method in teaching. A variety of multi-sensory stimulation techniques such as graphic and audio-visual aids including charts, diagram maps, pictures, slides etc. are advocated to educate the people and to develop their critical consciousness. Dialogue with students is the first step in education. Students should describe the world and reality around them, create values rather than receive them and thus develop their understanding and commitment for action. Their understanding needs only be recognized, interpreted, discussed and refined. Freire's ideas are too revolutionary. Theoretically they appear to be quite sound, but functionally they are 'Utopian' in nature. Of course, his methodology of education can be used with some modifications.

Other key terms related to Critical pedagogy

- **Culture Circle**: It is a discussion group in which educators use representation and themes from learner's everyday lives to imitate critical dialogue regarding the various factors that contribute to the real material, social and political contexts in which the learners are embedded. Through dialogue and collective reflection, the group of learners transforms their various observations and opinion to critical knowledge.
- **Culture of Silence:** It is a characteristic of oppressed people in colonized countries which do not have a voice in their society. The dominant culture silences the oppressed people through the cultural transmission of discourses in schools and other institutions that support its leadership. It also ignores other discourses that may challenge its authority.

Critical Pedagogy and Role of Teachers

Critical pedagogy is an educational philosophy and approach that aims to empower learners to critically engage with the world around them and to challenge existing social structures and inequalities. It emphasizes the development of critical consciousness, which involves understanding the social, political, and economic forces that shape society and being able to reflect on one's own position within these structures. The role of teachers in critical pedagogy is multifaceted and crucial. Here are some key aspects of their role:

- The role of teachers is to provide a safe space for children to express themselves, and simultaneously to build in certain form of interactions.
- Teachers need to step out of the role of 'moral authority' and learn to listen with empathy and without judgment, and to enable children to listen to each other.
- While consolidating and constructively stretching the limits of children's understanding, they need to be conscious of how differences are expressed.
- An atmosphere of trust would make the classroom a safe space, where children can share experiences, where conflict can be acknowledged and constructively questioned, and where resolutions, however tentative can be mutually worked out. In particular, for girls and children from underprivileged social groups, schools and classrooms should be spacious for discussing processes of decision-making, for questioning the basis of their decision, and for making informed choices. Teachers need to cultivate an understanding of the cultural and socio-economic diversity that learners bring with them to school.

Conclusion

In conclusion, the psychological dimensions explored in this chapter shed light on the intricate dynamics of physical science teaching. From behaviourism's focus on observable behaviours to the recognition of diverse intelligences through Gardner's theory, educators are presented with a myriad of approaches to cater to the needs of all learners. Moreover, cognitive and social constructivism underscore the importance of student-centred learning and collaborative inquiry in science education. Finally, critical pedagogy emerges as a powerful tool for instigating critical thinking and societal reflection among students. By embracing these psychological insights, educators can cultivate environments that foster curiosity, creativity, and deep understanding in the study of physical science.

Chapter - 2

Planning of Instruction

Introduction

Effective teaching begins with meticulous planning to ensure that instructional objectives are met and students' learning needs are addressed. In this chapter, we delve into the intricate process of planning instruction, examining the hierarchical structure of year plans, unit plans, and lesson plans. We also explore various approaches within lesson planning, such as the Herbartian Approach and the Constructivist Approach, which offer distinct perspectives on organizing and delivering lessons to engage and empower learners.

DIFFERENT TYPES OF PLANS: YEAR PLAN, UNIT PLAN AND LESSON PLAN

Teaching is an activity, which requires careful advance thinking and planning. *Instructional planning* is the ability of the teacher to visualize and forecast into the future of what, why and how of the teaching- learning process. Before undertaking a teaching-learning activity it is necessary that a teacher gets familiar with the content to be taught, behavioral outcomes to be expected, and learning experiences to be provided, evaluation activities to be administered etc.

Importance of Instructional Planning

- Provides logical sequencing and pacing of lessons
- Economizes time and energy
- Provides a variety of instructional objectives
- Creates the opportunity for higher level of questioning
- Provides direction for the teachers

- Correlates instructional events
- Develops a sequence of well-organized learning experiences
- Presents a comprehensive, integrated and meaningful content at an appropriate level
- Prepares students for the day's activities

Components of Instructional Planning:

- The teachers' attitudes, beliefs, orientations and teachers' social background
- The pupils' age, background knowledge, motivational level of interest
- The learning content, textbook and other instructional materials.
- Material resources which include equipment/tools for teaching
- Time frame which is considerable

Types of Instructional Planning

The teacher has to plan the teaching activity in three stages or levels. They are:

- **Year plan:** This plan is meant for the whole academic year. This determines the content to be taught in various periods of a year.
- **Unit plan:** This plan is for teaching a single unit. This includes organization of the selected materials into meaningful segments of activity and experience.
- **Lesson plan:** The plan is required to teach a lesson and for the daily work in the class room

YEAR PLAN

The most general type of planning one does as a classroom teacher is year planning. Year plan is the long-term planning of the instructional process. It is the process of arranging various units in a subject and the periods assigned to them in a year. Such a planning provides teachers with a design of the work to be executed during the year as a whole. A year plan act as a guide for the teacher to organize her day-to-day class work keeping in mind the long-term goals. The following are the factors to be considered while preparing the year plan:

- Units to be taught in the subject
- The number of periods available during the year
- The periods given for teaching, experimentation and testing
- The total number of periods assigned in each term

Steps in Year Planning

- Divide the content into units and sub-units
- Allot the periods for each unit depending on the scope and extent of content to be taught Decide weightage to the objectives to be realized
- Plan the practical activities like lab work, project, seminar etc. for the year Plan field trips, visit to museums, exhibitions etc.
- Plan the tests and examinations Annual plan in the required format

Table 2.1: Year Plan Format according to SCERT Syllabus Kerala

Subject: Chemistry

Standard: 8th

Term	*Month*	*Unit Number*	*Name of the Units*	*Periods*	*Modules and Total Number of Periods*	*Evaluation*
1.	June- July	1	Changes	10	4 (2+3+3+2)	CCE & TE
	August	2	Molecule, Atom	8	3 (3+3+2)	
	September	3	Structure of Atom	8	4 (1+3+2+2)	
2.	October	4	Stability	8	3 (4+3+1)	CCE & TE
	Nov-December	5	Metals	6	2 (4+2)	
3.	January	6	Water	7	3 (3+3+1)	CCE & TE
	February	7	Solution	6	3 (2+3+1)	
	March					

Importance of Year Planning

- The year plan helps teacher in the smooth conduct of the teaching activity
- Points out the way of achieving these objectives and the methods and approaches to be adopted for each topic
- It gives an overall view of content in terms of concepts, objectives, activities, time and many other things
- The entire syllabus to be covered in a year is divided into terms, months, periods etc., helps in easy preparation for the class
- Helps in allotment of periods required for teaching different units
- It helps in planning curricular and co- curricular activities like debates, excursions, discussions etc.

- Methodological year planning leads to effective teaching.
- It gives specified role for every teacher in the total educational system

UNIT PLAN

The second level of planning involves unit planning. A unit is a mutually related content area. A number of related lessons may be combined to complete one teaching unit. Each lesson is a part of the whole unit and leads to the development of next lesson in the unit. A careful unit planning is the road to successful teaching. According to Preston, "A unit is a large block of related subject matter over-viewed by the learner". According to Wisley, "The unit is an organized body of information and experience designed to effect significant out comes for the learner". Thus, unit is a related learning segment which consists of a few lessons along with an outline of its actual execution in the classroom. Hence unit is a large block of subject matter, which includes a series of meaningful activities designed to provide the appropriate learning experiences and bring about significant behavioral changes in the student. Therefore a 'unit' can be described as an integrated whole which includes a systematic arrangement of teaching methods, materials and learning experiences which brings about the desired behavioral changes in the learner.

Criteria of a Good Unit

- It should consider the needs, capabilities and interests of the pupils.
- It should permit a variety of learning experiences like field trips, experiments, demonstration and projects etc.
- It should take into account the previous experiences and background of the pupils.
- It should provide new experiences.
- The length of the unit should be such as to maintain the interest of the students till the last.
- The material of the unit should consist of familiar and related topics and not as remote and strange one.
- It should be flexible so as to allow the above average pupils to go beyond the limits of the unit.
- It should be related to the social and physical environments of the pupils.
- It should help anticipate and satisfy some of the future needs of the pupils.

Steps involved in Unit Planning

While planning the unit, the teacher should bear in mind the aims and the methodology of teaching. The teacher has to select the instructional objectives, analyze the contents, identify the appropriate teaching methods, and teaching aids and evaluate the learning out comes. The various steps involved in the unit planning are:

- **Content Analysis** (the ***What*** of the unit): In unit planning emphasis is placed on analyzing the content into terms, facts, concepts, situations, processes, generalizations, principles, laws etc. the analysis helps the teacher to get a thorough in-depth understanding of the subject and this also increases the confidence of the teacher.
- **Objectives with Specifications** (the ***Why*** of the unit): After analyzing the content, teacher should identify the general and specific objectives of the content.
- **Learning Activities** (the ***How*** of the unit): Keeping in mind the individual differences, the psychology of learning, the content and objectives, suitable learning activities can be planned to which the students will be exposed during the course of the unit. Activities like field trips, experiments, demonstrations and projects can be used in different settings. The experiences can be supplemented with reference books, films and slides.
- **Testing Procedures** (*evidence of achievement*): The last step is the choice of suitable evaluation tools and techniques through which teacher can evaluate the content coverage and teaching method used.

Format of a Unit Plan

- Preliminary Details: Name of the teacher, Subject, Topic, Standard, Duration
- Introduction: Need and Significance, Historical Background, Applicability, Resources
- Curricular Objectives
- Content Analysis
- Pre-requisites
- Body of the Unit Plan consists; Curricular Objectives, Content Outline, Learning Activities, Learning Strategies, Learning Materials, Duration, and Evaluation Strategies

- Follow up Activities
- Enrichment Activities for the gifted

Advantages and Limitations of a Unit Plan

- It is based on aims and objectives of teaching
- It makes the teaching-learning clear, precise and more comprehensive
- It breaks up the entire work into smaller sections, small enough so that pupils can easily grasp the scope of these during a brief overview. Short tasks are easily completed than long ones.
- It helps to cater the needs, nature and aptitude of the students
- It vitalized learning and makes the learning process more life-like.
- It develops the content knowledge of the teacher
- More disciplined teaching and learning is observed.
- It is economical in terms of time
- Since several activities are involved, it helps to develop the skills in the students
- It develops self confidence among students because it provides opportunities for meaningful experience wherein, they can organize and review their learning.
- It requires committed and hardworking teachers
- Confusion sets in when the topics are unrelated and unsystematically arranged
- Evaluation is difficult to do at lower stages.

LESSON PLANNING

Planning means thinking about something beforehand. The success of any work is ensured if it is planned properly. Without planning we cannot achieve our desired ends. A lesson is considered as the work to be covered in a class period which runs for about 40 minutes. A lesson can be considered to a good story. A good story is well organized; it has a beginning, a middle and an end. It engages the reader's interest in a series of interconnected events which are best understood in the context of the events that proceed and follow it. Teaching is a complex activity. It needs proper preparation and planning. Lesson plan is the blue print of those teaching activities that are to be done in the class-room. Every teacher tries to plan the content in his own style so that he can teach systematically and effectively at the right moment. Teaching is a process which involves those teaching activities which a teacher performs in the class-room. It is based on planning and specifically lesson planning. Thus, a lesson plan is a detailed plan prepared by the teacher in advance for the daily teaching. It helps the teacher in systematic and effective teaching.

Careful planning of classroom lessons is the key to successful teaching. Lesson planning means the planning of a daily lesson related with a particular unit of a subject to be covered by the teacher in a specified period for the realization of some stipulated instructional objectives. It gives an outline of the contents that are taught in a class room in a period. A lesson plan provides a guide line for planning the instructional strategies, teaching materials and the learning experiences to be provided to the students. It helps in evaluating the learning outcomes of the students. **Binning and Binning** says, "Daily lesson planning involves defining the objectives, selecting and arranging subject – matter and determining the method or procedure." **Lester B. Stands** defines a lesson plan as a "plan of action". **Cater V. Good** says, a lesson plan is, "a teaching outline of the important points of a lesson arranged in order in which they are to be presented to students by the teacher. It may include objectives, points to be made, questions to be asked, references to materials, assignments etc."

Thus, lesson plan is that pre-determined plan according to which the teacher presents the content regarding new knowledge or experiences by appropriate methods, strategies, tactics, techniques and instruments before the pupils in a particular period, in order to achieve the objectives of the lesson. It is the heart of effective teaching. Lesson plan is a teacher's mental and emotional visualization of class room activities. For successful and effective teaching, lesson plan is very essential. There can be as many lesson plans as there are teachers on a single topic.

Principles of a good lesson plan

The following are the important principles for a good lesson plan:

- A good lesson plan should proceed from simple to complex, known to unknown, concrete to abstract, whole to part and back to the whole.
- It should follow the instructional objectives and specifications
- The teaching aid should be generally and appropriately used
- The activities should be relevant and properly selected
- The evaluation procedures should be suitable to the lesson
- It should induce the power of reasoning, analysis and critical thinking among the students.
- It should indicate definite assignments for the students.

- There should be extra information about the topic and a note on other available reference materials

Significance of Lesson Planning

- Lesson planning helps us to achieve the pre- determined and well-defined objectives of the lesson.
- It helps us to make wise selection of different methods and techniques in order to carry out teaching systematically so that it becomes effective and fruitful.
- A good lesson plan helps the teacher to act orderly and proceed systematically while delivering the lessons. He / she will have a good control over the lesson delivery and haphazard teaching can therefore be avoided.
- It brings economy in the teaching learning process by keeping both the teacher and pupils on right track and there is no wastage of time and energy.
- It develops the habit of hardworking among teachers by daily planning of the lesson.
- It helps a teacher to make use of the principle of correlation and integration by linking new knowledge with previous knowledge, linking theory with its practical aspects etc.
- It helps the teacher to prepare tests for progress and to evaluate the teaching – learning process.
- It helps a teacher in developing his decision-making ability, teaching competency and teaching effectiveness.
- It develops confidence and self- reliance in the teacher which is of great value for successful teaching.
- Individualizes instruction at its best.
- It helps the teacher as well as taught in fixing the new learning by making adequate provision for revision, practice, drill work and home assignments.
- It helps the teacher to become aware of what, when and how much is to be done in the class. It engages pupils in their respective tasks and results into classroom discipline.
- Ensures the continuity of the lesson.
- It makes classroom teaching interesting, systematic and organized.
- A good lesson plan correlates with social and physical environment and also considers the needs and interest of the student.

- Lesson planning assures a proper connection of the new lesson with the previous lesson

Requirements for Planning a Lesson

A teacher needs to possess the following to plan her lessons:

- A mastery over the content
- A thorough knowledge of the process of teaching and learning
- An understanding of the relevant methods and techniques to be used in the class room
- An overview of the instructional objectives and specifications
- Knowledge of the individual differences and psychology of the learners.

Table 2.2: Difference between Unit Plan and Lesson Plan

The below Table 2.2 indicates the difference between unit plan and lesson plan:

Unit Plan	Lesson Plan
It is the plan of a unit.	It is the plan of a lesson
A unit may extend to 4-10 periods.	It is confined to one period
Brief and General	Detailed and Specific.
Units divide the year's work into discrete segments of study. It helps to bridge the gap between long-term planning and daily lesson plans.	Derived from the Unit Plan
Learning activities are briefly mentioned	Learning activities are mentioned in detail
Evaluation tools and techniques are only mentioned	Actual test items are given
The components (goals, objective, content, activities) are tied together in a logical coherent manner, providing structure for the new material to be learned.	Reflects individual needs, strengths, and interests of the teacher and students

APPROACHES IN LESSON PLANNING

Herbartian Approach

John Fredric Herbart was a great European educationist and philosopher of 19th century. He advocated that teaching should be planned actively if we intend to make it efficient. Based upon Educational psychology, Herbart's educational ideology advocated the following four elements for a successful teaching.

- **Interest**: The teaching process should be interesting. When the interest of pupils is created in some subject, their attention is attracted towards it. They acquire the new knowledge very easily.
- **Apperception:** The learner is like a clean slate and all the knowledge is given to him from outside. Apperception of this external knowledge occurs in the unconscious mind of the pupils. By relating new knowledge to the previous knowledge of the pupils, their learning is simplified. Hence, in order to make the learning process effective, the teacher should move from known to the unknown.
- **General Method**: Learning activity occurs in a definite sequence. Hence, the activities of the unit should be edited in a definite sequence and in a logical order.
- **Correlation**: Knowledge is one unit. All the subjects should be studied after correlating each other in the form of one unit.

John Fredric Herbart suggested the following six steps which are generally called as the Herbartian Steps of Lesson Planning.

- **Preparation (Introduction):** The student should be in a position to acquire the new knowledge that is imparted to him/her. This step is also called as introductory stage or motivation stage or creating a "will to learn" stage. Here the teacher prepares the minds of the learners in order to receive the new knowledge. The teacher performs different activities like asking questions related to previous knowledge, narrating a story related to the topic, using different types of teaching aids such as charts, maps or pictures etc. only to prepare their minds or to create interest among learners to become receptive for further learning. Once they are motivated and prepared mentally for studying the lesson, teacher introduces the lesson by taking care of the general and specific aims of the lesson.
- **Presentation:** The actual lesson commences here. After motivating the students, the teacher now presents the learning material before the students. This is the step where there is equal participation of students and the teacher in the teaching-learning process. While presenting the subject matter, the teacher uses different strategies like narration, question – answer method, demonstration, illustrations, explanation, and audio – visual aids etc. in order to make his teaching an interesting activity. The learners are fully involved in the lesson and they do not remain passive even for

a moment. Teacher represents the material in psychological and logical sequence keeping in view their individual differences. He never allows the teaching process to become just one-sided affair. Black board should be properly used.

- **Comparison and Association:** Here the teacher tries to compare and associate the newly learned matter with the one already learnt. Association means to link new knowledge with the old and with one another into a system. It is always desirable that new ideas or knowledge should be associated to daily life situation by citing suitable examples and by drawing comparison with the related concepts. No doubt newly learned material remains for the time being but soon it vanishes from the mind. When the teacher presents the materials, he asks them to compare it with another material and it helps them to retain the material for long time. Comparison and association remove doubts and confusions of the students. It strengthens their acquisition of new learning material. Therefore, the teacher should try to use the method of comparison and association.
- **Generalization:** Comparison and association help the children to find out certain conclusions which enable them to form general laws, principles or formula. It means arriving at a certain conclusion on the basis of comparison, contrast and associations observed in the learning material. The teacher should provide ample opportunities to learners in order to derive themselves some conclusions. This step is as a result of the reflective thinking of the students. This knowledge gained in the earlier steps is used in this step to draw generalizations, and rules with the help of comparison or abstraction. Sometimes the students may make incorrect generalizations, at that time; the teacher helps and guides them in order to correct those. Now, the students are ready to use the knowledge they have gained by applying them in real life situation.
- **Application:** The learners after deriving some rules, principles or laws then applies them to different situations and hence get more and more knowledge. By application the new facts get established in the mind of the pupil and become a part of his mental make-up. This step tests the validity of the generalization arrived at by the pupils. For application purpose, both familiar and unfamiliar situations should be provided to the learners. The more the application of the subject matter, the greater is the learning.

- **Recapitulation:** This is last step of the lesson plan. The teacher tries to ascertain whether the students have understood or grasped the subject matter or not by putting some suitable questions on the topic to the students. This will also help the teacher to find out whether his method of teaching is effective or not.

Advantages of Herbartian Approach

- **Organized Teaching**: Each step has been organized in a logical order which provides an opportunity to the fresh teacher to become aware of future mistakes. Originality is never affected and the teaching goes on in a very organized way.
- **Acquiring thoughts as apperception:** Herbart believed that when the new thought related to the thoughts lying in unconscious mind of the pupils are presented, the thoughts of unconscious mind come to the conscious mind, establish relationship with the new thought and again go to the unconscious mind. Herbart termed this material process of acquiring thoughts as apperception.
- **Use of Inductive and Deductive Methods**: While presenting the new knowledge, help of various examples is sought through 'generalization' and rules are derived. It is an inductive method. In the step application, these rules are to be executed, this is a deductive method. Thus, both indicative and deductive methods are used in this approach.
- **Recapitulation**: Such questions are asked while recapitulating which, on answering, result in the learning and application of the acquired knowledge in new situations.
- **Correlation Possible**: Herbart considered entire knowledge as a single unit. The knowledge of the pupils is acquired in a single unit. This allows establishing a correlation between previous and new knowledge and between all subjects of the curriculum.

Limitations of Herbartian Approach

- **Mechanical Method of Teaching**: The use of these steps takes away the freedom of the teacher as he cannot incorporate his independent thought in any step. This reduces his originality. Hence, Herbartian approach is a mechanical method of teaching.
- **No Place for Individual Differences:** While using Herbartian approach. Similar questions are asked to the entire students. This overlooks individual differences.
- **Teacher More Active**: In Herbartian approach, the teacher has

to be more active. It is more desirable if the pupils remain more active than the teachers. As this teaching method is not activity-centered, pupils don't get any motivation for learning.

- **No need of Generalization:** Generalization is not needed while teaching language, geography, history, music and arts etc. Thus, all the six steps are not needed while teaching.
- **Uninteresting**: This approach stresses upon the teaching of all the subjects of curriculum in a similar sequence. The entire teaching becomes monotonous. The pupil does not show any interest in acquiring new knowledge. Thus, Herbart's teaching method is not interesting
- **Difficulty of Correlation:** Considering the knowledge as a complete unit, Herbart emphasized correlation between different subjects for the unity in the mental life of the pupils. Correlation between various subjects is essentially difficult.

Constructivist Approach

Constructivist learning has emerged as a prominent approach to teaching during this past decade. The work of Dewey, Piaget, Bruner, and Vygotsky provide historical precedents for constructivist learning theory. Constructivism represents a paradigm shift from education based on behaviorism to education based on cognitive theory. Constructivist epistemology assumes that learners construct their own knowledge on the basis of interaction with their environment. **Four epistemological assumptions** are at the heart of what we refer to as "constructivist learning."

- Knowledge is physically constructed by learners who are involved in active learning.
- Knowledge is symbolically constructed by learners who are making their own representations of action
- Knowledge is socially constructed by learners who convey their meaning making to others
- Knowledge is theoretically constructed by learners who try to explain things they don't completely understand.

For constructing knowledge of the learner, the teacher may adopt or adapt various strategies of teaching-learning that come under the purview of constructivist pedagogy. Many constructivist pedagogies are available (Brooks and Brooks, 1993; Steffe & Gale, 1995; Larochelle, Bednarz & Garrisson, 1998) which share certain common principles and indicate that eight factors are essential in constructivist pedagogy, viz.

- Learning should take place in authentic and real-world environment;
- Learning should involve social negotiation and mediation;
- Content and skills should be understood within the framework of learners' prior knowledge;
- Content and skills should be made relevant to the learner;
- Students should be assessed formatively, serving to help them acquire further learning experiences;
- Students should be encouraged to become self-regulatory, self-mediated and self-aware of learning;
- Teacher should serve primarily as facilitator of learning, not instructor; and
- Teacher should provide for and encourage multiple perspectives and representations of content.

Over the past three decades, different researchers have proposed a number of teaching models for classroom teaching in the constructivist framework. Implementation of constructivist teaching practices in classroom teaching process is an issue of concern worldwide as it leads to meaningful learning. Structured strategies are followed in different sequential manner by many researchers which result in constructivist teaching models. However, all constructivist teaching models are guided generally by five basic elements (Tolman and Hardy, 1995) which are:

- Activating prior knowledge
- Acquiring knowledge
- Understanding knowledge
- Using knowledge
- Reflecting on knowledge

NCF-2005 has strongly recommended the use of constructivist approach to teaching-learning in schools. This approach is based on actively engaging students in situations that involve collaboratively considering their own explanations for phenomena, resolutions to problems, or formulation of questions. Students are asked to actively construct their own knowledge by making meaning out of the situation by themselves with support and guidance from the teacher. Teachers organize the situation and then provide encouragement and questions to groups of students who are trying to construct and to display their own explanations. The constructivist approach can be adapted to any subject area or curriculum by involving students as active participants in making meaning instead of passive recipients of information given to them by the teacher. Constructivist learning implies an initial concern with what knowledge is and how knowledge is actively constructed by the learner. Advocates of constructivism agree that acquiring knowledge or knowing is an active process of constructing rather than the passive receipt of information.

Role of the Teacher

Hence, from a constructivist perspective, the primary responsibility of the teacher is to create and maintain a collaborative problem-solving environment, where students are allowed to construct their own knowledge, and the teacher acts as a facilitator and guide. Brooks and Brooks (1993) suggest twelve strategies for teachers to exercise in order to move towards a more constructivist approach:

- Encourage and accept student autonomy and initiative;
- Use raw data and primary sources, along with manipulative, interactive, and physical materials;
- Use cognitive terminology such as "classify," "analyze," "predict," and "create";
- Allow student responses to drive lessons, shift instructional strategies, and alter content;
- Inquire about students' understanding of concepts before sharing their own understandings of those concepts;
- Encourage students to engage in dialogue, both with the teacher and with one another;
- Encourage student inquiry by asking thoughtful, open-ended questions and encouraging students to ask questions of each other;
- Seek elaboration of students' initial responses;
- Engage students in experiences that might give rise to contradictions to their initial hypotheses and then encourage discussion;
- Allow wait time after posing questions;
- Provide time for students to construct relationships and create metaphor;
- Nurture students' natural curiosity through frequent use of the learning cycle model. (The learning cycle model consists of discovery, concept introduction, and concept application);

Constructivist teachers must create opportunities for peer scaffolding and teacher-directed scaffolding which is the process of allowing interaction that stimulates knowledge building, and therefore bridges differences of knowledge levels within a classroom. The role of the teacher is no longer to be "the one" but to provide each one with opportunities to learn how to learn (Jarvinen 1998, Cohen 1993).

Format of a Constructivist Lesson Plan

- General Information
- Content Overview
- Content Analysis
- Learning Objectives (Five domains of learning followed by specific objectives)
- Learning Strategies
- Subjective Realities (Pre-requisites, Pre-conception and Misconception)
- Learning Resources
- Precautions /First Aid
- Class room Transaction (A Two column format showing process/ activities in various sessions in one column and response/ assessment regarding the sessions in the other column)
- Follow-up Activities (Activity assignment and written assignment)
- Reflection Notes (My findings and follow up/ remedial measures)

Conclusion

In conclusion, the planning of instruction is a cornerstone of successful teaching practice, serving as the blueprint for fostering meaningful learning experiences. By carefully crafting year plans, unit plans, and lesson plans, educators can scaffold students' understanding, promote critical thinking, and cultivate a supportive learning environment. Whether employing traditional frameworks like the Herbartian Approach or embracing more student-centered methodologies like the Constructivist Approach, educators play a vital role in shaping the educational journey of their students through thoughtful and intentional instructional planning.

Chapter - 3

Evaluation In Physical Science Teaching And Learning

INTRODUCTION

In this chapter, we explore the various methods and practices involved in evaluating teaching and learning in physical science education. Evaluation is essential for assessing students' understanding, identifying areas for improvement, and enhancing the effectiveness of teaching strategies. This chapter covers different types of evaluation tools and processes, including achievement tests, diagnostic tests, remedial teaching approaches, teacher evaluations, and student self-evaluations. Each of these methods plays a crucial role in gauging the progress and success of both students and teachers in the realm of physical science education. Through this exploration, educators can gain insights into the strengths and weaknesses of their instructional practices and make informed decisions to optimize the learning experience for their students.

CONSTRUCTION OF ACHIEVEMENT TEST

An achievement test is an instrument designed to measure relative achievement of students. It is an indispensable instrument in the teaching learning process. The achievement test measure knowledge and skills that are closely tied to school instruction. The achievement test focuses upon an examinee's attainments at a given point in time. Any test that measures the attainments or accomplishments of an individual after a period of training or learning is called an achievement test. Here main emphasis is given on content coverage or course material along with the realization of objectives. The characteristics of an achievement test given as under:

- It should have a description of measured behaviour

- It should contain a sufficient number of test items for each measured behaviour.
- A good achievement test is tried out and seeks on the basis of its difficulty level and discriminating power.
- In a good achievement test administration procedure, scoring key etc. everything is decided in advance
- A good achievement test is always accompanied by norms.
- A good achievement test is always accompanied by test manual.

Purpose of Achievement Test

- Provides an idea to the teachers about the progress and mastery of learning of the students.
- Provides feedback to teachers about how effective the teaching was, and whether the learning objectives have been achieved or not.
- It also provides teachers enough feedback to re-design his/her teaching and learning conditions to make it more effective.

According to Gronlund (1981) Achievement Tests can be used for a variety of instructional purposes. They are:

- To measure whether students possess the pre-requisite skills needed to succeed in a unit or course or to what extent students have already achieved the objectives of the planned instruction (Placement Evaluation)
- To monitor students' learning progress and to provide ongoing feedback to students and teacher about the success of the teaching-learning process (Formative Evaluation)
- To identify students' learning difficulties in any areas of learning, to investigate the causes of the learning difficulties and to provide adequate remedial instruction to maintain the gap of learning.
- To assign grades and certify the students at the completion of any semester, year or entire program (Summative evaluation)

Uses of Achievement Test

- To assess the current performance of the students.
- To assign grades on the basis of performance scores.
- To promote students to higher classes on the basis of test scores.
- To classify students into various courses.

- Used in guidance and counselling to understand various difficulties of students.
- Useful in helping students to choose their future vocational courses
- Used to measure the effectiveness of teachers and different kinds of instruction.
- Used as predictors of future behaviour or success in various vocations.

Uses of achievement test to a teacher

- The teacher comes to know about the general range of abilities of students in the class.
- In the light of above, s/he can select appropriate materials of instruction so that all individuals benefit from instruction to the maximum.
- The teacher can determine and diagnose the strengths and weakness of the students in various subjects.
- The teacher can spot out brilliant and backward children.
- S/he can determine the progress of the group in a particular subject over the period of time.
- By studying the results of the students on achievement tests and intelligence test, the teacher can determine whether or not the students are working at their maximum capacity.

Uses of achievement tests to administrators

- Tests help to discover backward children who need help and plans for remedial instruction for such students.
- Tests help to select talented peoples for special classes and courses.
- Tests help to decide proper classification of students.
- Test help to get a better understanding of the needs and abilities of pupils.
- Tests help to select students for the award of special merits or scholarships.
- Test help to group pupils in a class so that students are put in such a way that individual differences are as slight as possible.
- Tests help the parents in recognizing the strengths and weaknesses of their children so that they direct their energies on suitable goals only and do not put heavy demands on them.
- Test help to determine the efficiency of one school with the others.

- Tests help to determine the general level of achievement of the class may be judged on the basis of the achievement of the class in the beginning and at the end of the school year.
- Tests help to discover the type of learning experiences that will achieve these objectives with the possible results.
- To evaluate, revise and improve the curriculum in the light of these results.
- To evaluate the extent to which the objectives of education are being achieved.
- Tests help to classify school objectives.

Construction of an Achievement Test

Since evaluation is an integral part of teaching and learning, students are observed in various situations continuously with a view to assess their level of achievement in terms of what has been expected of them. Written examination is one of the most commonly employed and widely acceptable techniques for measuring student's achievement. Steps Involved in the construction of an Achievement test are discussed as under:

Planning of the test: A test is meant to serve many essential and important purposes. Therefore, it should be well planned and systematically developed. The first consideration which is of utmost importance is what the paper setter intends to find out through the achievement test. There are certain outcomes of learning which any teacher would like to realize by teaching every unit. The paper setter should aim at testing the achievement of these objectives. The next step is to determine the maximum time, maximum marks and the nature of the test. These should be decided in terms of the nature and scope of the sub units or units involved in the testing.

Preparation of a design for the test: After determining the broad scope of the test, a design has to be developed in tune with it. The objectives, content, forms of questions and the difficulty levels of items are the most important factors to be considered in such a design. The design presents an outline on the weightage given to each of these factors.

Weightage to Objectives: This indicates what objectives are to be tested and what weightage has to be given to each objective. The teacher should decide the relative importance of each of these objectives after carefully studying the prescribed syllabus and in tune with the nature of the content covered. This step will ensure objective basedness to the test, which is required for scientific evaluation

Sl. No.	Objectives	Marks	%
1.	Knowledge Domain	5	20
2.	Process Domain	6	24
3.	Application Domain	12	48
4.	Creativity Domain	2	8
	Total	25	100

Weightage to Content: The content refers to the topics in which the achievement test is to be conducted. Marks are distributed to the contents in each unit appropriately by which proper coverage is made possible. This indicates the various aspects of the content to be tested and the weightage to be given to each of these aspects.

Sl. No.	Content	Marks	Percentage
1	I	4	16
2	II	3	12
3	III	6	24
4	IV	7	28
5	V	5	20
Total		25	100

Weightage to Form of Questions: This indicates the forms of questions whether objective type, short answer type and essay type are to be included in the test and the weightage to each form of questions. The paper setter should select those forms of questions that are suitable to the objectives and content to be tested.

Sl. No	Form of Questions	No. of Questions	Marks	%
1.	Objective Type	10	10	40
2.	Short Answer	5	10	40
3.	Essay Type	1	5	20
	Total		25	100

Weightage to Difficulty Level: It is desirable to construct the test with some questions as easy, some difficult and the others of average difficulty. This would help us to discriminate between the bright, average and the dull students.

Sl No.	Difficulty Level	Marks	%
1.	Easy	6	24
2.	Average	12	48
3.	Difficult	7	28
	Total	25	100

Preparation of Blue Print: Blue print of the test may be defined as the final and detailed plan of the test prepared on the basis of the already made design to test the learning outcome in a balanced manner. It is a three-dimensional chart indicating the distribution of questions-objective wise, content wise and forms of questions. The blue print reveals the actual lay out of the question paper. It is at this stage the paper setter decides how many questions are to be included under different instructional objectives.

Objectives	**Knowledge Domain**			**Process Domain**			**Application Domain**			**Creativity Domain**			**Total**
Form of Questions ☞	O	SA	E	O	SA	E	O	SA	E	O	SA	E	Marks
Content I													4
Content II													3
Content III													6
Content IV													7
Content V													5
Grand Total	5			6			12			2			25

Note: O Stands for objective type questions, SA indicates short answer type question, E stands for Essay type questions. Figures outside the bracket indicates the mark allotted to questions Figures inside the bracket indicates the number of questions.

Writing of Items: The paper setter writes items according to the blue print. This is an important step because every question tests a definite ability or skill. The standard rules for the same given as under:

- Questions should measure the learning outcomes.
- The language used should be simple, clear, and within the comprehension level of the students.
- The difficulty level has to be considered while writing the items.
- It should also check whether all the questions included can be answered within the time allotted.
- Also avoid providing any clues to answers in the items.

Preparation of the Question Paper: After writing the items, they need to be relooked, modified and finalized. Then the finalized questions are assembled in a question paper. The following should be done:

- Write general instructions clearly so that the students get a clear idea about magnitude of task before them
- These instructions should be as specific as possible. Any specific

instruction related to a particular question or a group of questions must be written before these questions

- There are a number of ways of assembling questions according to suitable criteria. It can be according to form of questions, instructional objectives, content units, difficulty level or according to the convenience of administration
- Arrangement of questions in a question paper should be such that it facilitates the examinees as well as evaluation process.

Preparation of Scoring Key and Marking Scheme: Scoring key is prepared for the objective questions and a marking scheme is made for the essay and short answer questions. A marking scheme is essential as it indicates the number of points or steps expected in the answer, the outline of each point or step expected in the answer and the weightage to each of these points or steps. The detailed making scheme developed minimizes the variability in marking and increases reliability and objectivity.

Scoring Key

Qn. No.	1	2	3	4	5
Answer	a	b	Power	Joule	0.76m

Marking Scheme

Qn. No.	Value Points	Marks Allotted to Each Value Point	Total Marks
11	Definition Examples	1 1	2

Question Wise Analysis: In order to avoid all loopholes, the paper setter prepares a table containing all relevant details of all the items of the test. This is done by making an analysis of each item in terms of content, objectives, specification, and form of questions, difficulty level, marks and estimated time. This analysis is very helpful to check whether all the aspects envisaged in the design and blue print are satisfied by the test in its final form. If some mistakes are noticed it should be rectified at this final stage.

Qn. No.	Content	Objectives	Specifi-cation	Form of questions	Difficulty level	Marks	Time in Minutes
1	I	Knowledge	Recalls	Objective	Easy	1	1

Sample Achievement Test in Physics

Standard: IX
Score: 25
Time: 40 Minutes

Part A: Fill in the blanks. Each question carries one mark (3x1=3).

1. According to the second law of motion, force is equal to ....
2. The inertia of an object depends upon it's ....
3. Fill in the blanks by identifying the correct relationship. In polar region: The value of g is more. So, in the centre of the earth: ....

Part B: Match the Terms in Column A against those in Column B & C. Each correct answer carries one mark (4x1=4).

A	B	C
4. Weight of the Object	m/s2	Henry Cavendish
5. Mass of the Object	Newton	GM/R2
6. Gravitational Constant	Kilogram	The force with which Object is attracted towards the Centre of Earth
7. Acceleration due to gravity	Nm2/kg	The Quantity of matter contained in an Object

Part C: Short Answer Type Questions. Each question carries two marks (3x2=6).

8. State Newton's firs law of motion. Give one example.
9. Passengers are not allowed to travel standing in the upper deck of a double decker bus. Give reason.
10. If a body of mass 40 kg is kept at a distance of 5 m from a body of mass 60 kg. What is the mutual force of attraction between them?

Part D: Descriptive/Essay Type Questions. Each question carries three marks (3x4=12).

11. Draw a velocity – time graph using the below given data.

Time (s)	0	2	4	6	8	10
Velocity (m/s)	10	15	20	20	20	15

12. A car travels with a uniform velocity of 15 m/s gives an acceleration of 2 m/s2 in a time of 5 seconds. What is the velocity after 5 seconds? What is the distance travelled by the car when it is subjected to acceleration?

13. What is meant by the terms mass and weight? Are they vector or scalar quantities? Why?
14. The mass of a body is 30 kg. What is its weight on earth? What is its weight on the moon? (g = 1.62 m/s2)

CONSTRUCTION OF A DIAGNOSTIC TEST

Diagnosis means the art or act of finding out the root cause or cause for defective learning to adopt remedial teaching. When a student does not make progress in his studies, there must be a cause for it. This cause can be physical, mental, emotional etc. Teacher should find out the exact cause for these so that appropriate remedial measures may be taken. Educational diagnosis is the use of technical procedures designed to locate specific learning and instructional difficulties, and if possible, to determine their causes.

Diagnostic Test is a test designed to locate specific learning difficulties of the students at a specific stage of learning so that specific efforts could be made to overcome the difficulties. It helps a teacher to identify the status of a learner at the end of a particular lesson or unit as to what specific teaching or learning points have been properly grasped by the learner. A test designed to identify and investigate the difficulties, disabilities, inadequacies and gaps of pupils in specific curricular areas with a view to help them overcome those difficulties through remedial instruction are called a diagnostic test. The teacher then takes suitable remedial measures to overcome the deficiencies thus discovered. Diagnostic test can be formative or summative. Diagnostic test becomes relevant on two occasions, i.e. Before introducing a new unit, after teaching a unit.

Diagnostic tests are not administered to all students. Before the administration of diagnostic tests, the students' achievement usually is established as deficient relative to other students. The diagnostic test is expected to indicate the specific skills in which the student is deficient. To accomplish this, a diagnostic test must have the following characteristics:

- It should reveal the students' progress in terms of objectives.
- The test should be designed to detect faulty learning and difficult elements.
- It should provide specific remedial procedures for each error detected.
- The test should reveal the mental process of the learner sufficiently to detect points of error.
- Diagnostic test led to remedial teaching.

Diagnostic tests can indicate what a student's deficiencies are and why these deficiencies have occurred. A diagnostic test, however, is used to find a way to resolve the difficulty a student is having. A diagnostic test might identify important specific: skills the student has yet to achieve, but it will not indicate why these skills have not yet been achieved or what action, if any, will help the student to overcome these difficulties.

Steps in the Construction of a Diagnostic Test: The steps of preparation of a diagnostic test are given as under:

- **Planning**: The area of learning difficulty identified, on which a diagnostic test is based, requires a detailed exhaustive content analysis. It is broken into learning points without omitting any point. The diagnostic procedure is based on the premise that mastery of the total process cannot be stronger than that of the weakest link in the chain of related concepts and skills. Accordingly, each concept, skill or learning point, is identified at the time of constructing the test. As far as a diagnostic test is concerned, it is not very necessary to know the relative importance of the learning points. All the learning points have to be covered in an unbroken sequence. Each learning point should have an adequate number of questions to help identify the area of weakness.
- **Writing Items**: All the forms of questions (Essay, Short answer and Objective Types) can be used for testing different learning points. However, it appears for diagnostic purposes, short answer questions involving one or two steps, are used widely. Whatever be the form of questions, they should in general be easy, suitable for average students of that age or grade. The questions have to be specifically related to the learning points and should be such as to throw light on the weakness of the students. The questions should be written in simple language. The questions are clubbed around the learning points, even when they are of the different forms; the learning points are arranged sequentially from simple to complex which ensures that students do not have to change their mental sets very frequently.
- **Assembling the test:** Preparation of blue print may altogether be avoided. No rigid time limit needs to be specified, though for administrative case a time limit may be set. It is not the balance of objective, content, type, time and marks maintained in this test but it is the mastery of each and every teaching point is considered.
- **Providing directions and preparing scoring key:** A set of instructions clear and precise, is drafted. It should also be provided

with a scoring key and marking scheme. Scoring key and marking scheme are to be prepared for test to ensure objectivity in valuation and correctness of the information required from their responses.

- **Reviewing the test:** Before printing the test, it should be carefully edited and reviewed. This ensures that any inadvertent errors are eliminated. An analysis of the test and listing down learning points with corresponding questions may be prepared for future reference.

Administration of Diagnostic Test: The following points need to be kept in view:

- The first task of the teacher is to win the confidence of the students and reassure them that test is to help them in the improvement of their learning rather than for declaring pass or fail.
- It should be administered in a relaxed environment.
- Students should be seated comfortably.
- Students should be asked not to consult each other while taking the test.
- If any student is not able to follow something, he should be allowed to seek clarification from the teacher.
- The teacher may ensure that the students taking the test attempt all questions.
- Time schedule should not be enforced strictly. If any student takes a little more time, he should be allowed to do so.

Use of Diagnostic Tests: The important uses of diagnostic tests are;

- Items, units or skills, which are understood by a majority of students, can be located and teaching can be adjusted to the situation
- Items, units or skills which are not understood by a majority of pupils can be located and there by special emphasis in these aspects can be attempted
- The causes for the difficulty in certain items can be found out, for which remedial measures can be taken
- Individual weaknesses can be found out which would serve as the baseline for individual correction work and personal guidance
- Diagnostic test may be used for prognosis. It helps to predict the possible success in certain type of courses or vocation and therefore it helps in providing guidance and counselling

- Diagnostic tests can be made the basis of individualized instruction. Differentiated teaching methods, ability grouping, differentiated assignments etc. can be attempted on the basis of the results of diagnostic tests
- Diagnostic test measures 'real understanding' as opposed to superficial mastery of subject areas measured by achievement of pupils in subject areas
- Diagnostic tests can assist the pupil in locating one's weakness and so they can be corrected with maximum ease and economy
- Diagnostic tests can indicate the effectiveness of specific methods of teaching in dealing with specific teaching situations
- Diagnosis of pupils' weakness and self-discovery can lead to motivation and interest can generate cooperation in future teaching learning situation

Diagnostic Test Versus Achievement Test

Diagnostic Test	Achievement Test
Measure how much a student has not achieved	Measure how much a student has achieved
Diagnostic tests are used to identify difficulties and weaknesses of students.	Achievement tests are used to evaluate the achievement level of the students.
Diagnostic test leads to remedial teaching or special coaching. Marks are not very important	Achievement tests are used to compare achievement of students and also for grading.
Diagnostic tests concentrate on difficult areas.	Achievement tests relate to the entire unit covered.
Diagnostic tests are not usually used to evaluate the efficiency of teachers and the system.	Achievement tests at various occasions determine the effectiveness of the teacher in the teaching -learning process
Time factor is not important	Time factor is important in answering
Construction is comparatively difficult	Construction is comparatively easy

REMEDIAL INSTRUCTION (REMEDIAL TEACHING)

Remedial instruction is the process of instruction that follows immediately after diagnostic testing. Cognitive development is a continuous process. Any gap in this will be a hindrance to achieve knowledge. If the learner lacks the pre-requisites such as required knowledge, competencies, skill etc., compensatory education should be given to fill up the gap. When the exact nature of the difficulties and the reasons there of, are known the teacher has to take steps for remedial teaching. This may be at the group level or individual level, depending on the scope of the diagnosis and spread the difficulty within the group. These types of instruction are not given in a general class. In remedial classes, resistant children become acceptable to the group. Therefore, both diagnosis and remedial instruction should be continuous process and an integral part of effective instruction. Diagnosis relates to the process by which we try to know the real cause of the obstacles in education and adjudge their nature. Remedial teaching aims at correcting the error of past and thus it also prevents future errors. Special classes are held for remedial teaching definitely proves useful for remedial teaching. It removes the obstacles lying in the way of acquiring knowledge by the child. It also facilitates the progress of the child and the teacher.

By giving successful experiences to the slow learner, the teacher is taking a great step towards re-building his morals and integrating his personality. By the success in remedial classes, resistant children become self-confident, socially maladjusted students become acceptable to the group. Once the nature of difficulties and reasons are known through a diagnostic test, the teacher has to take steps for remedial instruction. It provides additional learning experiences in order to reduce the learning difficulties. It is an extensive effort to improve motivation, correct emotional difficulties and to overcome deficiencies in learning. Diagnosis and remedial instruction should be continuous and integral part of effective instruction. Learners are motivated and learning becomes meaningful and interesting. Learning becomes a continuous process. Since the stumbling blocks are removed, learning becomes smooth and easy.

TYPES OF TEST ITEMS – MERITS AND DEMERITS

Class room test and assessments play a central role in the evaluation of student learning. The main goal of classroom testing and assessment is to obtain valid, reliable and useful information concerning student achievement. Achievement tests are conducted using different types of test items. Quality of an achievement test is determined by the quality of its items. Hence science teacher should master the skills of constructing test items. A constructor should take the following precautions while framing the test items. The items should cover as far as possible, the whole range of topics prescribed in the syllabus.

- No item or part of the item should be set which is outside the syllabus
- More items should be set to test higher objectives. For this purpose, items should be in the context of new situations

- Items should provide clear direction to the students regarding the scope and length of responses
- The language of the items should be simple and within the easy grasp of students

Objective Type Test Item

Objective type test items are highly structured test items. Objective type questions are questions that require a specific answer. An objective question usually has only one potential correct answer and they leave no room for opinion. An objective type test item is one in which the response will be objective. The responses are made fixed and hence the freedom of the respondent to deviate subjectively is restricted. It requires the pupils to supply a word or to select the correct answer from a number of alternatives. The answer of the item is fixed one. According to Linn and Miller (2005), objective test items are highly structured and require the students to supply a word or two or to select the correct answer from a number of alternatives. Objective type items are most efficient to measure different instructional objectives. An Objective test is so named because the system of scoring is objective rather than subjective. Objective type test item can be broadly classified into two, [1] Supply Type (Recall Type), [2] Selection type (Recognition Type).

Supply Type (Recall type, free response type)

Supply type items are those in which answers are not given in the question. The students supply their answer in the form of a word, phrase, number or symbol. These items require student to supply the answer. This is also known as simple recall items. In such items, the teacher asks a short question expecting a quick one-word answer or completion of a statement. These items are also called as 'free response' type items. Supply type items are further classified into: (a) Simple Recall Type Test Items. This test requires the respondent to recall a response to a direct question. The typical response should be short preferably a word, a number or a small phrase. It eliminates the chance of guessing.

Completion Type Test Item

A completion type item consists of a series of sentences in which certain words are omitted and replaced by blanks. The respondents are expected to fill in the blanks with a word or a number or at the most a phrase. The probability of guess work is completely eliminated. Examples: What is the composition of water? (Answer: H2O). The name of the person who invented telephone is ---------. (Answer: Alexander Graham Bell)

Selection type (Recognition Type, Fixed Response type)

In the recognition type items the answer is supplied to the examinee along with some distractors. The examinee has to choose the correct answers from among them. So that these tests are known as 'Selection type'. As the answer is fixed and given, some call it as 'Fixed response type' items. Selection type items are considered as carrying the quality of objectivity. Scoring to such type items are considered easy and objective. Selection type items are further divided into the following: (a) True or False Items (Alternate Response Type), (b) Matching type items, (c) Multiple choice type items.

True or False Items (Alternate Response Type)

A true or false item consist of a statement or proposition which the examinee must judge and mark either true or false. The respondent is asked to read a statement and indicate in some specific manner suggested, whether it is true or false, right or wrong, correct or incorrect, agree or disagree, yes or no. It tests the ability to discriminate between misconceptions and scientific truth. It is suitable for young children who have poor vocabulary.

Multiple choice Test Items (Changing Alternative type)

These are items presenting four or more responses in which one is either correct or definitely better than the others. The examinee has to find this and record this in the manner required in the paper. Here the chances of guess work are minimized. Multiple choice items consist of two parts. The first part of the item is called stem presented in the form of a direct question or incomplete statements. The second part of the item is called options or alternatives or responses, usually four or five in number among the options one is the keyed response and others are called distracters or misleads. The stem gives data for the selection of the keyed response. The respondent has to read the stem and options and to select the correct or best alternative. The different forms multiple choice test items in vogue are correct answer form, best answer form, multiple response form, etc.

Matching Type Test Item

This is a modified version of the multiple-choice test items. In fact, matching type is an economized form of combining a number of multiple-choice items in the same question. It consists of two parallel columns, with each phrase, word or number or symbol in one column (Usually the first) being matched to a word, phrase or sentence in the other column. The items in the column for which a match is sought are called premises or stem and items in the column from which selection is made is called responses or options. The respondent is required to make some sort of association between each premise and each response in the two columns. While writing various types of selection type items for an objective type test, one should keep the following points in mind:

- **In true-false/two alternative response items:** Double negatives must be avoided. The statement must be either entirely true or entirely false. The statement must not be complex and indirect. The number of true statements and false statements should be approximately equal. True statements and false statements should be approximately equal in length.
- **In matching items**: Homogeneous content should be used in a single matching exercise. An unequal number of responses and premises should be included and the student should be instructed that one, more than one or no response may be used. All the items for one matching type item must be placed on the same page.
- **In multiple choice items:** An item should contain only one correct or the best answer. There should be no verbal association between the item and the correct answer. The correct answer should appear in each of the alternative positions equal number of times but in random order. The length of the alternatives should be approximately equal. Weak distracters must be avoided. The stem should not be ambiguous and all the alternatives should be grammatically consistent with the stem of the item.

Advantages of Objective Type Items

- As a large number of questions are set, a wide coverage of the syllabus is possible.
- It possesses objectivity of scoring. The answer in objective type test is fixed and only one and it is predetermined. So that different persons scoring the answer script arrives at the same result.
- It is easy to score. Scoring is made with the help of scoring key.
- They are more valid and reliable, since the response/ answers are definite
- There is greater administrative use and control
- They have higher diagnostic value
- They are less time consuming

Disadvantages of Objective Type Items

- Such tests do not encourage verbal fluency or a student's ability to develop argument
- Chances of guessing are high
- Emphasis on testing superficial knowledge
- Inefficiency in testing complicated skills
- Objective type items are often ambiguous, particularly for the better students
- Such tests when over used can have a negative effect on teaching, since they encourage the student to learn bits of knowledge rather than the whole.

Short Answer type test item

The length of the answer expected from a short answer question is very short. This diminishes subjectivity. In this way it is an improvement upon essay type questions. Such questions are of great help in having a wide coverage of content and each item can be set to a test a definite objective. A question requiring value points at the most may be defined as a short answer question. The term value point indicates a point to be given credit in the expected answer. Because of these reasons, a fair proportion of such questions should be included in a test.

Advantages

- Questions of this form can be made stimulating
- Students can be trained to select relevant information and present it in a few short, crisp sentences
- Short answers are easy to score
- Reliability of scoring is high
- Questions can cover a wider content area than essay type test items.
- The short answer test gives little opportunity for bluffing
- The short answer test is especially useful in diagnosis.

Disadvantages

- It is more subjective than the objective type of items
- It is excessive use may encourage a student to memorize facts and develop poor study habits
- Mechanical scoring is not possible because of the subjectivity involved

Essay Type test item

According to Good, essay test is a type of examination in which the subject or examinee is asked to discuss, enumerate, compare, state, evaluate, analyse, summarize or criticize and involves writing at specific length on a given topic involving the processed listed above. The essay type questions get its name from the manner in which the examinee responds. The term essay implies a written response which may consists of many sentences to several pages. The student is allowed freedom with respect to what his answer will include, its wording length and organization.

Advantages

- They are easy to construct
- They can be used to test the student's language mastery, expression and organizational ability of a student
- Chances of copying are minimal
- A student's ability to use knowledge effectively can be assessed. It helps to develop a variety of skills. In addition to self-expression, students have to select pertinent material, organize this material into a coherent discussion and arrive at conclusions.
- It encourages good study habits. A student preparing for an essay test is likely to highlight important units, look for relationships and exercise judgment in deciding points of emphasis.

Disadvantages

- Subjective bias could creep in as these tests are based on the examiner's moods and whims
- Essay type encourages rote memory. The higher levels of the cognitive domain cannot be completely assessed by this method
- There is danger of bluffing. It requires a discerning teacher to realize that nothing much is been said.
- Unreliability of scoring restricts the use of essay type tests. Different teachers scoring an essay type question may arrive at different results even the same teacher scoring it at two different times get two different scores.
- Essay type tests can cover a limited range of course content as well as instructional objectives

TEACHER EVALUATION

Criteria for Evaluating Teaching Competence

Teaching is a demanding and complex profession. Meeting the demands of the teaching profession requires tremendous will, ability, and preparation. It also requires continuous learning and support. As the most significant resource in schools, teachers are critical to raise education standards. Improving the efficiency and equity of schooling depends, in large measure, on ensuring that teachers are highly skilled, well resourced, and motivated to perform at their best. Raising teaching performance is perhaps the policy direction most likely to lead to substantial gains in student learning (Organization for Economic Co-operation and Development, OECD, 2005). In turn, the effective monitoring and evaluation of teaching is central to the continuous improvement of the effectiveness of teaching in a school. It is essential to know the strengths of teachers and those aspects of their practice which could be further developed.

Teacher Evaluation is a procedure which assesses individual performance of a teacher over a period of time, identifies the qualities of educational practices and teaching performance, and provides detailed information for personnel practices relating to renewal, assignment and dismissal. Meaningful teacher evaluation involves an accurate appraisal of the effectiveness of teaching, its strengths and areas for development, followed by feedback, coaching, support and opportunities for professional development. It is also essential to celebrate, recognize and reward the work of teachers. Research results reveal that the great majority of teachers report that the appraisal and feedback they receive is beneficial, fair and helpful for their development as teachers (OECD, 2009b).

In general, teacher evaluation refers to the formal process an institution uses to review and rate teachers' performance and effectiveness in the classroom. Ideally, the findings from these evaluations are used to provide feedback to teachers and guide their professional development. Traditionally, teacher evaluation systems relied heavily on classroom observations conducted by principals or other school administrators, sometimes with the help of rubrics or checklists. Samples of students' work, teachers' records and lesson plans, and other relevant factors were also often taken into account. The core purpose of teacher assessment and evaluation should be to strengthen the knowledge, skills, dispositions, and classroom practices of professional educators. This goal serves to promote student growth and learning while also inspiring great teachers to remain in the classroom. Comprehensive systems of continuous teacher education and professional growth help teachers master content, refine their teaching skills, critically analyse their own performance and their students' performance, and implement the changes needed to improve teaching and learning.

Need and Purpose of Teacher Evaluation

- To screen out incompetent and unqualified persons from certification and selection processes and thereby aid institutions.
- To provide constructive feedback to individual educators.
- To recognize and help reinforce outstanding service.
- To provide direction for staff development practices.
- To provide evidence that will withstand professional and judicial scrutiny.
- To unify teachers and administrators in their collective efforts to educate students.

Importance of Teacher Evaluation

- Reliable feedback helps teachers to get rid of uncertainties and distortions of self-image perceived by the self.
- Helps give parents assurance about teaching competence and student welfare.
- Helps in taking decisions regarding personal decisions with respect to selection, contract renewal, promotions, reassignment, certification, staffing, retirements, leave of absence and in-service education.
- Vital in giving detailed information to administrators and supervisors

Aims and Objectives of Teacher Evaluation

- Ultimate aim is improving quality of education and learning outcomes.
- To help teachers realize their potentials.
- To assist in planning in-service training and professional development of teachers.
- To enhance overall management and development of school.
- To provide reassurance for 'teacher audiences'- parents, elected representatives, society and administrative professionals.
- To help in staffing and decision-making regarding retaining, remediating or terminating.

- To enable teachers competently solve their professional problems.
- To promote co-operative work among teachers.

Types of Teacher Evaluation

A comprehensive teacher assessment and evaluation system should have two distinct components: (1) **Formative**: Ongoing, consistent, formative assessments of performance for the sole purpose of fostering professional growth and improved practice; and provides teachers with feedback on how to improve performance and what types of professional development methods will enhance their performance. (2) **Summative**: Periodic summative evaluations of teacher performance for the purpose of approving continued employment. Used to make final decisions on factors such as salary, tenure, personal assignments, transfers or dismissals. Determines whether performance has improved from status of previous evaluation, whether the teacher should remain in current position or be rewarded for performance.

Steps involved in Teacher Evaluation

- **Preparation:** It is a planning conference held with the teacher to discuss and set goals to focus for professional growth.
- **Observation**: The evaluator observes classes taken by the teacher for firsthand information. Observations can be formal/pre -planned or informal/unannounced.
- **Data Collection:** Vital data is collected through methods like student feedback, peer evaluation, self-evaluation etc. Tools like Rating Scales, Checklists etc. can also be used.
- **Reporting:** Based on data collected, a formal report is prepared. Evaluator can include additional appropriate comments also.
- **Follow-Up:** It is a meeting with teacher post observation. Feedback is provided on strengths and weaknesses of the teacher. Feedback must be positive and balanced between praise and criticism. It should offer ideas for future improvement.

Methods of Teacher Evaluation

- **Pupil Rating**: Students are in the unique position to rate teachers. They can rate the extent of change in motivation towards the subject-They are direct observers of teacher's punctuality, enthusiasm, subject knowledge, handling methods etc.
- **Peer Rating:** Teachers use their direct knowledge and experiences

in assessing and judging the merits and values of fellow co-workers.

- **Community Rating:** Ratings of parents and community is obtained through formal and informal contacts made by the school management.
- **Supervisor Rating**: Teachers are evaluated by a panel of experts
- **Self-Rating**: Teachers assess their own performance with help of self-assessment preforms.

Characteristics of Fair and Effective Teacher Evaluation Systems

A successful system of teacher evaluation is based on a comprehensive review of effective teaching behaviours. Such a review identifies the knowledge, dispositions, pedagogical skills, and other commitments to learning characteristic of highly skilled teachers. A successful system relies on a wide range of evidence, including classroom observations, teacher-developed materials, student products and performances, student feedback, and quantitative measures of student achievement. A successful system aligns quality assurance purposes with professional growth. It is useful and practical for teachers and evaluators. It promotes professional learning, encourages teacher agency and is differentiated for teachers based on their professional needs. A successful system is fair and nonthreatening. It is based on clearly defined standards of teacher performance and is implemented by well-trained and ethical evaluators who follow common procedures. Evaluators consider the context of evaluation and promote a culture of inquiry.

Instruments and Information Sources

Gathering multiple sources of evidence about teacher practice meets the need for accuracy and fairness of the evaluation process, taking into account the complexity of what a 'good' teacher should know and be able to do. A range of instruments and information sources are typically used to evaluate teachers.

- **Classroom observation**: Teaching practices and evidence of student learning are likely to be the most relevant sources of information about professional performance. As a result, teacher evaluation is typically firmly rooted in classroom observation. Most key aspects of teaching are displayed while teachers interact with their students in the classroom.
- **Objective setting and individual interviews**: Most teacher evaluation models require the individual teacher to set performance

objectives for a given period of time in agreement with the school management. The evaluation then assesses the extent to which such objectives were met. The settings of objectives, as well as the evaluation itself, typically involve individual interviews which are an opportunity to trigger critical reflection between evaluators and teachers.

- **Teacher self-evaluation**: Another common instrument used in teacher evaluation is teacher self- evaluation. The perspective of the teacher being evaluated is essential, because it allows teachers to express their own views about their performance, and reflect on the personal, organizational and institutional factors that had an impact on their teaching.
- **Teacher portfolio**: An instrument which typically complements teacher self-evaluation is a teacher portfolio, providing evidence about key aspects of the teacher's teaching. Different elements can compose teacher portfolios, including: lesson plans and teaching materials, samples of student work and commentaries on student assessment examples, teacher's self-reported questionnaires and reflection sheets. It should be noted that portfolios are not only a tool for evaluation per se, but also play a role in supporting a reflective approach to teaching practice that is a hallmark of effective teachers.
- **Standardized form to record teacher performance across a range of dimensions:** Comprehensive models of teacher evaluation involve the use of standardized forms to record teacher performance across the aspects being evaluated. These are key tools used in the evaluation process which seek to capture performance across the range of domains under evaluation.
- **Teacher testing**: In some countries, for particular purposes such as the access to a permanent position or entry into the profession, teachers are the subject of testing to assess their general and subject-matter competencies. In some instances, the results of such tests can be used for teacher evaluation.
- **Student results**: Student results are not commonly used as sources of evidence for teacher evaluation in countries (OECD, 2005; UNESCO, 2007). Because a wide range of factors impact on student results, identifying the specific contribution of a given teacher is faced with numerous challenges.
- **Surveys of students and parents**: An instrument that is rarely used in the context of individual teacher evaluation is surveys

collecting the views of students and parents. Parent's surveys are more relevant for whole-school evaluation than for individual teacher performance evaluation.

Criteria for Evaluating Teaching Competence

Competency is the conscious use of one's own knowledge, abilities, skills, talents, values, attitudes and behaviour patterns, in order to resolve issues and problems, overcome challenges, fulfilling one's duties and achieving the aims proposed. Competent teachers are teachers who deploy their knowledge, abilities, skills, talents, values, attitudes and behaviour patterns to meet the challenge of educating their students. They possess the professional skills needed and adequate to perform their assigned duties and attain the educational goals. Teachers must educate students by enabling them to develop the basic skills they need to design a life project of their own, endowed with intrinsic value, and become capable of fulfilling it without irksome constraints within their living environment. Being a teacher at any level requires a significant amount of knowledge and skill. Paying attention to the core competencies for educators helps to ensure that all teachers and others who work in education are prepared to make school a positive experience for students and their families.

- **Subject Matter Knowledge:** Teaching requires a myriad of knowledge and skills, knowledge about pupils, systems and structures, knowledge about styles of teaching and learning, knowledge about management, resources and assessment as well as knowledge about the subject. That subject matter is an essential component of teacher knowledge is neither a new nor a controversial assertion. After all, if teaching entails helping others learn, then understanding what is to be taught is a central requirement of teaching. The myriad tasks of teaching, such as selecting worthwhile learning activities, giving helpful explanations, asking productive questions, and evaluating students' learning, all depend on the teacher's understanding of what it is that students are to learn.
- **Interacting with Students:** Educators must be able to positively interact with all students. This includes difficult students, students who work below grade-level and students whose personalities just grate on a teacher. Teachers must put aside their prejudices and feelings in order to treat all students with respect, provide them with equal opportunities for learning and make them feel confident.

- **Create a Learning Environment**: Creating a safe learning environment that is conducive to learning is essential. Educators must set high expectations for student performance and behaviour. All rules must be enforced consistently and fairly. Students should not have to worry about being bullied in the classroom and should feel comfortable when speaking up.
- **Good at Lesson Plan Design:** All educators must be capable of designing lesson plans to meet student needs and cover the standards. This requires knowing how to choose and create instructional materials to accommodate students at different levels. It also requires creating a scope and sequence that provides students with enough time to master the standards.
- **Able to Employ Varied Teaching Strategies:** Best practices and other appropriate teaching strategies allow competent educators to effectively teach the curriculum. Competent educators may lecture, but they also incorporate a variety of strategies, including non-traditional teaching strategies, to help students with multiple learning styles learn and stay engaged. Educators also attend regular professional development sessions to learn new strategies and the latest best practices.
- **Use of Assessments:** Educators must design or select and administer effective assessments. An assessment must accurately measure what has been taught and what students have learned. Competent educators combine informal and formal assessment techniques to monitor student performance. They also incorporate technology, portfolios and other creative methods to assess students.
- **Able to Identify Student Needs:** Being able to identify and address student needs is a crucial component of an educator's job. This is done by partly using formal and informal assessments to help guide instruction. However, it also involves getting to know students beyond an instructional level, learning about their interests, recognizing changes in mood and making sure students are mentally and emotionally focused on learning.
- **Communication Skills:** Communicating effectively with parents and other stakeholders in a child's education is a key component of an educator's job. A quality educator provides regular updates on a child's progress and immediately addresses any concerns that may arise. The educator also knows how to calmly discuss issues with difficult parents and how to come to decisions that have the best interests of the child in mind.

- **Able to Collaborate:** Educators must be able to collaborate with other teachers and school staff. Teachers can learn from one another and grow into better teachers through collaboration. They can also collaborate to make the school a safe, effective learning environment for all students and to improve the overall image of the school and the instruction that takes place there.
- **Maintaining a Professional Appearance:** Being an educator requires maintaining a professional appearance at all times. This includes dressing appropriately and acting professionally. Educators often serve as role models for students. Actions such as using foul language, gossiping about teachers and students or dressing inappropriately can cause students to lose respect for an educator.
- **Demonstrating a Commitment to the Profession:** Educators must make a commitment to education and professional development. Subject matter knowledge fades, teaching strategies change and new research is always modifying the way students learn and teachers teach. By furthering their education and taking part in professional development sessions, educators can continue to improve the quality of the education they provide. Effective teaching contributes to student learning, regardless of the circumstances and conditions. Teachers are responsible for making their own practice as effective as possible. Teachers also need to take control of their own profession and share in the school system's responsibility for transforming education. Identifying a comprehensive, rigorous process for assessing, supporting, and evaluating teachers is a critical first step toward reclaiming the profession of teaching. With the appropriate framework for support and feedback, teachers will be able to make continual improvements in their practice and continue to ensure that every student has access to a great education.

In short, promoting teacher evaluation is clearly in the national interest as well as serving students and their families and communities. Teachers need feedback on their performance to help them identify how to better shape and improve their teaching practice and, with the support of effective school leadership, to develop schools as professional learning communities. At the same time, teachers should be accountable for their performance and progress in their careers on the basis of demonstrated effective teaching practice.

STUDENT SELF-EVALUATION

Self-assessment is the involvement of learners in making judgments about their achievements and the outcomes of their learning and is a valuable approach supporting student learning, particularly when used formatively. Self-assessment supports student learning and is one of the most important skills that students require for future professional development and life-long learning, as it develops their capacity to be assessors of learning. Self-assessment is a powerful technique for self-improvement.

Klenowski defines self-assessment as "the evaluation or judgment of 'the worth' of one's performance and the strengths and weaknesses. Airasian and Gullickson (1994) define self-assessment as "the process of making judgments about the appropriateness or effectiveness of one's own knowledge, performance, beliefs, products, or effects, so that they can be improved or refined". Boud and Falchikov (1989) define self-assessment as the involvement of learners in making judgements about their achievements and the outcomes of their learning and identifying standards or criteria to apply to their work and making judgments about the extent to which they have met these criteria and standards. Thus, self-assessment is intimately bound up with issues of power, control and authority and the extent to which these are transferred from academic staff to students (Brew, 1999). Student self-assessment involves students in evaluating their own work and learning progress. Self- assessment is a valuable learning tool as well as part of an assessment process. Student self-assessment occurs when learners assess their own performance. Through self-assessment, students can:

- Objectively reflect on and critically evaluate their own progress and skill development
- Identify gaps in their understanding and capabilities
- Learn independently and think critically
- See where to focus their attention in learning
- Set realistic goals
- Revise their work
- Track their own progress
- Discern how to improve their performance

This process helps students stay involved and motivated and encourages self-reflection and responsibility for their learning. It is also useful in preparing students for life-long learning, through discussions about their skills and competencies (including the ability to assess), not just knowledge (Brew, 1999). For self-assessment to be effective, students should first become familiar with the concept. The term 'self-assessment' is used to cover all judgments by learners of their work: it is related to and incorporates terms such as 'self-evaluation' and 'self-appraisal'. There are several purposes of self-assessment; viz. (a) to evaluate understanding of the content, (b) to demonstrate the achievement of outcomes and goals and, (c) the self-development of the learner. These three aspects of self-assessment are all inter-linked and will receive different emphases at different times during the process of learning. There are a number of benefits, along with barriers to and issues associated with self-assessment that is outlined below:

Benefits of Student Self-Evaluation

- Enhances learning, including deep and lifelong learning
- Makes students feel that they have some control over their own evaluation
- Develops learner autonomy, cognitive abilities and meta-cognitive engagement
- Makes them aware of and more responsible for their own learning processes
- Promotes active engagement with learning
- Promotes better understanding of content and increased quality and thoughtfulness on assignments
- Enhances personal or intellectual development or social competencies
- Develops important meta-cognitive skills that contribute to a range of important graduate capabilities. All professionals must be able to evaluate their own performance, so this practice should be embedded in higher education learning as early as possible.
- Increasing self-awareness through reflective practice, making the criteria for self-evaluation explicit, and making performance improvement practices intrinsic to ongoing learning.
- Contributing to the development of critical reviewing skills, enabling the learner to more objectively evaluate their own performance
- Possibly, in the long run, reducing the teacher's assessment workload

Barriers of Student Self-Evaluation

- Some students are reluctant to self-assess; they feel they lack the necessary skills, confidence or ability to judge their own work
- Students prefer and expect to be assessed by experts and see it as the teachers' responsibility
- Students are afraid of being wrong or are too harsh on themselves and are uncomfortable with the responsibility
- Students do not like it and do not see benefit in it
- Students cannot be bothered arguing that they have "enough to think about as it is"
- For some student's cultural issues impact on self-assessment because giving themselves a good grade is considered inappropriate or boasting

Who is the 'self' in 'self-assessment'? It involves one part of the self-assessing another part of the self's actions and outcomes - 'it raises some deep questions about the nature of the self, self- awareness and self-monitoring'. It encourages the internalization of accountability and may be linked to notions of surveillance and social control. In order to become lifelong learners, students need to learn the importance of self-evaluation. They can do this by filling out self-evaluation forms, journalizing, taking tests, writing revisions of work, and asking questions, and through discussions. When students evaluate themselves, they are assessing what they know, do not know, and what they would like to know. They begin to recognize their own strengths and weaknesses. They become more familiar with their own beliefs, and possibly their misconceptions. After they self-evaluate, they will be able to set goals that they feel they can attain with the new knowledge they have about themselves.

Teachers should encourage self-evaluation because self-assessment makes the students active participants in their education (Sloan, 1996). There are a variety of ways for teachers to provide the students with self-assessments. Research suggests that the simplest tools to encourage student self-assessment are evaluative questions that force students to think about their work (Hart, 1999). Teachers need to show their students that it is important for everybody to self-evaluate by doing their own self-evaluation. Self-assessment is one of the most important skills that students require for future professional development and life-long learning, as it develops their capacity to be assessors of learning. It is important that teaching staff consider how they might share some of the feedback and assessment processes with students to facilitate student learning.

Tools and Strategies for Self-assessment

The ability to self-assess effectively develops over time and with experience (Cassidy, 2007). With this in mind, it is helpful for teachers to select tools and strategies that can be used in the classrooms. The tools and strategies suggested below should be adapted by teachers to suit the various needs of their diverse student population. Each allows for self-assessment of both process and product, and focuses on assessment for learning. Each demand that students revisit their own work, engage in reflection and set goals for improvement. Following are all tools that can help students with self-assessment.

- **Checklists:** Checklists are easier to construct and use. A checklist spells out what needs to be included in a piece of work. As students work on assignments, checklists serve as useful reminders of specific expectations and can help students stay focused and on task when working independently. Students can only be reminded of what they already know so be sure that checklists contain items that you've already introduced to them. Use checklists when a process or product can be broken into components; they are quick and useful in situations involving a large number of criteria. Align checklists closely with tasks.
- **Rubrics:** Rubrics are tools designed to provide constructive feedback for students through self, peer, or teacher assessment in order to further develop skills or knowledge (Creighton, 2000). A rubric demand reflecting on and describing performance with some precision; creating a rubric teaches us to think (Spandel, 2006). Rubrics help students assess how well students have met expectations. A rubric lists the criteria for good work and levels of performance. Criteria on a rubric allow students to make choices in their learning and bring their own voice into their work. Involve students in the creation of rubrics. When students help to create rubrics, they increase their understanding of lesson goals and expectations and are more interested in the lesson and in performing at a high standard. Constantly modify them with student input and use student- friendly language. When students have a chance to analyse examples with varying levels of quality, they can understand what "proficient" work looks like and get a concrete idea of what they can do to stretch themselves to achieve that level of work.
- **Reflection:** Reflection helps students to make sense of both content and process. To be effective with self- assessment, students

need to develop their ability to think critically about the work they're doing. To help students learn and practice critical thinking skills, reflection can be used. Reflection can be used along with checklists and rubrics. Reflection formats provide structure for students' thinking about their work.

- **Portfolio Assessment:** A student portfolio is a systematic collection of student work and related material that depicts a student's activities, accomplishments, and achievements in one or more school subjects. The collection should include evidence of student reflection and self-evaluation, guidelines for selecting the portfolio contents, and criteria for judging the quality of the work. The goal is to help students assemble portfolios that illustrate their talents, represent their writing capabilities, and tell their stories of school achievement.
- **Reflective Journal:** Students producing a reflective journal about their own learning and achievements are a logical way to engage them in self-assessment, as it gives both them and their assessor(s) insights into the process. The reflective journal can be extended to include their thoughts on how they can improve their performance. Students can keep a daily or weekly journal to record reflections on their own learning, challenges, and accomplishments, in response to prompts provided by the teacher.
- **Self-assessment Schedule:** One version of this type of assessment task is the "self-assessment schedule" (Boud, 1992), a formal document prepared by the student that presents their achievements alongside their learning goals and comments on what they feel they have achieved.
- **Online Tools:** Some teachers use online tools such as blogs or shared documents as a way for students to record their reflections. These can be set up to be private between the student and teacher or shared with the classroom community. For more objective tasks, such as scientific or mathematical calculation, online automatically marked tests could be provided where students can test their skill. Invite students to create questions to contribute to the test database; this adds a meta-cognitive layer to the exercise. Online tool such as the Moodle Learning Management System (LMS) allows the compilation of question banks, and self-assessment can be incorporated into a Workshop activity.

In short, students are an intrinsic part of the information sharing process. They can reflect on their learning and be involved in a number of ways.

Effective reporting involves each child in taking increasing responsibility for their own learning. Involving students in the assessment process helps them to become lifelong learners. Peter Senge (2000) says, "A cornerstone of lifelong learning is the capacity for objective self-assessment – the ability to judge for yourself how well you are doing."

Conclusion

In conclusion, the evaluation process in physical science teaching and learning is multifaceted and crucial for fostering student growth and understanding. Achievement tests provide valuable insights into students' grasp of content knowledge and their ability to apply it. Diagnostic tests offer educators a deeper understanding of individual student needs, allowing for targeted instruction and intervention through remedial teaching strategies. Teacher evaluation is essential for ensuring the effectiveness of instruction and identifying areas for professional development. By assessing teaching methods, content delivery, and classroom management, educators can continuously improve their practice to better meet the needs of diverse learners.

Moreover, empowering students through self-evaluation encourages metacognitive awareness and accountability for their own learning. When students take an active role in assessing their progress and understanding, they become more engaged and motivated learners. Overall, a comprehensive evaluation framework that incorporates achievement tests, diagnostic assessments, remedial teaching, teacher evaluation, and student self-evaluation is essential for promoting meaningful learning experiences and academic success in physical science education. By continuously assessing and reflecting on teaching and learning practices, educators can create dynamic and effective instructional environments that nurture students' curiosity, critical thinking skills, and passion for science.

Chapter - 4

Techno Pedagogic Content Knowledge

INTRODUCTION

In the rapidly evolving landscape of education, the integration of technology has become paramount for effective teaching and learning. This integration not only demands a deep understanding of pedagogy and content but also necessitates the seamless incorporation of technology into instructional practices. Chapter 4 delves into the intricate interplay between pedagogy, content, and technology, focusing specifically on the concept of Techno Pedagogic Content Knowledge (TPACK). The chapter begins by elucidating the foundational components of pedagogical knowledge and pedagogical content knowledge, highlighting their significance in instructional design and delivery. It then transitions into an exploration of TPACK, a framework that synthesizes the complex interactions between pedagogy, content, and technology, providing educators with a comprehensive model for effective technology integration.

Furthermore, the chapter delves into various strategies and methodologies for linking technology to pedagogical content knowledge, emphasizing the importance of aligning technological tools with educational objectives and content-specific needs. Through practical examples and case studies, educators are guided on how to leverage technology to enhance pedagogical approaches and facilitate deeper understanding of subject matter. Finally, the chapter underscores the role of the teacher as a Techno Pedagogue – an educator equipped with the knowledge, skills, and mindset to effectively integrate technology into teaching practices. By embracing this role, teachers can harness the power of technology to create dynamic and engaging learning experiences, ultimately fostering meaningful learning outcomes for students.

Throughout this chapter, readers will gain insights into the theoretical underpinnings and practical applications of Techno Pedagogic Content Knowledge, empowering them to navigate the complex intersection of pedagogy, content, and technology in the modern educational landscape. Technology has become an increasingly important part of students' lives beyond school, and even within the classroom it can also help increase their understanding of complex concepts or encourage collaboration among peers. Because of these benefits, current educational practice suggests that teachers implement some form of technology in their classrooms – but many teachers face difficulties in doing so. Cost, access, and time often form considerable barriers to classroom implementation, but another obstacle is a lack of knowledge regarding how technology can best be used to benefit students across diverse subject matter.

PEDAGOGICAL KNOWLEDGE

Pedagogical Knowledge is the deep knowledge about the processes and practices or methods of teaching and learning and how it encompasses overall educational purposes, values and aims. This is a generic form of knowledge that is involved in all issues of student learning, classroom management, lesson plan development and implementation, and student evaluation. It includes knowledge about techniques or methods to be used in the classroom; the nature of the target audience; and strategies for evaluating student understanding. A teacher with deep pedagogical knowledge understands how students construct knowledge and acquires skills; develop habits of mind and positive dispositions towards learning. As such, pedagogical knowledge requires an understanding of cognitive, social and developmental theories of learning and how they apply to students in their classroom.

Pedagogical Components of Pedagogical Knowledge

- Knowledge of teaching methods: having a command of various teaching methods, knowing when and how to apply each method;
- Knowledge of classroom assessment: knowledge of different forms and purposes of formative and summative assessments, knowledge of how different frames of reference (e.g., social, individual, criterion-based) impact students' motivation;
- Structure: structuring of learning objectives and the lesson process, lesson planning and evaluation
- Adaptivity: dealing with heterogeneous learning groups in the classroom

- Knowledge of classroom management: maximizing the quantity of instructional time, handling classroom events, teaching at a steady pace, maintaining clear direction in lessons;

Pedagogical Content Knowledge (PCK)

Pedagogical knowledge means the "how" of teaching, generally acquired through education coursework and personal experiences. Content knowledge, on the other hand, is the "what" of teaching. In 1986, Lee Shulman claimed that the emphasis on teachers' subject knowledge and pedagogy were being treated as mutually exclusive. To address this dichotomy, he introduced the notion of *pedagogical content knowledge* (PCK) that includes pedagogical knowledge and content knowledge, among other categories. Shulman argued that having knowledge of subject matter and general pedagogical strategies, though necessary, were not sufficient for capturing the knowledge of good teachers. To characterize the complex ways in which teachers think about how particular content should be taught, he argued for "pedagogical content knowledge" as the content knowledge that deals with the teaching process, including the "the ways of representing and formulating the subject that make it comprehensible to others". If teachers were to be successful, they would have to confront both issues of content and pedagogy simultaneously, by embodying "the aspects of content most germane to its teachability". This form of practical knowledge entails, among other things:

- Knowledge of how to structure and represent academic content for direct teaching to students
- Knowledge of the common conceptions, misconceptions, and difficulties that students encounter when learning particular content
- Knowledge of the specific teaching strategies that can be used to address students' learning needs in particular classroom circumstances.

PCK is concerned with the representation and formulation of concepts, pedagogical techniques, and knowledge of what makes concepts difficult or easy to learn, knowledge of students' prior knowledge and theories of epistemology. It also includes what the students bring to the learning situation that might be either facilitative or dysfunctional for the particular learning task at hand. This acknowledges students' strategies, prior conceptions; misconceptions about a particular domain and potential misapplications of prior knowledge.

Techno Pedagogic Content Knowledge

Teaching with technology is complicated further considering the challenges newer technologies present to teachers. Newer digital technologies present new challenges to teachers who are struggling to use more technology in their teaching. Teachers often have inadequate experience with using digital technologies for teaching and learning. At the heart of good teaching with technology are three core components: content, pedagogy, and technology, plus the relationships among and between them. The idea of PCK was first described by Lee Shulman in 1986 and TPACK builds on those core ideas through the inclusion of technology. Punya Mishra and Mathew J. Koehler (2009) Professors at Michigan State University found the absence of sufficient theory to explain or guide technology integration in teaching and have done extensive work in constructing the TPACK framework.

The TPACK Framework

The TPACK framework for education and teaching is formed around the idea that, according to Mishra and Koehler, there is no singular 'best' way to integrate technology into the classroom; integration should be done reflexively and creatively to fit within the specific subject matter being taught and the context of the learning, making technology integration a challenging, though malleable, task. An understanding of the three key components to teaching, pedagogy, content, and technology, as well as the educators' knowledge of these components, will allow teachers to best recognize where technological advances may be made within their respective classrooms.

These three knowledge bases (content, pedagogy, and technology) form the core of the technology, pedagogy, and content knowledge (TPACK) framework. Also, of importance is how and where the teachers' areas of knowledge (Technological Knowledge, Pedagogical Knowledge, and Content Knowledge) interact and intersect with one another, within the context of the classroom. Understanding these dynamics will allow for more flexibility and preparedness in various subjects and class settings, to appropriately and effectively bring technology forward for students. At the heart of the TPACK framework, is the complex interplay of three primary forms of knowledge: Content (CK), Pedagogy (PK), and Technology (TK). The TPACK approach goes beyond seeing these three knowledge bases in isolation. The interactions between and among the three components, playing out differently across diverse contexts, account for the wide variations seen in the extent and quality of educational technology integration. Equally important to the model are the interactions between and among these bodies of knowledge, represented as PCK (pedagogical content knowledge), TCK (technological content knowledge), TPK (technological pedagogical knowledge), and TPACK. Technological Pedagogical Content Knowledge (TPACK) attempts to identify the nature of knowledge required by teachers for technology integration in their teaching, while addressing the complex, multifaceted and situated nature of teacher knowledge.

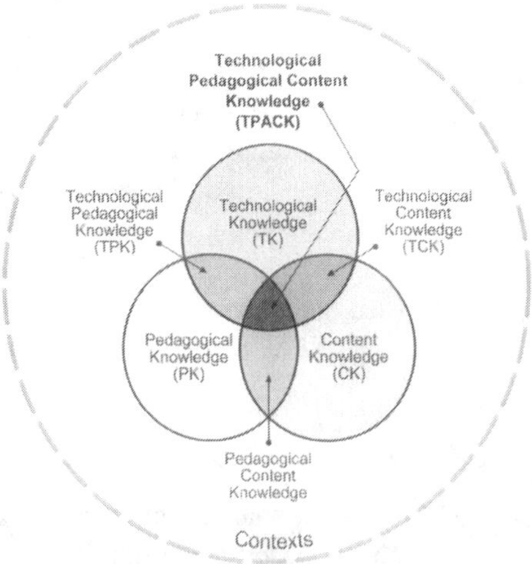

Figure 4.1 The TPACK framework and its knowledge components

Content Knowledge (CK)

CK refers to the teacher's knowledge about the subject matter to be learned or taught. This includes the knowledge about scientific terms, facts, concepts, laws, principles, hypotheses, theories, ideas as well as established practices and approaches towards developing such knowledge. In short, CK represents the subject competency of the teacher.

Pedagogical Knowledge (PK)

Pedagogical knowledge is the set of skills that teachers must develop in order to manage and organize teaching and learning activities for intended learning outcomes. It is the teacher's deeper knowledge about the processes/practices and methods/techniques of teaching and learning. This knowledge involves, understanding how students learn, understanding of classroom management activities, the role of student motivation, lesson planning, proper use of improvised learning aids for knowledge construction and assessment of learning. In short PK refers to the conducive way of planning, organizing and executing the teaching learning process so as to ensure maximum output.

Technological Knowledge (TK)

This goes beyond traditional notions of computer literacy to require that persons understand information technology broadly enough to apply it productively at work and in their everyday lives, to recognize when information technology can assist or impede the achievement of a goal, and to continually adapt to changes in information technology. Acquiring TK in this manner enables a person to accomplish a variety of different tasks using information technology and to develop different ways of accomplishing a given task. TK includes an understanding of how to use computer software and hardware, presentation tools such as document presenters and projects, and other technologies used in educational contexts. The overlapping knowledge components of the TPACK framework are discussed in detail as below:

PEDAGOGICAL CONTENT KNOWLEDGE (PCK)

Forming the basis for traditional teaching contexts, and following Shulman's original research and observations, the intersection of pedagogy and content knowledge results in the transformation of subject matter through educators' teaching styles, abilities, and understanding. By utilizing their pedagogical training and experiences, teachers are able to adapt various materials, subjects, and educational resources to suit their students' needs. Pedagogical content knowledge is knowledge about how to combine pedagogy and content effectively. This is knowledge about how to make a subject understandable to learners. PCK includes knowledge of what makes a subject difficult or easy to learn, as well as knowledge of common misconceptions and likely preconceptions students bring with them to the classroom. PCK refers to the knowledge of understanding the unique interplay between content and pedagogy. The nature of the subject/topic, psychology of the learner, psychology of learning etc. are the important factors that determine the appropriate selection of the methods/techniques for teaching. (e.g.; art, drama, puppetry, role play, nature rambling, field trips, laboratory method, project method etc.). The teacher interprets the subject matter (CK- facts, concepts, principles etc.), finds multiple ways to represent it (method), and adopts most suitable instructional materials (learning aids), based on students' prior knowledge. This promotes fruitful learning by interlinking pedagogy, assessment and curriculum.

Technological Content Knowledge (TCK)

Mishra and Koehler noted the distinct relationship between subject matter and the rise of technology, with technological advances affecting a wide range of fields, including history, physics, and medicine. In the digital age, information is presented in new and dynamic ways through a variety of sources, which must be properly understood by educators prior to their teaching. Teachers must, the researcher's state, do more than 'master' their particular subject matter, and be able to reflect on and comprehend how technology affects representations of topics at hand. Ultimately, while technology can alter the form of content and the methods of receiving and processing it, the inverse is true; content dictates the technology being used, and not all technologies will be appropriate or sufficient enough for the subjects covered within a particular classroom. Technological content knowledge refers to knowledge about how technology may be used to provide new ways of teaching content. For example, digital animation makes it possible for students to conceptualize how electrons are shared between atoms when chemical compounds are formed. TCK describes knowledge of the reciprocal relationship between technology and content. An understanding of the manner in which technology and content influences one another. Teachers must have deep understanding of the manner in which the subject matter can be changed by the application of particular technologies. Teacher should be aware of the innovative technologies available in the global market for the effective transaction of the subject matter. E.g.: Edubuntu, Virtual Labs, Virtual field trips, e-brary, educational software like Kalzium, Dynamic periodic table, Celestia, Rasmol, PhET etc.

Technological Pedagogical Knowledge (TPK)

Having both strong technological knowledge and pedagogical knowledge, educators can understand how technologies will affect both learning and teaching in the classroom. This includes both the positives of technology's integration in the classroom, such as replacing the immobile whiteboard with projectors to enhance teaching presence and practices, as well as the negatives or limitations of technology, including the rigid business-oriented structure of particular software and the potential pitfalls and distractions of allowing students access to social networking. This overlapping of knowledge must be met with creativity and flexibility to ensure the appropriate technology is used not for its own sake, but for the purposes of furthering student learning.

TPK identifies the reciprocal relationship between technology and pedagogy. An understanding of how teaching and learning can change when technologies are used in particular ways. This includes knowing technological tools for appropriate pedagogical designs and strategies. Technological pedagogical knowledge makes it possible to understand what technology can do for certain pedagogic goals, and for teachers to select the most appropriate tool based on its appropriateness for the specific pedagogical approach. For example, collaborative writing can take place with Google Docs or Google Hangouts instead of face-to-face meetings, extending collaborative activities over distances. The advent of online learning is an outcome of techno-pedagogical knowledge. Incorporating technological knowledge in pedagogical designs and strategies. LMS, MOOCs, MOODLE etc. are best examples.

TECHNOLOGICAL PEDAGOGICAL CONTENT KNOWLEDGE

The pinnacle of the TPACK framework, the intersection of technological, pedagogical, and content knowledge provides teachers with an understanding of how technology affects both pedagogies and subject matter, and how technology integration in the classroom may best be used to further student learning while developing new areas and outlets for students' own knowledge. This incorporation of all three areas of knowledge is radically different from each one individually, but provides teachers at this intersection of the framework with the ability to adapt to a variety of educational settings and contexts. It includes an understanding of the complexity of relationships between students, teachers, content, practices and technologies.

Things are rarely that simple, particularly when newer technologies are employed. The introduction of the Internet, for example – particularly the rise of online learning – is an example of the arrival of a technology that forced educators to think about core pedagogical issues, such as how to represent content on the Web and how to connect students with subject matter and with one another (Peruski & Mishra, 2004). Teaching with technology is a difficult thing to do well. The TPACK framework suggests that content, pedagogy, technology, and teaching/learning contexts have roles to play individually and together. Teaching successfully with technology requires continually creating, maintaining, and re-establishing a dynamic equilibrium among all components. TPACK focus upon how technology can be uniquely crafted to meet pedagogical needs to teach certain content in specific contexts so as to ensure fruitful learning. TPACK is used for effective learning;

- As a knowledge for the representation of concepts using technologies.
- As a knowledge about pedagogical techniques that use technologies in constructive way to teach the content.
- As a knowledge of how technology makes concepts difficult or easy to learn and how technology can help to redress some of the problems that learners' face.
- As a knowledge of students' prior knowledge and theories of epistemology and knowledge of how technologies can be used to build on existing knowledge to develop new epistemology or strengthen old ones.

The outer-dotted circle labelled "contexts" emphasizes the realization that technology, pedagogy, and content do not exist in a vacuum, but rather, are initiated in specific learning and teaching contexts. For instance, consider two different classrooms - one where each and every learner has a laptop or a mobile device with access to the Internet and another, which is equipped with just one desktop machine at the front of the class. Clearly the kinds of instructional moves the teacher has to come up with would be very different in these two contexts. Similarly, school and national policies that allow or block certain websites (such as Face book or YouTube) change how teachers can structure their lessons and activities. Teaching with technology is difficult to do well. The TPACK framework suggests that content, pedagogy, technology, and teaching/learning contexts have roles to play individually and together. Teaching successfully with technology requires continually creating, maintaining, and re-establishing a dynamic equilibrium among all components.

Table 4.1: Definition and examples of TPACK Dimensions

TPACK Dimensions	Definition	Example
TK	Knowledge about how to use ICT hardware and software and associated peripherals	Knowledge about how to use hardware devices / Web 2.0 tools (e.g., TV, Radio, LCD, Computer / Blogs, Wiki, WhatsApp Facebook)
PK	Knowledge about the students' learning, instructional methods, different educational theories, and learning assessment to teach a subject matter without references towards content	Knowledge about how to use problem-based learning (PBL)/ collaborative learning in teaching

CK	Knowledge of the subject matter without consideration about teaching the subject matter	Knowledge about Science or Mathematics or Social Science or Language subjects
PCK	Knowledge of representing content knowledge and adopting pedagogical strategies to make the specific content/ topic more understandable for the learners	Knowledge of using analogies to teach electricity
TPK	Knowledge of the existence and specifications of various technologies to enable teaching approaches without reference towards subject matter	The notion of WebQuest, using ICT as cognitive tools, computer supported collaborative learning
TCK	Knowledge about how to use technology to represent/research and create the content in different ways without consideration about teaching	Knowledge about online dictionary, SPSS, subject specific ICT tools e.g. Geometer's Sketchpad, topic specific simulation
TPACK	Knowledge of using various technologies to teach and/represent and/ facilitate knowledge creation of specific subject content	Knowledge about how to use Wiki as a communication tool to enhance collaborative learning in social science

Implications of the TPACK Framework

- Educators should keep the TPACK framework in mind whenever they are going to use technology in their classroom, as it provides the appropriate context and foundation for utilizing technology alongside pedagogies and content, simultaneously or separately, depending on the present setting.
- The TPACK framework seeks to assist the development of better techniques for discovering and describing how technology-related professional knowledge is implemented and instantiated in practice.
- By better describing the types of knowledge teachers need (in the form of content, pedagogy, technology, contexts and their interactions), educators are in a better position to understand the variance in levels of technology integration occurring.
- TPACK framework offers several possibilities for promoting research in teacher education, teacher professional development, and teachers' use of technology.
- The allocation of a teacher's current placement within the TPACK framework is dependent upon how well he or she understands those three components of the classroom in relation to one another, and where there may be areas in need of improvement.
- Moreover, it allows teachers, researchers, and teacher educators to

move beyond oversimplified approaches that treat technology as an "add-on" instead to focus again, and in a more ecological way, upon the connections among technology, content, and pedagogy as they play out in classroom contexts.

- Regardless of the technology available to teachers, the TPACK model conforms to all settings and contexts. This allows its incorporation into schools with advanced technological access, such as personal laptops or tablets for students, and institutions where technology is more limited.
- All curriculums can be paired with the TPACK framework, as teachers develop their understanding of technology's connection to the specifics of both their classroom and teaching practice. The use of this model, however, will differ between teachers and schools, serving as a malleable outline through which educators may better combine technology and education.
- Teachers should, hypothetically, be constantly aware of the relationship between pedagogical practices and the content being taught, as noted above this forms the basis for instructional design and teaching. Educators who are familiar with technology may then move further throughout the TPACK model, increasing their flexibility in various educational situations requiring the inclusion of technology into the classroom. Ultimately, teachers must not insert technology into their curriculums without planning and preparatory work to determine how the technology will fit into their respective class structure.
- If the teachers need to adequately integrate technology across different subject areas in the school curriculum, they need to demonstrate a firm mastery of TPACK. TPACK is an amalgamation of teachers' knowledge of curriculum content, general pedagogies, technologies, and contextual factors that influence learning in the specific context. One approach through which teachers can acquire skills to effectively adopt technology in the classroom is by working through different stages of professional development to blend technology, content and pedagogy

Ways and means to link Technology to Pedagogic Content Knowledge

We live in an era characterized by the rapid development of technology. Computer technology and digital media have fundamentally transformed all aspects of our lives, including education. Use of technology can help to improve and enhance the acquisition of knowledge and skills and to gain competencies to function in a 21st society and workforce. Technology is ubiquitous, touching almost every part of our lives, our communities, our homes. Properly used, technology will help students acquire the skills they need to survive in a complex, highly technological knowledge-based economy. Science teaching is such a complex, dynamic profession that it is difficult for a teacher to stay up-to- date. For a teacher to grow professionally and become better as a teacher of science, a special, continuous effort is required (Showalter, 1984, p. 21). To better prepare students for the science and technology of the 21st century, the current science education reforms ask science teachers to integrate technology and inquiry- based teaching into their instruction (American Association for the Advancement of Science, 1993; National Research Council [NRC], 1996, 2000).

Technology also changes the way teachers teach, offering educators effective ways to reach different types of learners and assess student understanding through multiple means. It also enhances the relationship between teacher and student. When technology is effectively integrated into subject areas, teachers grow into roles of adviser, content expert, and coach. Technology helps make teaching and learning more meaningful and fun. Learning with technology has become essential in today's schools. Developing students' knowledge and skills related to ICT in the school years provides an important grounding for later in life. It also provides equity of opportunity, regardless of background. Technology is a critical component in designing instruction for students in the digital age. Depending on the demographics of our students, we might have some students who are complete digital natives, or at least more fluent in the use of technology than ourselves. Whatever our own or our students' level of expertise, technology skills are key to both delivering and learning new information. This is why teachers must find ways to integrate these skills into our science curricula. Mobile tablet devices and smart phones provide users with continuous and ubiquitous access to the Internet with the emphasis being on finding information efficiently and ensuring constant social presence with other people (Pachler, Bachmair, & Cook, 2011Pachler, Norbert; Bachmair, Benand Cook, John. (2011).

"Students in today's Web-dominated environment need to learn how to prioritize and manage a dizzying array of information coming at them through Web sites and e-mails, how to think critically about what they find, and how to use multiple media to communicate well, among other skills" (Vadero, 2007, p. 32). "Educators must prepare for a technology-rich future and keep up with change by adopting effective strategies that infuse lessons with appropriate technologies." (North Central Regional Education Laboratory NCREL, 2005, paragraph 1).

The Potential Technology Offers

Because technology is both highly customizable and intrinsically motivating to students, it is particularly well-suited to expand the learning experience. Technology can:

- Help diagnose and address individual needs: Technology can equip teachers to assess an individual student's strengths and needs.
- Equip students with skills essential for work and life in a 21st century global society: Using technology for purposes, such as writing, research and analysis, rather than simply drills and practice can enhance student competencies that surpass the knowledge and skills typically measured in achievement tests. These competencies include problem solving, creativity, collaboration, data management and communication.
- Provide an active experience for students: Technology can equip students to independently organize their learning process. So, instead of being passive recipients of information, students using technology become active users.
- Technology transfers some responsibility for learning to students: Through online learning (which provides increased access to course content, more scheduling flexibility, and better access to alternative education choices) and alternative media (such as digital games and project- based learning), students have the flexibility to direct their individual progress.

WAYS AND MEANS TO LINK TECHNOLOGY TO PEDAGOGICAL CONTENT KNOWLEDGE (PCK)

- **Multimedia Approach**: This method is a blend of text, audio, animation, video, still images or interactivity content forms to teach diverse difficult to understand concepts in science. The educator can convey vast information using advanced media, devices and techniques, and involve a wide range of activities to provide a meaningful learning experience.
- **Video clips:** This teaching technique makes use of instructional video clips available online or in libraries to show and teach a new concept. The animation of a process or evolution can be conveyed better with videos. It can also be videos of demonstration of an

idea or an application side of a theory or an interview with a scientist, tutorial by a subject expert and more.

- **Power Point Presentations:** Instead of the conventional talk and chalk methods, teachers now include power point presentations in their classroom sessions to make it more interesting. They connect the computers to projectors to address a larger classroom and include interesting slides with diagrams and flow charts to make the teaching more interactive.
- **Science movies:** Teachers take initiatives to take them for science movies in theatres or in school halls that clearly showcase the application side of scientific concepts. More than just entertaining them, many science movies captivate their attention and illustrate diverse science concepts in the real world. Science and nature-focused documentaries is one of the best ways to introduce science to kids than spoon feeding them with text book content.
- **Science games:** Kids always love to play and that is why smart teachers introduce science to them with interesting games. They can learn more about science and technology with fun. A wide range of games are available online that showcase the concepts of animals, plants, space, forces, light, sounds, magnets, electricity, weather and gases. There are games with multiple levels and passing each level teaches a new concept and illustrates scientific experiments.
- **Educational apps for Science:** One of the great aspects of having tablets, laptops, and smart phones in the classroom is the availability educational apps. With these apps, students can individually learn, practice, study, and have fun with different subjects and concepts. A number of apps are available online for elementary, middle school and high school students as well as for those undergoing advanced studies. Today's kids are tech savvies and they love to learn science using their gadgets. The advanced mobile apps built with innovative features in fact turn students into scientists. This lets them hold science in their hands and explore it with just a few taps. The popular apps in the category include Human Body, Cozmic Zoom, Earth Primer, Video Science, Science360, NASA GLOBE Observer, Periodic table, curiosity, Scratch, Science 360, Khan Academy, The Chemical Touch, Physics Calculator and a lot more.
- **Flipped Classroom:** Flipped classroom is an instructional strategy and a type of blended learning that reverses the traditional

learning environment by delivering instructional content, often online, outside of the classroom. In this innovative teaching technique, students are asked to go through video instructions or tutorials in the initial stage, i.e. digital learning. The second stage will be in classrooms where they involve in challenging tasks and assignments based on the information gathered through video assets. This flipped learning frees up class time for activities such as hands-on labs, guided practice or online simulations. In a flipped classroom, students watch online lectures, collaborate in online discussions, or carry out research at home and engage in concepts in the classroom with the guidance of a mentor.

- **Digital Books:** Laptop computers, tablet, smart phone and e-Readers, such as the Kindle and the iPad, allow students to access digital textbooks and library books anytime and anywhere. Further, as more and more books are transferred to digital platforms, they are re-designed to include more multimedia content to complement the text. Multimedia-enhanced digital books provide accessible content for learners who might be less comfortable with text-heavy materials. In addition, eBooks allow readers to annotate content and then share and archive their comments online. Websites such as *CAST's UDL book builder* allow teachers and students to create their own digital books, which can be customized to meet the needs of individual readers. Digital books are becoming more and more popular as it attempts to cut down the use of paper, as well as cut publishing costs, but have not yet been used widely in school settings (Johnson, Levine, Smith, & Stone, 2010).
- **Cloud Computing:** Cloud computing refers to digital programmes and storage that live in networked computers (rather than a local server), and that can be accessed anywhere using personal computers or mobile devices. Many applications that people use every day, such as Gmail or Google Docs, are cloud applications. Cloud computing means that instead of all the computer hardware and software you're using, sitting on your desktop, it's provided for you as a service by another company and accessed over the Internet, usually in a completely seamless way. Exactly where the hardware and software are located and how it all works doesn't matter to you, the user - it's just somewhere up in the nebulous "cloud" that the Internet represents. Cloud computing can bring otherwise out of reach resources into classrooms and into students' hands. For example, *iLab Central* makes authentic experimental

laboratories accessible for students to use and access through the Internet. And because they live on the network, applications in the cloud make it easy to share documents, collaboratively edit, and effectively manage versions, both locally and at a distance.

- **Mobile Devices:** Newly released, large screen mobile devices, or tablets, such as the Apple iPad, Google Tablet, and HP Slate, along with cell phones, iPods, and mp3 players that students are already using, offer a variety of educational affordances. In addition to mobile capabilities that might be used in the classroom such as Twitter to facilitate in class discussions, poll anywhere (pollanywhere.com) to turn a mobile device into an automated response system, or Internet browsing - this new generation of mobile devices can store digital textbooks and library books for students to access anywhere and at any time, run augmented reality programs, and allow students to more easily take notes and share digital resources (Johnson et al., 2010).
- **Augmented Reality:** Augmented reality (AR) is emerging as a popular technology for learning. It involves the use of smart phones or GPS equipped devices to explore real world spaces, such as historical sites, artifacts in a museum, or different trees in a local park, while receiving text, video, images, or other input that are associated with their location. The origin of the word augmented is augment, which means to add or enhance something. In the case of Augmented Reality (also called AR), graphics, sounds, and touch feedback are added into our natural world to create an enhanced user experience. AR lends itself well to students working in teams and solving problems in a real-world environment. As teams of students explore a location, they are provided with different clues in a jigsaw-puzzle style in order to promote collaboration and critical thinking skills necessary to problems solve in a group setting (Lemke, Coughlin, & Reifsneider, 2009). Research has shown that AR experiences can successfully engage students in scientific argumentation and collaborative investigation not often achieved through typical classroom activities (Johnson et al., 2010). Unlike virtual reality, which creates a totally artificial environment, augmented reality uses the existing environment and overlays new information on top of it.
- **Gesture - Based Computing:** Gestures can originate from any bodily motion or state but commonly originate from the face or hand. Current focuses in the field include emotion recognition

from face and hand gesture recognition. Users can use simple gestures to control or interact with devices without physically touching them. Human-computer interactions are moving away from the standard keyboard and mouse, and towards more intuitive gesture-based communication systems that adapt to, or are even designed for interpreting natural human movements. Gesture recognition enables humans to communicate with the machine (HMI) and interact naturally without any mechanical devices. Using the concept of gesture recognition, it is possible to point a finger at the computer screen so that the cursor will move accordingly. This could make conventional input devices such as mouse, keyboards and even touch-screens redundant. For example, the iPhone responds to the gliding of fingers across its screen, as well as the tilting and shaking of the device itself. Larger displays allow multiple users to collaborate on the computer at one time. One such display, the *Microsoft Surface*, has been installed into school study areas, with schools reporting that students appear to enjoy using them to collaborate on projects. Researchers and designers believe that the move away from keyboards and mice to gesture-based controls will provide opportunities for kinaesthetic learning. Learners move through learning activities using their whole bodies, and receive haptic feedback (touch or motion based) letting them know how well they are doing (Johnson et al., 2010).

Online Learning

Typically, communication in online learning environments is broken down into either synchronous or asynchronous. Often, online courses will use a combination of asynchronous and synchronous communication tools.

Synchronous Instruction refers to online teaching and learning that happens in real time via the Internet. Synchronous instruction methods afford life interactions between teachers and students, and student with each other, similar to face-to-face interactions. For example, using a synchronous communication tool, a teacher might deliver a lecture or facilitate a class discussion, or share online media or data. Synchronous communication tools also allow teachers to deliver immediate feedback to students in an online environment (Barbour & Reeves, 2009; Watson, 2009). There are a variety of synchronous communication tools, including: live chat, audio and video conferencing, shared screens, and virtual hand-raising. Students can interject questions in order to request clarify or ask for more in-depth coverage of relevant topics. Virtual hand-raising makes it possible to adjust the pace and content of a class to match the skills and goals of the students.

Asynchronous instruction refers to online teaching and learning that utilizes Internet-based, time- delayed communication tools. Typically, student's login to a course website that contains a course syllabus, course calendar, assignments, content resources, and communication tools such as message boards and file sharing utilities. Based on the syllabus and calendar, the student will use the available online resources, as well as, perhaps, supplementary texts and other media to complete weekly assignments, which he or she will hand into the teacher through the Course Management System. Assignments may vary and include written reports, posting on the class message board twice a week, or posting a weekly synopsis of course-relevant news articles, for example. Teachers provide feedback about written work to individual students, and monitor activity on the message boards to ensure that students are participating in group discussions (Barbour & Reeves, 2009; Watson, 2009). One of the benefits of asynchronous teaching and learning is that it allows students to work at their own pace to a greater degree. For instance, a student who is struggling with the course material can take more time to work through a problem set or a difficult assignment, while a more advanced student can complete assignments at a faster pace and move ahead in the syllabus without having to wait for the rest of the class. Asynchronous communication tools include e-mail, threaded discussion, news groups, bulletin boards, and file attachments.

Blended Learning

Blended learning opportunities incorporate both face-to-face and online learning opportunities. The degree to which online learning takes place, and the way it is integrated into the curriculum, can vary across schools. The strategy of blending online learning with school-based instruction is often utilized to accommodate students' diverse learning styles and to enable them to work before or after school in ways that are not possible with full-time conventional classroom instruction. Online learning has the potential to improve educational productivity by accelerating the rate of learning, taking advantage of learning time outside of school hours, reducing the cost of instructional materials, and better utilizing teacher time. These strategies can be particularly useful in rural areas where blended or online learning can help teachers and students in remote areas overcome distance.

Open Educational Resources (OER)

Open educational resources are teaching, learning, and research resources that reside in the public domain and are freely available to anyone over the Web. They are an important element of an infrastructure for learning and range from podcasts to digital libraries to textbooks and games. The term can include textbooks, course readings, and other learning content; simulations, games, and other learning applications; syllabi, quizzes, and assessment tools; and virtually any other material that can be used for educational purposes. OER typically refers to electronic resources, including those in multimedia formats. It is critical to ensure that open educational resources meet standards of quality, integrity, and accuracy as with any other educational resource and that they are accessible to students with disabilities.

Digital Resources

Schools can use digital resources in a variety of ways to support teaching and learning. Electronic grade books, digital portfolios, digital notebooks, learning games, and real-time feedback on teacher and student performance, are a few ways that technology can be utilized to power learning. Technology can also help students' process information and make sense of their topics. Start by identifying the different digital tools students can use to organize information. For example, there are tools that allow students to create and organize virtual note cards. Web-based programs also allow students to create graphic organizers and map out all of the information they have gathered for their projects. Students can also use digital notebooks, or digital binders, to organize information, which may be available for free, and are appropriate for students at higher level. As a digital tool, it allows students to collaborate more easily in team-based investigations by creating and sharing their notebooks with other members. Digital notebooks also allow team members to consolidate and organize information gathered through research or lab investigations. These options easily allow you to integrate other tools, such as those used to create digital graphs and graphics. If your students don't have access to the Internet outside of class, you have to decide to which degree you will incorporate digital tools to process the information they have collected. If your classroom demographics favour students with access to the Internet access both inside and out of the classroom, technology can open the door to a new level of collaboration.

Virtual Laboratory Environments

The Virtual Laboratory is an interactive environment for creating and conducting simulated experiments, a playground for experimentation.

WebQuests

WebQuests were created as a learning activity not long after the initial development of the worldwide web. A WebQuest is an inquiry-based activity that embeds the use of a variety of learning resources – with most being digital learning resources available on the internet. The inquiry activity may take the form of tasks such as a problem to be solved, a position to be taken, a product to be designed or a work to be created. Teachers can create their own WebQuests that address curriculum outcomes and draw upon resources they have identified and evaluated. Or teachers can choose to use a WebQuest that someone else has created. WebQuests have a consistent structure:

- *Introduction:* Orients students to the activity
- *Task:* Clearly and concisely describes the outcome of the learning activity
- *Process:* Lists the steps learners will take to accomplish the task and the digital, web-based and other learning resources that support learners in this process
- *Evaluation:* Provides a rubric to indicate how learners' performance will be assessed
- *Conclusions:* Summarizes what students will have covered and learned.

Blogging

Blogs (a short form of the weblog) are personal journal websites on which a user can type an entry, add images, video and links to other websites. Readers of a blog usually can post comments. For primary school students, the use of blogs has been found to be an engaging and effective way to promote writing skills (Richardson, 2006), particularly when student peers provide feedback to the blog's writer (Chen et al., 2011). It is exactly this feedback and sharing mechanism that makes the blog different to the traditional journal. In the notebook-and-pencil version, the contents of the journal are private to the student, apart from the teacher and whomever the student decides to share the journal with. With the blog, access can be provided to the teacher, the class, the student's parents and the world.

GOOGLE APPS FOR EDUCATION (GAFE)

Google Apps for Education (GAFE) is a widely used service offered by Google. In addition to e- mail, Google offers its suite of productivity tools including Docs, Sheets, and Slides and unlimited storage in its cloud-based service known as Google Drive. Google apps are Collaborative, Customizable, Free, Secure, without ads, Usable on any device, provides a simple tool for groups to collaborate on developing web pages or whole websites. Google is more than a search engine-it offers many tools that give people the opportunity to work virtually from anywhere, with anyone, at any time they choose. And these tools are available to teachers and students for free. Google Apps is a student-centred tool and can help shift a classroom toward a more student-centred environment. Google Apps is a wonderful free resource for educators to create engaging lessons, activities, and assessments. Google Apps provides users with the awesome opportunity of collaboration via the web.

- **Google Drive:** Google Drive is an online storage service.
- **Google Forms:** Google forms are free e tool, easy to use, variety of templates to create, can be used on web sites, via e-mail and webinars. It is a Google app that can deliver data for decision making. This tool is ideal for gathering data from students and the community as well as delivering online assessments to students.
- **Google Docs:** Google Docs, an online word processing application, is a promising tool for collaborative learning.
- **Google Calendar:** Google calendars are web-based calendar that lets users make appointments, scheduled meetings, set due dates, and share the information with others in a live online calendar. Teachers can create class calendars and share them with the specific students or with groups of contacts organized by class period, making it easy to share materials with large number of students.
- **Google Presentation:** Google presentations are a powerful presentation maker that is part of Google apps for education. Slide transitions, animations, inserting images, and video are all part of Google presentations.
- **Google Spreadsheets:** Google spreadsheets are a fully integrated spreadsheet programme that brings data alive in Google apps for education.
- **Google+:** Google+ was launched in 2011 and may be seen as Google's social networking alternative to Facebook.
- **Google Hangouts:** Google Hangouts is a video chat and an instant messaging platform established by Google and launched in 2013. Google Hangouts is similar to Skype, as it provides a free audio/ video conference along with a text chat capability.

- **YouTube:** YouTube is a popular video sharing website where users can upload, view, and share video clips. YouTube has become an enormously popular form of web 2.0 new media.

Google Classroom

As the classroom is becoming more and more paperless, teachers have to start finding solutions to hand out assignments, manage their classroom, and communicate with students, and so on. A rapidly growing number of teachers are finding their way to Google Classroom. Google Classroom is a free application designed by Google. Google Classroom helps teachers and students to communicate and can be used to organize and manage assignments, to go paperless, for collaboration between students and between teachers, and so on. It is a learning management system that allows you to digitally create and manage assignments as well as to provide feedback to your students. Google Classroom works particularly with Google Apps for Education, a suite of productivity tools (Drive, Docs, Gmail, etc.) that you may already use in your school. Google Apps for Education allows teachers to bring that environment into the classroom and make students' educational experiences more relevant and better mirror their day-to-day lives. Classroom is a free service for schools, and anyone with a personal Google account. Classroom makes it easy for learners and instructors to connect - inside and outside of schools. Classroom saves time and paper, and makes it easy to create classes, distribute assignments, communicate, and stay organized.

Ways to Integrate Google Apps in the Classroom

The following are the some of the strategies of integrating Google apps in the classroom.

- **Test/Exam** - Teachers can use Google Form to create test with multiple choices or texts-based questions with a class separately or embed entire test/exam on Google Sites and publish the same for viewers within class.
- **Time Table/ Events** - Teachers can use Google Calendar and add all the classes or time table or upcoming events and then it can be either shared with selective users or kept public for class to subscribe. (Secondary Calendar with Public Access)
- **Discussion** - Google Groups can be used to create a group mail id with all students as its members. Collaborative inbox within Google groups works wonder to track all previous and recent discussions in that forum.

- **Documentation** - Google Docs is very interactive documentation app with lots of new innovative features such as research, add-on, embed gadgets and more. End user can create documents, store it online in drive and share with others with multiple choice of access (view, edit or only comment).
- **Reports/Presentation** - Google Sheet and Slides are very wonderful apps and one of the most used apps today. Sheets can be used for more calculation-oriented information and slides for presentations and animations. Like Docs, they also have sharing options and access control.
- **Tutorials/Webinar** - Google Hangout can be used by end-users or teachers for taking online classes, recording and saving them in class-specific YouTube channel. Tutorials/Webinar is best way for student to learn and interact.
- **Feedback** - Google Forms can be created to take feedback or survey from parents or students as per the requirement. Google forms lets you create a questionnaire using text based or multiple-choice questions and then it can be shared with others.
- **Control** - Google Apps admin can control entire applications, access and sharing settings for their institute. This gives powerful control in the hands of admin to manage and monitor the use of the application.
- **Collaboration** - Multiple users can-do real-time document editing at the same time and can even start instant chat within document with colleagues. This kind of innovative team/class collaboration makes it very powerful application.
- **Communication** - End users can now communicate with colleagues and others via email or text/audio/video chat. Multiple Party web conference via Google Hangout can be done.

Benefits of Google Apps

- Easy to set up – Teachers can add students directly or share a code with their class to join. It takes just minutes to set up.
- Saves time – The simple, paperless assignment workflow allows teachers to create, review and mark assignments quickly, all in one place.
- Improves organization – Students can see all of their assignments on an assignments page, and all class materials (e.g., documents, photos, and videos) are automatically filed into folders in Google Drive.

- Enhances communication – Classroom allows teachers to send announcements and start class discussions instantly. Students can share resources with each other or provide answers to questions on the stream.
- Affordable and secure - Students can work on and turn in assignments, even from their smart phones. And teachers can grade them online – no red pens needed. That's a valuable time-saver. Teachers also can email reminders and announcements directly to parents, decreasing the likelihood that important permission slips get lost in backpacks on the way home.

But the app's greatest potential to change how education works lies in how it allows teachers and students to collaborate. Teachers can customize assignments based on students' needs and interests. Multiple students can work on an assignment at once, and teachers can watch remotely as students collaborate – making them more like guides for where to find information than the ultimate sources of it.

WEB RESOURCES FOR EFFECTIVE LEARNING, TEACHING AND EVALUATION

E-Books

http://www.gutenberg.org/

https://www.free-ebooks.net/

http://www.bookrix.com/

http://www.obooko.com/

http://www.e-booksdirectory.com/

http://www.getfreeebooks.com/

http://www.freebooks.com/ebooks/

http://www.forgottenbooks.com/

http://bookboon.com/

http://www.openculture.com/

Audio Books

http://www.learnoutloud.com/

http://www.openculture.com/

https://librivox.org/

http://www.loyalbooks.com/

http://www.readingfanatic.com/

http://freeclassicaudiobooks.com/

http://www.audiobooksforfree.com/

http://www.audiobooks.org/

http://www.audiobooks.com/

http://www.librophile.com/

Blogs

http://www.bloggeries.com/

http://www.bloglisting.net/

http://globeofblogs.com/

http://www.blogarama.com/

http://www.bloggingfusion.com/

http://portal.eatonweb.com/

For Creating Blogs

www.blogspot.com

www.wordpress.com

Podcasts

http://podcasts.ox.ac.uk/

http://www.bbc.co.uk/podcasts

http://www.npr.org/podcasts/

http://loc.gov/podcasts/

http://www.ipodder.org/

Wikis

http://educationalwikis.wikispaces.com/

http://wikieducator.org/

http://wikieducator.org/India

http://en.wikibooks.org/

Videos / Video Lessons / E-Content for Learning

http://www.learnerstv.com/

http://webcast.berkeley.edu/

http://cosmolearning.org/

http://www.world-lecture-project.org/

http://cec.nic.in/

http://nptel.ac.in/

http://epgp.inflibnet.ac.in/

http://www.co-learn.in/

Virtual Labs / Interactive Simulations

http://www.vlab.co.in/

http://aview.in/aview

http://www.pbs.org/wgbh/nova/ancient/explore-ancient-egypt.html

http://micro.magnet.fsu.edu/primer/java/scienceopticsu/powersof10/index.html

Digital Libraries

http://www.loc.gov/

http://library.clark.edu/

http://www.dli.ernet.in/

http://www.loc.gov/education/

MOOCs - Massive Open On-line Courses

https://www.swayam.gov.in

https://www.coursera.org/

https://www.edx.org/

http://www.alison.com

http://ocw.mit.edu/

http://www.open.edu/itunes/

http://nptel.ac.in/cerified_nptel_courses.php

Testing and Evaluation Tools

http://www.easytestmaker.com/

http://www.hotpot.uvic.ca/

http://quizstar.4teachers.org/

In short, the technology ushers in fundamental structural changes that can be integral to achieving significant improvements in productivity. Used to support both teaching and learning, technology infuses classrooms with digital learning tools, such as computers and hand-held devices; expands course offerings, experiences, and learning materials; supports learning 24 hours a day, 07 days a week; builds 21st century skills; increases student engagement and motivation; and accelerates learning. Technology also has the power to transform teaching by ushering in a new model of connected teaching. This model links teachers to their students and to professional content, resources, and systems to help them improve their own instruction and personalize learning. Online learning opportunities and the use of open educational resources and other technologies can increase educational productivity by accelerating the rate of learning; reducing costs associated with instructional materials or program delivery; and better utilizing teacher time.

TEACHER AS A TECHNO PEDAGOGUE

"21st century's teacher should be a techno-pedagogue"

Techno-pedagogy is the art of incorporating technology in designing teaching learning experiences so as to enrich the learning outcome. Technology has changed the way we communicate, socialize and work in ways that would have been unimaginable years ago. Today's children are well equipped with the new technologies and they are called "digital natives". Teachers are "digital immigrants" standing on shifting sands as new technologies appear regularly on the classroom horizon. Ongoing professional learning is essential for teachers to enable them to keep abreast of new and emerging technologies. Professional learning also needs to address the changes in pedagogical practices needed to support the integration of technology into the classroom in such a way that it impacts positively on student learning. To reflect on the rapid changes in the technology, teachers should change their way of teaching by integrating pedagogical knowledge with technological knowledge. Acquiring techno-pedagogical proficiency will make teaching and learning a pleasurable exercise as it would lessen the pressure on the teachers and enable the students to develop deeper domain of knowledge. The education system is now witnessing a paradigm shift from the traditional chalk-and-board teaching methodology to digitizing the pedagogical approach through technical devices. Such a transformation would not only increase the capability of the teachers but also widen the knowledge base of students so as make them competitive in the international arena

Techno-pedagogic Skills/Competencies

- Skill to assess the potential and limits of technologies for learning.
- Skill to carry out a need analysis to introduce technologies in a pedagogical sequence.
- Skill to handle basic tools and applications, and solve simple technical problems.
- Skill to design appropriate tasks.
- Skill to design for intersections within and outside the classroom.
- Skill to invest new and interactive technologies congruence with the nature of the subject.
- Skill to manage time and optimize the integration of technologies.

Role of Teacher as a Techno Pedagogue

In education, teachers facilitate student learning. The objectives of learning are typically accomplished through either an informal or formal approach to learning, including a course of study and lesson plan that teaches skills, knowledge and thinking skills. Different ways to teach are often referred to as pedagogy. When deciding what teaching method to use teachers consider students background knowledge, environment, and their learning goals as well as standardized curricula as determined by the relevant authority. Most of the teachers follow the traditional ways of teaching. But, the increasing use of technology, specifically the rise of the internet over the past decade, has begun to shape the way teachers approach their roles in the classroom. Since teachers can affect how students perceive the course materials, it has been found that teachers who showed enthusiasm to use technology in class integrated with their pedagogical skills can produce a positive learning experience to the students. Therefore, it is important for teachers to have pedagogical skills and technological knowledge along with content knowledge.

In confronting the ways in which technology, content, and pedagogy interact in classroom contexts we see an active role for teachers as designers of their own curriculum. Like all design tasks, teachers are faced with an open-ended and ill-structured problem in the process of crafting their curricula. This requires teacher educators to adopt, identify and select methods to develop technology integration knowledge by starting from already-existing bodies of teacher knowledge in a gradual manner. Teachers should act as a techno pedagogue in this present era of technology revolution. Technological Pedagogical Content Knowledge helps the teachers by giving proper guidance on class room teaching as a techno pedagogue. It is a framework to understand and describe the kinds of knowledge needed by a teacher for effective pedagogical practice in a technology enhanced learning environment. The idea of PCK was first described by Lee Shulman in 1986 and TPACK builds on those core ideas through the inclusion of technology. Punya Mishra and Mathew J. Koehler, Professors at Michigan State University Have done extensive work in constructing the TPACK framework.

Dozens of methods have been proposed for this development of TPACK and they vary in their effectiveness. Among various approaches, an emphasis upon how teachers integrate technology in their practice is more important than the emphasis upon what teachers integrate in their practice. For example, approaches that develop technological knowledge in isolation, where technology literacy is the goal, fail to assist teachers in the development of the educational uses of those tools. Similarly, approaches that develop only pedagogy or content-or even pedagogical content knowledge-do not capture the scope and unique flavour of knowledge needed to effectively teach with technology.

In the TPACK framework, what teachers need to know is characterized by three broad knowledge bases-technology, pedagogy, and content-and the interactions between and among these knowledge bases. In this approach, technology in teaching is characterized as something well beyond isolated knowledge of specific hardware or software. Rather, technology that is introduced into teaching contexts "causes the representation of new concepts and requires developing sensitivity to the dynamic, transactional relationship between all three components". Good teaching with technology, requires a shift in existing pedagogical and content domains.

- The Curriculum Guide and Syllabus for Information Technology in Schools developed by NCERT, India, describes competencies of teachers to achieve the objectives of ICT education at the secondary level; viz.
- Understanding the role of technology in change and the implications of technology-mediated changes for education.
- Creating interest in learning among students through unique utilities like animation, simulation, the Internet, etc.
- Demonstrating a sound understanding of basic IT concepts and operations.
- Planning and designing effective learning environments with necessary technology support.
- Making the best use of technology-enhanced lessons to enrich student learning.
- Adopting assessment strategies to evaluate (a) student competencies in IT skills and (b) student learning in the new environment.
- Using technology to enhance our own creativity and professional practices.
- Demonstrating understanding of social, ethical, legal, and human issues surrounding the use of technology in schools.
- Fashioning a climate of values that encourage questioning, exploration, problem solving, decision-making, and group co-operation.
- Striving for education to emerge from its disciplinary narrowness.
- Identifying useful learning material from various sources.

Technology is a literacy need by the teachers of this era as students are well equipped with modern technologies. Therefore, teachers should act as techno pedagogue by incorporating modern technologies in teaching. Teachers have an inevitable role as a techno pedagogue to improve students' achievement by introducing new gadgets and techniques for learning.

Conclusion

In the ever-evolving landscape of education, the integration of technology has become more than just a trend; it has become a necessity. Chapter 4 has provided an in-depth exploration of Techno Pedagogic Content Knowledge (TPACK) and its significance in modern pedagogy. We began by dissecting the fundamental components of pedagogical knowledge and pedagogical content knowledge, recognizing their pivotal roles in effective teaching and learning. From there, we delved into the TPACK framework, which serves as a guiding light for educators seeking to harmonize pedagogy, content, and technology in their instructional practices. Throughout this chapter, we have explored various strategies and methodologies for linking technology to pedagogical content knowledge. From leveraging Google Apps for Education (GAFE) to harnessing web resources for effective learning, teaching, and evaluation, educators have been equipped with a myriad of tools and techniques to enhance their teaching practices. Furthermore, we have emphasized the critical role of the teacher as a Techno Pedagogue – an educator who not only possesses technological proficiency but also understands how to leverage technology to enhance pedagogical approaches and facilitate deeper understanding of content. As we conclude this chapter, it is evident that the integration of technology into pedagogy is not merely about adopting the latest gadgets or software; it is about transforming teaching and learning experiences to meet the needs of 21st century learners. By embracing Techno Pedagogic Content Knowledge, educators can empower themselves to create dynamic and engaging learning environments that prepare students for success in an increasingly digital world.

Chapter - 5

Curriculum

INTRODUCTION

Chapter 5 delves into the critical aspects of curriculum design and development in education. It begins by exploring the fundamental concepts of curriculum, providing various definitions and establishing its foundational principles. The chapter then examines the relationship between curriculum and syllabus, elucidating how these components work together to shape educational experiences. Curriculum planning is a central focus, highlighting the processes and strategies involved in designing effective curricula to meet the needs of learners. Additionally, the chapter discusses curriculum evaluation, emphasizing the importance of assessing curriculum effectiveness and making necessary adjustments for continuous improvement. Furthermore, it explores the diverse factors that influence curriculum planning, design, and development, including educational philosophies, societal needs, technological advancements, and cultural considerations. By understanding these influences, educators can create relevant and meaningful curricula that facilitate learning and promote student success.

CURRICULUM: MEANING, DEFINITIONS AND FOUNDATIONS

Curriculum is the crux of the whole educational process. Without curriculum, we cannot conceive any educational endeavour. The term curriculum has been derived from a Latin word *Currere* which means a *race course* or *a runway* or *path* on which one runs to reach a goal. In this sense curriculum is the path through which the student has to go forward in order to reach the goal envisaged by education. All these activities and instructional material are covered under a broad concept called curriculum. It is derived from the Latin word 'currere' which means "a course to run".

All the activities going on the school or outside of the school is called curriculum. It is basic to the intellectual, physical, moral and emotional development of the child. A curriculum is the instructional and the educative programme by following which the pupils achieve their goals, ideals and aspirations of life. It is curriculum through which the general aims of a school education receive concrete expression.

Definition of Curriculum:

The term curriculum has been defined by different writers in different ways:

- Cunningham – "Curriculum is a tool in the hands of the artist (teacher) to mould his material (pupils) according to his ideas (aims and objectives) in his studio (school)".
- Morroe – "Curriculum includes all those activities which are utilized by the school to attain the aims of education.
- Curriculum is the totality of experiences that pupils receive through the manifold activities that go in the school, in the classroom, library, laboratory, workshop, playground and in the numerous informal contacts between the teachers and pupils. - *The Secondary Education Commission (1952-1953)*
- Crow and Crow – The curriculum includes all the learners' experience in or outside school that are included in a programme which has been devised to help him developmentally, emotionally, socially, spiritually and morally".
- T.P. Nunn - "The curriculum should be viewed as various forms of activities that are grand expressions of human spirit and that are of the greatest and most permanent significance to the wide world".

Brubacher (1969) referred to curriculum as the ground which pupils and teachers cover in order to reach the goal of education. In other words, it can be regarded as a total experience with which the school deals with educating young people. That is all the experiences both curricular and co-curricular which children pass through to become what is known as an educated person. The concept if Curriculum is dynamic as the changes that occur in society. In its narrow sense, curriculum is viewed merely as a listing of subject to be taught in school. In a broader sense, it refers to the total learning experiences of individuals not only in schools but in society as well. Thus, Curriculum is a comprehensive Plan for an educational/ Training programme/course to offer new/improved manpower to fulfil the rising needs of a dynamic society.

Characteristics of Curriculum

Education is expected to preserve and reform society to the extent that it is a congenial place for individual members to live and work happily. It is supposed to familiarize members with the physical features of the society together with its cultural patterns and practices as well as the effect of these on the individual's behaviour and competence. If education is concerned with the advancement of man and the society in which he finds himself, the curriculum planned to actualize this must possess the following characteristics:

- **Purposeful aims and objectives** – The aims and objectives must be clearly and precisely stated bearing in mind the societal values and the needs of the child. In selecting and stating the aims and objectives, consideration should be given to the learner's age level of development, needs and interests. The economic attainment, religion, philosophy and norms of the people should also be put into consideration.
- **Functionality** – The curriculum planned must be workable, practicable and feasible. For a curriculum planned to be called functional, it must be stated in clear and understandable terms. Practicability is another criterion for judging the functionality of a curriculum. The curriculum should be able to succeed with the human and economic resources available. It should also be acceptable by the people in a given society. It should strike a balance between theory and practice.
- **Flexibility** – The curriculum must be capable of adapting to the needs of the changing learner and the society. Since education is not static, it should change with the society. It must be flexible and be able to create an avenue for growth and development to attain the predetermined objectives. In order words, it should be sufficiently flexible to enhance its adaptation to the changing condition and needs of the people.
- **Relevance** – It should emphasize those aspects that will be of benefit to the learner and the society. The curriculum should assist in helping to ease contact between the learner and his studies, socialize him and facilitate the transfer of knowledge and developmental skills to the entire populace.
- **Evaluation** – It should be subjected to evaluation to ensure that there is progress and that such a progress is in the desired direction. Evaluation as a characteristic could facilitate learning and

teaching. It could produce records appropriate to the purpose for which records are essential and provide feedback for curriculum planners and teachers.

Foundations of Curriculum

Any curriculum, if it is to serve the purpose for which it is constructed must be based on sound foundations. Foundations are the forces that influence the minds of curriculum developers. In this way they affect the content and structure of the curriculum. The curriculum reflects the society and culture of a country and it is the desire of a society that their children should learn the habits, ideas, attitudes and skills of the society and educational institutions are the proper way to impart these skills. The needs, knowledge and information of the society provide foundation in the formation of curriculum.

Philosophical Foundation

Philosophy means the love of wisdom; it searches for truth, not simple truth. It searches for eternal truth, reality and general principles of life. Curriculum helps in the practical use of knowledge in real life situations and understanding realities and ideas of life and that why curriculum is called the dynamic side of Philosophy. Curriculum is used for the modification of the behaviour of the students and philosophy help in the process of finding new ways and basis for teachers and curriculum planner to modify their behaviour. Philosophy also helps in the exploring new methods of teaching and how to apply in the classroom situation for better achievement of the teaching learning process. It also provides new ways and methods for the evaluation of student's achievement and evaluation of curriculum. Philosophy of education provides rules and principles which lead the decision-making regarding educational practices and polices planning. It guides the curriculum planner on the bases of the philosophical and ideological belief of the society in constructing of subject matter keeping in view the future demands and needs of the schools and help in the promoting of human life through social change in the behaviour of the students. For Example: In some countries, the ideological beliefs of the society are based on Islam. Therefore, the curriculum planner introduces such curriculum in education system, which inculcate true knowledge of Islam and preserve the culture of Muslim society in new generation and the Islamic curricula should be based on the ideology of Islamic laws and principles. Thus, Philosophy has direct effect in curriculum planning because it guides the curriculum planner in the selection of the objectives and it provides guidelines in the selection of objectives, learning experiences and content of the curriculum, and how to evaluate the curriculum, learning experiences and achievements of the students. For example, educational philosophies of Plato (Idealism), Aristotle (Realism), and John Dewey (Pragmatism) have also influenced educational curricula the world over. Education in our country has been greatly influenced by the thoughts of Tagore and Mahatma Gandhi. Indian philosophers like Vivekananda, Tagore and Sri Aurobindo considered education as a means of individual development and perfection. Mahatma Gandhi, the father of our nation, maintained that education should provide for all-round development of a child and it should also help him/her to earn a meaningful livelihood.

Psychological Foundations

Curriculum is influenced by psychology. Psychology provides information about the teaching and learning process. It seeks answers as to how a curriculum be organized in order to achieve students' learning at the optimum level. Psychological foundation is based on the individual differences, every student has its own unique personality and they have differences in their abilities and skills. They are different in nature so they can't be treated alike in teaching learning process, some may be fast learner while other slow. Therefore, the curriculum should be based on the above facts, and it should be design to support the capacity and potentialities of all the students. Psychology plays a vital role in the teaching learning process. It is the foundation for all type of educational related programmes. The methods of teaching, the selection of content of subject and the methods and theories of learning, the overall development of the students and to inculcate the norms of the society in the students. Psychology helps in all the processes above in the development process of the curriculum.

Today psychology is the core and foundation element of all the learning processes; curriculum development, Child mental development, teaching methods, learning theories, administration of education system and planning, character building of the students, attitude of students and teacher, the society, the use of different technologies. Psychology helps in all fields of education; it not just adds to knowledge; psychology is applied in practical class room situation as well as in the curriculum development process. Some of the basic human needs to be put into consideration while developing a curriculum include:

- The need for love, belonging, affection and security.
- The need for new experiences.
- The need for praise and recognition.
- The need for responsibility.

- The need for achievement.
- The need for self-actualization.

Therefore, it is said that the impact of psychological sources on the foundations of curriculum is more than significant and still on the rise. The role of psychology in the development of curriculum is vast and with each day it is becoming increasingly more meaningful and unavoidable.

Sociological Foundation

When a child is born, he is born into a family. The family, therefore, becomes the first agent of socializing him. As he grows up, it is noted that the school comes in as another agent of socialization. With time, it will be seen that the world of the child is larger than the home and the school and that world influences both his interests and attitude. The society maintained the school partly to help the growing child adapt to and prepare for life in the larger society. For this, curriculum developers must put into consideration the characteristics of the contemporary society as well as, that of the future in which the child of today will live most of his life as a mature adult. Children of today and adult of the future have a lot to do in making the society a place worth living. Depending on the type of education the school provides, it becomes a major factor in the improvement of society. It helps young people to develop the capacity to respond intelligently to social problems. In this way, the curriculum serves not only the needs of the learner but also those of the society. Being a part of the society, sees the purpose the school can serve. Curriculum developers, therefore, need to decide what kinds of skills, knowledge and attitudes are needed by the society. Whether they should plan what will conform the existing social order/values, encourage questioning of those values, what issues and facts should be studied in schools should be their major concern when planning the school curriculum. Other social issues, according to Beane et al. (1980) that curriculum planners should address are:

- Technology.
- Family structure.
- Working in the information society.
- Changing sex roles.
- Cultural Diversity and Pluralism.
- Changing Lifestyles and values.
- Futuristic transformation.

Sociological factors have highest impact on the content of curriculum and that is the reason that curriculum developers and planner both reflect and transfer their own culture in curriculum. Curriculum developers are the part of the society therefore they are indirectly affected by the society and culture. Their cultural standards, attitudes and beliefs leave deep impact on the individuals because the curriculum designers influence the selection of objectives, subject matter, teaching learning methods and the process of evaluation. Some social values, changes and conditions are included into some extent in some of the curriculum projects in the context of current social issues and problems, such as rapid growth of population, democratic values, urbanization, and management problems could be found in proposed program. Some vital problems and topics are considered in relation to concepts and key ideas drawn from the disciplines. Curriculum developer is the part of that society and culture therefore they should keep in mind that their decision could affect their culture and society. Therefore, their decision should be related to the needs and values of the society. The goals of education emerge from the needs of the society. When a society urge a need or a goal it becomes an educational objective and the school and they attempt to attain that goal by putting it into school objectives. And when a societal goal become an educational objective then the school, teacher and student must make their efforts to achieve it and for that purpose appropriate educational facilities and methods must be planned. Educational aims are based on the study of sociological and political condition of the society and the main purpose of the curriculum is preservation and advancement of the that society.

Economical Foundations

The economical foundation of curriculum gives importance to the vocational aspect of the curriculum. The economic condition of a nation or a society guide the curriculum of the country, because the stakeholder of the education wants to employ such a curriculum which help them to build their economy and the people have better jobs when they finish their schooling. In this kind of situations, the curriculum become job or market oriented. In this curriculum the curriculum developer gives importance to skills acquisition which is the demands of the time. The financial condition of a country reflects its curriculum because without proper funding one can't achieve the outcome of a good curriculum. It is the financial aspect of a country which guide them to adopt which type of curriculum, for example activity based or learner centred curriculum need more money in the process of the implementation of the curriculum then subject matter curriculum. Lack of resources due to financial constraints effect the developing and planning of the curriculum. The lack of skilled manpower due to financial constraints, without proper financial support it is hard to train the people to support the teaching learning process. Teachers are the core of education system and without proper training one can't implement a curriculum and to support the curriculum one need to train the entire teachers on that style of curriculum. The lack of labs and libraries also affect the curriculum development process because without proper computer labs in cities and villages one can't implement computer education curriculum all over the country. In the same way without proper libraries in all school one can't implement a curriculum which needs supporting or reference books. The overburden of the population is also one of the factors that affect the financial support of the curriculum development, lack of facilities and implementation of the curriculum in the country. In short, we can say that economy play a vital role in the curriculum development and implementation process in the country and it is the foundation of the successful curriculum. Without a good economic background, a country can't afford a curriculum which needs huge financial support.

CURRICULUM AND SYLLABUS

Syllabus refers to a list of topics or collection of outlines of what pupils should study in a subject for a specified period of teaching. Broadly speaking, the syllabus is that aspect of curriculum that lists subjects to be taught in a given course or programme. The outline of the syllabus is meant to guide the teacher on the extent of work involved in a particular class. Sometime, the syllabus often gives detailed instructions on what is to be taught in each term of each year of a course, what books are to be used and even what methods are appropriate (Farrant, 1980). Syllabus is a part of curriculum. Curriculum is the overall learning experience that a student goes through during the particular course of study. It contains the teaching methods, lessons, assignments, physical and mental exercises, activities, projects, study material, tutorials, presentations, assessments, test series, learning objectives, and so on. Syllabus is made available to the students by the teachers to bring their attention towards the subject and take their study seriously. The below table provides the comparison between curriculum and syllabus.

Aspect	Curriculum	Syllabus
Definition	Comprehensive educational plan outlining the scope and sequence of learning goals, objectives, content, and assessments for an entire educational program or course.	Specific outline or plan detailing the topics, units, lessons, and activities to be covered within a particular course or subject area.

Scope	Encompasses all aspects of the educational program, including goals, content, teaching methods, assessments, and resources.	Focuses on the content and organization of a particular course or subject, detailing what will be taught and learned within a defined timeframe.
Flexibility	Generally, more flexible, allowing for adaptation and customization based on educational objectives, student needs, and societal changes.	Typically, less flexible, as it outlines specific topics and content to be covered within a predetermined timeframe.
Long-term Focus	Often long-term in nature, providing a framework for overall educational planning and development.	Usually short to medium-term, focusing on the immediate instructional goals and content delivery within a specific course or subject area.
Development	Developed at the institutional or district level by educators, administrators, and curriculum specialists, often in alignment with educational standards and guidelines.	Developed at the course or subject level by individual educators or instructional teams, based on curriculum frameworks, standards, and educational goals.
Integration	Requires integration of various components such as goals, content, teaching strategies, assessment methods, and resources to ensure cohesive and effective instruction.	Typically focuses on the organization and sequencing of content, with less emphasis on integration of teaching methods, assessments, and resources.
Examples	National curriculum frameworks, state curriculum standards, district curriculum maps, and school curriculum guides.	Course outlines, unit plans, lesson plans, and instructional materials

CURRICULUM PLANNING

The Curriculum is likely to be good one if there is good curriculum planning. A good understanding of curriculum planning is essential for good teaching. "Unplanned teaching and learning are a recipe of wasting time". Curriculum planning develop well-coordinated, quality teaching, learning and assessment programs, which build students' knowledge, skills and behaviours in the disciplines, as well as their interdisciplinary and/or physical, personal and social capacities. Curriculum planning is a complex activity involving the interplay of ideas from the curriculum field and other related disciplines. However, the ultimate purpose of curriculum planning is to describe the learning opportunities available to students. A curriculum Plan is the advance arrangement of learning opportunities for a particular population of learners. It is the process of preparing for the duties of teaching, deciding upon goals, determining curriculum content, selecting learning resources and classroom procedures, evaluating progress, and looking toward next steps. 'Curriculum planning' as a continuous process in which participants contribute at various levels towards making decisions about: (a) the purposes of learning, (b) how that purpose might be carried out through teaching – learning situations, (c) Whether the purpose identified and the means selected are both appropriate and effective.

Curriculum planning is a blanket concept that may describe activity ranging from the identification of broad goals to the description of experiences for specific teaching/learning situations. The planning of learning experiences is one of the most important professional activities in education. It is an important activity since it largely determines the day-to-day life of learners. There are four major stages which are interdependent and interrelating in the process of curriculum development namely; (1) the selection of aims, goals and objectives; (2) the selection of appropriate learning experiences and content for the achievement of the aims, goals and objectives; (3) organisation of learning experiences; and (4) Evaluation of the extent to which the objectives identified have been achieved.

Curriculum Planning

The planning phase lays the foundation for all of the curriculum development steps. Planning to determine the need and purposes, identification and analysis of existing situation have to be done. The steps in this phase include: (a) Identify Issue/Problem/Need, (b) Constitute a committee for curriculum preparation, (c) Conduct Needs Assessment and Analysis.

Characteristics of a Good Planning Process

- It is using leadership to motivate people and to coordinate their activities
- It is reflecting on what has been planned already and how it is working
- It includes the periodic recording of planning decision for future reference.
- It should stimulate change and improvement
- It is organized thinking that helps in deciding what needs to be done, how it will happen, and who will do it.
- It should raise awareness about what is being done and why
- It should build a trail of activities over time so one can look at what has worked well and what has not
- It should decrease fear about the process of change and its result
- It is the setting of priorities in the use of resources: people, money, time and materials

- It is trying to anticipate the future.
- It is adapting and modifying steps or processes until they work out

Importance of Curriculum Planning

Curriculum planning ensures:

- Optimum coverage of all domains within the curriculum
- Continuity of learning between domains across years
- Addressing the full range of learning needs of students
- Students are given opportunities to develop deep understanding
- Cohesiveness in teaching, learning and assessment practices
- Elimination of repetition of learning activities
- Improved student learning outcomes.

Curriculum Design

- Analysis of social needs and translating the needs into course/ general/learning/terminal objectives
- Splitting the objectives into specific objectives
- Grouping the specific objectives into subjects
- Deriving the subjects from the above classification
- Instructional development
- Materials and media development
- Methods of teaching & testing
- Unitising each subject matter
- Specification of required time
- Curriculum formulation

Producing curriculum incorporates the following:

- Step 1: Diagnosis of need (What needs to be taught?)
- Step 2: Formulation of objectives (What objectives should be taught?)
- Step 3: Selection of content (What information or data will be taught and where will it come from?)
- Step 4: Organization of content (How will the information be organized? Will it be in a textbook, using the internet, etc.?)
- Step 5: Selection of learning experiences (What learning experiences {role play, cooperative or team learning, lecture, etc.} will the instructor incorporate into the subject taught?)

- Step 6: Organization of learning experiences (How will these learning experiences be organized?)
- Step 7: Determination of what to evaluate and of the ways and means of doing it. (How will learning be assessed?)

Implementation of the Curriculum

In the implementation phase, identify sufficient resources, support, and others to successfully implement the curriculum. Here the schools conduct the course and carry out a plan to evaluate how well the methods and materials work in practice. It includes;

- Instructional scheme of each subject to be completed in the semester/year.
- Planning the lessons as per the timetable
- Using the transactional strategies
- Using the appropriate media
- Providing the learning resources
- Promoting classroom learning experiences
- Progressive testing

CURRICULUM EVALUATION

Evaluation describes how to assess the nature, impact and value of an activity through the systematic collection, analysis and interpretation of information with a view to making an informed decision. Evaluation involves three activities; (a) Outlining clear purposes, (b) Gathering evidences, (c) Judgment. Curriculum evaluation is an integral part of curriculum development. Curriculum evaluation is used not only to determine the attainment of the purposes but also "to gauge the value and effectiveness of any particular piece of educational activity undertaken by pupils" (Kelly1989). In relation to curriculum, evaluation is the process of making value judgments about the merit or worth of a part or the whole of a curriculum. Evaluation is part of development rather than apart from it. In the evaluation plan, the schools will determine whether or not the course and its components worked. The evaluation plan addresses both the course as a whole and the individual lessons and units within the course. The focus of the evaluation study is to compare the expectations for the course and the reality from teaching it. It includes;

- Intra-curricular evaluation
- Teacher evaluation of students
- Student evaluation of teachers

- Materials evaluation
- Verification of methods
- Evaluation of tests and examinations
- Checking the learning outcomes
- Curriculum review/ improvement/ change/ modification
- System revision

Evaluation of curricula is typically concerned with the:

- Impact of the curriculum: on individual students, their needs, their level of engagement and their performance; on society, including the appropriateness of values communicated and attitudes fostered, and the level of public satisfaction; on the economy including labour markets as an indicator of economic development;
- Process through which the curriculum was developed;
- Content and design of the curriculum compared with: recent social, technological, economic or scientific changes; recent advances in educational research and educational paradigms;
- Possible future directions for curriculum change.

Curriculum evaluation ranges from estimating the performance of a single child in a course through the evaluation of specific instructional materials, methods, activities and techniques to the evaluation of an entire curriculum. A comprehensive curriculum evaluation is concerned with the worthwhileness of the curriculum components, and the information provided is for the sake of facilitative decision making at the various stages of curriculum development (Alade, 2006).

Use of Curriculum Evaluation

Teachers should be consulted about curriculum evaluation because they are ultimately responsible for translating its objectives into specific lessons. Teachers are ethically and legally bound to routinely assess students and report their progress. A curriculum should help teachers do this by providing a realistic set of goals and suggested techniques to assist students at all ability levels. When decisions are made about changes in content, teachers can provide feedback based on their direct interaction with students.

- A teacher could use curriculum evaluation to improve his teaching.
- A school may use curriculum evaluation to appraise the quality of the teaching staff.

- Principals may use curriculum evaluation to provide information to help them make decisions
- Governing agencies may use curriculum evaluation for accountability and control purposes.
- During the early stages of curriculum development, formative evaluation helps the curriculum developer to determine the effectiveness of new procedures and identify areas where revision is needed.
- When the curriculum has been fully developed, summative evaluation makes it possible to determine the effectiveness in meeting the instructional objectives.

Need for Curriculum Evaluation

- To restructure the curriculum according to the needs of learners and society.
- To eliminate unnecessary units, teaching methods and contents.
- To introduce latest and update methods of teaching and content, new knowledge and practices.
- To add or delete number of hours of instruction.

FACTORS INFLUENCING CURRICULUM PLANNING, DESIGN AND DEVELOPMENT

Cultural Factors: The society and culture exercise massive powers on the formation of curriculum and the reason behind that it was society who created schooling to safeguard the survival of their cultural heritage, and survival of their species. The purpose of curriculum planner and developers is to translate traditional norms, philosophies, ethics, knowledge and attitudes in the objectives of curriculum, the content, learning processes and the evaluation of elements of the curriculum. Therefore, a curriculum without the reflection of culture is not possible for that reason one should consider what characteristics of the culture should be the part of curriculum and what not. Though schools are formal institutions that educate the people, there are other units of society that educate or influence the way people think, such as families and friends as well as communities. Since the society is dynamic, there are many developments which are difficult to cope with and to adjust to. But the schools are made to address and understand the changes not only in one's country but in the world as well. Therefore, schools must be relevant by making its curriculum more innovative and interdisciplinary. A community may include Christians, Muslims, Hindus and adherents of other religions. Their views must be considered when designing a curriculum. The design of curricular materials and their presentation should accommodate the culture of the society that the curriculum is seeking to serve. We may have a curriculum that is gender biased against female children because it includes instructional materials that portray negative attitudes towards women and girls. It is therefore possible for culture to have both positive and negative influences on the curriculum.

Historical Factors: The history of the curriculum:

- Tells the curriculum planner how to develop and modify the curriculum, what to teach and what should be the core material of the subjects, what objectives they want to achieve through the curriculum.
- Tells them how the teacher should teach, what are the best practices they need to incorporate in curriculum teaching and what kind of teaching need to be avoid.
- Explains the teacher psychology at different time and how to improve their teaching styles.
- Provides a detail about the learner behaviour at different times. It also provides information about the psychology of the students, how they learn and what they want to learn.
- Changed teaching methods, now every researcher is finding new ways to teach and it is also becoming the part of curriculum history.
- Guides the future plans because curriculum is always based on the future demands of the country and the lesson learned through history, tell the curriculum developer not to repeat the mistake of the past and develop a curriculum which is based on the future need of the society and international demands.
- Tells the curriculum developer what not to include in the curriculum. What of lessons can bring no good to the curriculum and what type of contents material are good for the teaching learning process, so history of the curriculum eliminates all those useless traditions from the modern curriculum and help the developer to incorporate what is needed for the curriculum.

Economic Factors

The economical foundation of curriculum gives importance to the vocational aspect of the curriculum. The economic condition of a nation guides the curriculum of the country, because the stakeholder of the education wants to employ such a curriculum which help them to build their economy and the people have better jobs when they finish their schooling. In this kind of situations, the curriculum become job or market oriented. In this curriculum the curriculum developer gives importance to skills acquisition which is the demands of the time. Undeveloped nations try to prepare skilled work force and send it to other countries for jobs. Here are some economical factors which influence the curriculum development process.

- *Allocation of funds*: The financial condition of a country reflects its curriculum because without proper funding one can't achieve the outcome of a good curriculum. It is the financial aspect of a country which guide them to adopt which type of curriculum, for example activity base or learner centred curriculum need more money in the process of the implementation of the curriculum than subject matter curriculum.
- *Lack of skilled manpower*: The lack of skilled manpower due to financial constraints, without proper financial support it is hard to train the people to support the teaching learning process. Teachers are the core of education system and without proper training one can't implement a curriculum and to support the curriculum one need to train the entire teacher on that style of curriculum. So, the skills of the teachers also guide the direction of the curriculum, and to develop these skills in the teachers need funds.
- *Lack of labs due to financial problems*: The lack of labs and libraries also affect the curriculum development process because without proper computer labs in cities and villages one can't implement computer education curriculum all over the country.

Political Factors

National ideology and philosophy have a tremendous influence on the education system because:

- Politics determine and define the goals, content, learning experiences and evaluation strategies in education.
- Curricular materials and their interpretation are usually heavily influenced by political considerations.
- Political considerations may play a part in the hiring of personnel.
- Funding of education is greatly influenced by politics.
- Entry into educational institutions and the examination systems are heavily influenced by politics.

Geographical Factors

To discuss the geographical factor, the economic nature of the country, its regions, climate, natural resources, production etc. should not be ignored. a) The economic nature of the country and its geographical location - If the country is agricultural, its education system should place emphasis on agricultural education because the economics of the country is essentially based on the natural resources of that country. As an example - India is still a predominantly agricultural country. A large part of Indian population still depends on agriculture for earning livelihood. Naturally the educational policy should have agricultural base. In the same manner an industrialised country demands different types of education which would help the country to develop more engineers and technological experts. If the country possesses extensive mineral resources, the education system will place an emphasis on mining education in order to develop the economy of the country. A coastal country will teach how to utilise the sea resources properly. The naval training and fishing industry should be given priority to harmonise with the geographical factors.

Technological Factors

The latest technological innovation t will have a significant impact on education and society. Curriculum designers cannot afford to ignore technology and its influence on the curriculum.

Environmental Factors

Over time, people have become insensitive to their surroundings and natural resources. This has affected the sky, the land and the sea. The end result is that humanity is being adversely affected by these in-considerations. Industrial wastes have polluted the world. For example, the ozone layer in the atmosphere, which protects us from harmful radiation from the sun, is being depleted. People want this redressed. It is through education that remediation can be affected. Consideration for the environment influence curriculum design to ensure the survival of future generations.

CONCLUSION

In conclusion, the curriculum is the backbone of any educational system, providing a framework for what students are expected to learn and how it will be taught. It encompasses various elements such as goals, objectives, content, teaching methods, and assessment strategies. Curriculum planning involves a systematic process of designing, implementing, and evaluating educational programs to ensure that they are effective and meet the needs of students, teachers, and society. Factors influencing curriculum planning, design, and development include societal needs, cultural values, educational philosophy, student characteristics, teacher expertise, and available resources. Continuous evaluation and adaptation are essential to keep the curriculum relevant and responsive to changing educational contexts and learner needs. Overall, a well-designed curriculum serves as a roadmap for quality education and meaningful learning experiences.

Chapter - 6

Curriculum Organization

INTRODUCTION

Curriculum is the crux of the whole educational process. Without curriculum, we cannot conceive any educational endeavour. The term curriculum has been derived from a Latin word *Currere* which means a *race course* or *a runway* or *path* on which one runs to reach a goal. In this sense curriculum is the path through which the student has to go forward in order to reach the goal envisaged by education. The Secondary education commission (1952-53) says, "Curriculum does not mean only the academic subjects traditionally taught in the school, but includes the totality of experiences that pupil receives through the manifold activities that go on in the classroom, library, laboratory, workshop, playground and in the numerous informal contacts between teachers and pupils". In this sense, the whole life of the school becomes the curriculum which can touch the life of the students at all points and help in the evolution of balanced personality. Crow and Crow say "The curriculum includes all the learners' experience in or outside school that are included in a program which has been devised to help him developmentally, emotionally, socially, spiritually and morally".

Children are individuals with their own intellectual and biological needs, capabilities and potentialities. Every aspect of their need and development should be taken care of while framing curriculum for them. Similarly, we are living in a developing nation which has its own demands for scientific and technological developments. These demands are to be fulfilled by the younger generation when they enter the society as responsible citizens. Another important aspect of curriculum is the subject matter or the medium through which these demands of the child or society are to be fulfilled. Now the question arises as to how to plan a curriculum that caters to the needs of pupils, society as well as that of discipline/subject matter. There are some principles to be followed while constructing the curriculum.

PRINCIPLES OF CURRICULUM ORGANIZATION

Curriculum organization is a scientific process which involves basic principles on which its credibility exists. The review of the present curriculum reveal that it is subject oriented, examination ridden, not in conformity with the aims and objectives of teaching science, rigid and outfits the different age group. So, it is imperative that the present curriculum should be reorganized in the light of the principles mentioned below.

- **Principle of Child Centeredness:** Curriculum is mainly for the students. Foremost consideration should be given to the child. Curriculum should properly suit their age, needs, abilities, capacities, interests, mental development and previous experience. Educational activity should be meaningfully appropriate for the child for his all-round development. The child should occupy a central position in the entire teaching learning process and he should actively participate in it. It becomes obligatory on the part of curriculum planners to provide means and material to satisfy the child's need for proper growth and development.
- **Principle of Variety and Flexibility:** The curriculum should not be rigid, but should be flexible to suit the changing needs of the individual and the society. There must be variety in the curriculum in order to cater to the needs of the individuals with different taste, skills and intelligence. The learners should be given freedom of choice in selecting subjects. Individual differences among the students must be taken proper care of. The materials and activities included in the curriculum should have rich variety to prevent boredom. Ours is a diverse society in terms of culture, occupation, social and economic conditions, religion, castes, rural/ urban etc. We also have differences in geographical conditions. It is impossible to set a rigid national curriculum for our country. Also, the knowledge is changing with such a rapid rate that every year, new discoveries are either replacing old knowledge; or improving it so it is necessary to keep the curriculum flexible in order to make it effective.
- **Principle of Activity:** Curriculum should be activity based. Children are quite active by nature. Child learns more from activities. The curriculum must have scope for varied and

interesting activities. There should be emphasis on learning by doing. Children always take interest, pay attention and are benefited by those learning experiences that involve activities, learning by doing and living on their part. More provision should be made for individual work and other field experiences. Simple scientific activities performed in the classroom, in laboratory, or at home enable the child to go beyond the verbal information. Growth and learning take place where there is activity.

- **Principle of Utility:** This principle states that children should be taught those useful things that are really necessary in life. The curriculum must include speaking, reading and writing one's language simple arithmetic and measurement, physical education and care of health and some craft. Curriculum should be of practical use to the pupil and hence should maintain vocational and technical base. Emphasis should be given to work experiences.
- **Principle of adjustment to one's Environment:** The curriculum should be so framed that the student may acquire the ability to study the real aspect of any situation and if unfavourable circumstances arise, he may adjust with them. Rusk analyses man's environment into two - material (physical) and cultural (spiritual). The latter has been classified into three - intellectual, aesthetic and moral. The curriculum must represent all these.
- **Principle of Community centeredness:** School is said to be the 'epitome of the life." The curriculum must be vitally related to community life, interpreting for the child its salient, significant features allowing him to come in contact with some of its important activities. The activities of the community life must be introduced in the school. The school must become the centre of community life. The fundamentals of the community's life should be taught according to mental development of children. Children may learn a lot through the various useful and relevant resources available in the community. Curriculum should be very much linked with the study of the community and its people and their interrelationships. Hence the curriculum should be planned in such a way that it could equip children with knowledge and competencies expected to play their role in the society. They should fulfil the needs of the society. The requirements of society have to be fulfilled by educated citizens.
- **Principle of Conservation of Culture:** The curriculum should include such experiences by which the student should cultivate

a sense of respect for his traditions and culture. Students should know about their past culture and traditions. We know that culturally India is a very rich country and over the years, people of India have preserved it. Only through education the values, morals, attitudes and customs which are part and parcel of culture can be preserved and transmitted to next generation concerned.

- **Principle of Creativity:** Children by nature are very energetic. They are always active and on observing their activities we can find out that most of them are very creative. To keep this ability alive, there should be a conscious effort on the part of planners to make the curriculum creativity oriented. Curriculum should provide experiences that place the pupil in the place of discoverer. Activities should be included which enable the child to exercise his creative and constructive Power. This will help the child to try out new methods and techniques when he will be in actual field of work in the society. It will help him to take part in the development of society.
- **Forward Looking Principle:** Children of today are the future citizens of tomorrow. Education should give them a foundation of knowledge and the capability of adjustment in different circumstances of life. Education must prepare the child of shouldering future responsibilities. It should equip him to face the challenges that come in his future life. The curriculum should include such elements by which students may prepare themselves for their future life i.e., they may be able to learn their livelihood sufficiently and adjust themselves with the society successfully.
- **Principle of Leisure:** Education must prepare persons, not only for the serious business of life, but also for leisure. Hence the curriculum must include cultural pursuits and hobbies which will provide for recreation and enjoyment. It should therefore, include a variety of aesthetic, physical, social and cultural activities. This will not only make a school life pleasant and meaningful for the students, but also provide excellent training for leisure, which greatly determines a man's capacity to work. So, curriculum prepare individual to use their leisure time effectively.
- **Principle of Correlation:** Correlation is the corner stone of education. The subjects in the curriculum should not be divided into a number of isolated, un-coordinated water-tight compartments. Subjects should be interrelated and within each subject, the contents should so far as possible be envisaged as

"broad fields" units which can be correlated better with life rather than narrow items of information. The principle of correlation asks for teaching subjects in such a way as its link its study (1) with the study of other subjects and activities of the school curriculum (2) with the physical and social environment of the students (3) with the day-to-day life activities of the students. Curriculum provides appropriate opportunities to the students to acquire the desired knowledge and experiences in a correlated and integrated manner for being utilized properly in their life.

- **Principle of Scientific thinking:** Curriculum should enable the students to think scientifically. It should allow pupils to learn by problem solving method. It should train pupils to develop scientific attitude through activities.

Integration of these fundamental principles and using them in curriculum making and in the instructional activity are crucial to educational improvement.

APPROACHES TO CURRICULUM ORGANISATION

After the topics have been selected according to the relevant fundamental principles they have to be systematically arranged so as to facilitate its meaningful and effective transaction. The content should be arranged in a systematic manner. Curriculum practitioners and implementers may use one or more approaches in planning, implementing and evaluating the curriculum. The decision regarding the use of an approach for the organization of some particular subject material and learning experience for a particular class depends on the situations and circumstances available at the time of the development of the curriculum. They are several approaches to curriculum organization. Some of them are discussed as below:

CONCENTRIC APPROACH

Concentric circles have a common centre but radius goes on changing. In concentric approach, knowledge widens slowly and steadily just as concentric circles go on extending and widening. It is a system of arrangement of subject-matter. The whole curriculum is spread over a number of years. A topic is divided into a number of portions which are then allotted to different classes. A general treatment of almost all the topics is attempted at the beginning and it is developed in successive years according to the mental development of the pupils. The criterion for allotment of a particular portion of the course to a particular class is the difficulty of portion and power of comprehension of students in that age group.

The concept of concentric curriculum design is based on the cognitive psychological theories of Jerome S. Bruner. Bruner believed that there are three distinct stages in the human cognitive process: the enactive phase, in which the learner interacts with and uses objects or processes; the iconic phase, in which the learner manipulates images of these objects or processes; and the symbolic phase, in which abstract representations of them can be utilized. Concentric curriculum design attempts to leverage this understanding of cognition into a deeper understanding of the subject at hand.

In the beginning of the course, the whole aspect is given to pupils in a simplified way. In the next year more and more details of its parts are added. It follows the maximum of teaching, such as from whole to part, simple to complex, easy to difficult etc. To begin with, a simple presentation of the subject is given and further knowledge is imparted in following years. Thus, beginning from a nucleus, the circles of knowledge go on widening year after year and hence the name concentric approach. In this method the contents are arranged based on the child's developmental stages. The interests change by age so also the activities. So, contents must be based on this principle. The whole syllabus is arranged in concentric manner. The topics are introduced gradually. The complexity of the concepts and the quantity increases by age. In dealing with a subject; very little is taught at first, then the scope is extended in the next stage. Thus, keeping the subject as the centre or core, ever widening concentric circles of experience are provided.

While conceiving it as concentric only the widening of the scope is indicated but the linkage is not taken care of. E.g. Consider the topic acids. In the first year, food items having sour taste can be familiarized. In the second year the common properties of acids can be included. In the successive years, strong and weak acids, monobasic and dibasic acids, electronic concept of an acid, etc. can be included. Thus, method of arranging the course is based on the maxims of teaching from whole to parts and simple to complex. E.g. Consider the topic water. In the first-year pupil learn an outline consisting of sources of water, storage, its distribution, uses etc. During second year purification of water, method of purification, composition of water etc., third year types of water, hardness of water, causes of hardness, removal of hardness etc. For instance, it is very important that children should know our freedom struggle. In the primary classes the information about this unit will be imparted through some of the more important leaders. In the middle stage, the information will be imparted through events – The Indian National Congress, Partition of Bengal, The Gandhian Era, the civil disobedience, the INA, Quit India Movement. In the secondary stage, the pupils will learn to compare and contrast the freedom movement in our country with other countries of the world. E.g.: analogy of Painting. In Painting several coats are to be applied to get a permanent effect, from primer to final touch. Concentric approach is really a very good approach to be adopted. Teachers have to be careful so that portion is neither too long nor too short. In every consecutive year positive points can be added, if same teacher, teaches the particular content every year.

SPIRAL APPROACH

This approach is almost similar to the concentric approach, but here connected facts are grouped around one central theme. In concentric approach only the widening of the scope is indicated while the linkage is not taken care of. Spiral curriculum ascends and enlarges as it climbs. The upward and outward curriculum organization acknowledges the gradual nature of development of knowledge and also the development of learner. The spiral view accounts for the more refined wisdom distilled from the experience over time. Gradation of linkage too is taken care of and the continuity of the topic concerned is never broken. The spiral approach is a technique often used in teaching where first the basic facts of a subject are learned, without worrying about details. Then as learning progresses, more and more details are introduced, while at the same time they are related to the basics which are reemphasized many times to help enter them into long-term memory.

Basic idea behind spiral progression approach is to expose the learners to a wide variety of concepts/topics, skills and attitudes that are deemed of "continual concern of everyone "until they are mastered. A spiral curriculum design is one in which "key concepts are presented repeatedly throughout the curriculum, but with deepening layers of complexity." After a mastery of the initial topic, the student "spirals upwards" as the new knowledge is introduced in next lessons, enabling him/her to reinforce what is already learned. In the end, a rich breadth and depth of knowledge is achieved. The term spiral gives the additional implication that while attempting gradation the linkage too is taken care of and the continuity of the topic concerned is never broken. With this procedure, two purposes are served: The previously learned concept is reviewed hence improving its retention; The topic may be progressively elaborated when it is reintroduced leading to a broadened understanding and transfer of learning.

A spiral curriculum can be defined as a course of study in which students will see the same topics throughout their school career, with each encounter increasing in complexity and reinforcing previous learning. Spiral system is based on the principle that a subject cannot be given an exhaustive treatment at the first stage. To begin with, a simple presentation of the subject-matter is given, gaps are filled in the following year and more gaps a year or two later, in accordance with the amount of knowledge which pupils are capable of assimilating. Spiral method demands the division of the topic or the subject into number of smaller independent units to be dealt with in order of difficulty suiting the mental capacities of the pupils. Spiral approach is more natural and less tiring to the pupil.

Spiral curriculum is probably most easily seen in mathematics because most topics in math build off of each other with increasing complexity. For example, in first grade and the beginning of second grade, students learn simple addition and subtraction facts. Addition and subtraction are then made more complex by introducing two-digit numbers. Students need to rely on their knowledge of the facts they have memorized in order to do the more complex problems. Accordingly, concepts incorporating addition and subtraction become more complex as students move through the grades. The early skills of adding and subtracting in elementary school grow and spiral as the years go by, to be used in algebra in high school.

For the topic heat, in the first-year pupil study about the uses of heat, in the second-year pupil study about the transference of heat, third year about measurement of heat, at a later stage law of heat. Thus, method of arranging the course is based on the maxims of teaching from whole to parts and simple to complex. Plant biology, for instance, is a terrific place for spiral curriculum methods to be put into action. A lesson in first grade might focus on what plants need to grow, including sunlight. In third grade, students will then learn about photosynthesis, which explains why plants need sunlight to grow. In sixth grade, students will learn about the cellular structure of plants, which will give them a more complex picture of plant biology. Finally, students in high school will learn about organic chemistry in plants, completing the picture.

Merits of spiral and concentric approaches

- Continuous learning of the subject matter through primary to the secondary stage.
- Based on psychological principles
- Complexity as well as gradation in the content will challenge the students so to motivate them.

- Greater opportunity for revision of topics may form the background for additional knowledge to be gained.
- The system is most successful when the teaching is in hands of one teacher because then she can preserve continuity in the teaching and keeps the circle expanding. Unnecessary repetition can be avoided. If same teacher takes topic continuously every year, he/she knows weak points of students and thus can bring necessary modifications in topics, to make base of the content strong in students.
- Since the same topic is learnt over many years so its impressions are more lasting.
- Since only small portion of topic is taken, interest of student is maintained. Teaching does not become dull. Every year there are new problems to solve and new difficulties to overcome.
- Teacher can make use of different techniques, to introduce and deliver the content.

Limitations

- Students get disinterested by repeated dealing of the same content every year. The presentation being devoid of freshness and novelty fails to arouse curiosity and a sense of wonder in the pupil.
- Hurried and passing references will not be of help in understanding complex problems.
- A sense of boredom and dullness is inevitable because the children have gone through the whole course more than once. They develop a sense of familiarity without the fullness of knowledge.
- For the success of this approach, we require really capable teachers. If a teacher becomes over ambitious and teaches all the possible interesting illustrations in the introductory year then the subject loses its power of freshness and appeal and nothing is left to create interest in the topic in subsequent years.
- In case the topic is too short or too long then also the method is not found to be useful. A too long portion makes the topic dull and a too short portion fails to leave any permanent and lasting impression on the mind of the pupil.
- If topic is not divided properly, into its sub units, it may prove harmful.

TOPICAL APPROACH

In this type of organization, the subject matter is arranged under *topics*. The whole course is divided into a number of topics. In applying this approach, therefore a few topics of science may be marked for being included in the curriculum of a particular grade and then it is expected to cover all the contents or learning experiences related to that topic in that grade or class and not allowing their repetition in any way in the junior or senior grades. Thus, topic marked for particular grade must not be touched in another grade. It is opposite of concentric method. Concentric method involves the breaking up of a topic into suitable portions, whereas topical method aims at keeping it intact. In topical method a topic is taken as unbreakable unit. It is based on the principal that any topic when begun should not be left half done. It should be finished in its entirety, before the next topic is taken. Thus, a topic marked for a particular grade must have the beginning and end in that grade itself. We have different sets of topics for their inclusion in the curriculum of different grades of secondary stages of school education.

In this method, instead of classifying the subject matter as physics, chemistry and biology, the topic under consideration will combine the three subjects and present the subject matter in a correlated and integrated manner. Each concept will be interrelated and forms a topic. The selected topic becomes the centre of correlation. For e.g.: the topic 'Osmosis' whether it is from Physics or Chemistry or Zoology, there can be only one discussion. A topic 'air' can include a number of lessons such as its physical properties, chemical properties, its components, respiration, ventilation, barometer and pumps. E.g.: If we include the topic 'climate' in the curriculum of social science of class VII. Hence, we must include all what is taught on this topic to the students during the entire stage of secondary education, in this way we are required to have different sets of topics for their inclusion in the curriculum of different grades of elementary and secondary stages of school education. For example: While dealing with the Unitary method, the students can be acquainted with time and work, simple interest, average, percentage and even extended to simple equation of algebra. In this approach, selected topics of study suitable for the age ability and interest of children are included in the curriculum and each topic is dealt with completely in the class. This method of curriculum organization is advantageous as it brings the different branches of science together and in close relationship. The knowledge imparted becomes well integrated and correlated thereby making the subject matter more interesting and real to pupils.

Merits of topical approach

- It illustrates the advantage of correlation.
- Helps to deal with the simple topics in the earlier grades and difficult one in the higher grades.
- Focuses only on a few topics included in their present curriculum while leaving the rest to the earlier or later grades.
- This approach can be adapted according to the age ability and aptitude of the children.
- This approach provides an action plan for dealing with vast material in a logical and rational way. It helps the pupils to understand the facts appropriate to their developmental stage.
- It imparts a sense of purpose to the pupils because of the total perception attempted.
- This approach enables the teacher to control the subject matter and adapt it to the varying needs of the children
- Each topic has transfer value for other topics
- The topical arrangement is helpful in avoiding the duplication in the curriculum

Continuous teaching of topic not only save the student from divided attention, but may ensure their full and whole – hearted concentration on the topic. A natural link and sequence will exist in the day today work in class room. The student's complete attention, ability and capacity will be directed exclusively to the topic under study for a sufficiently long time.

Limitations

- It destroys the continuity of subject matter
- Since many aspects involved in a topic may be beyond the cognitive competencies of pupils in lower classes a complete study of the topic will not be possible because of the above reason.
- Generally speaking, when a topic is complex and very large and involve units posing varied levels of difficulty it will be advisable not to have topic approach.
- Sometimes topic is not selected carefully to avoid duplication.
- As there is no agreement as to what constitutes a suitable topic, therefore some topic included are trivial and others are all inclusive.
- Lack of efficient teachers for proper selection of topics.

- The interest of the student may go away within a month, if we focus on only on a particular topic.
- This method does not provide any opportunity for year-to-year revision.
- Keeping psychological reason in view, it will be foolish to take a topic like area in grade four and try to finish in at one stretch. The student may be able to understand the elementary portion, but will certainly not be able to attempt its most difficult question.

In topic approach, certain topics of study make up the whole syllabus. The only advantage of this method is that a topic is made a centre of other topics, which can provide good step towards correlation. As a method, it is only an idea, which should be kept in mind to be used only at the appropriate opportunity.

Topical *Versus* Spiral or Concentric

Topical: A topic is taken up and is treated exhaustively. It gives mastery over the topic. The disadvantage is that a good deal of time is wasted on unnecessary matter for which the pupil has no time or no need or the use of which he/she cannot appreciate. Secondly, if once a topic is taken up, it must be completed exhaustively before passing on to another. It is a false idea.

Spiral or Concentric: A topic is taken up in a simpler form. As the pupil's advance, the treatment of the topic is to be exhaustive. The topics should be graded and each should be introduced when it is needed. In doing so the parts should be neither too long nor too short. If it is too long, interest will be lost and it is too short, no lasting impression can be made. The time gap between one part and the other part of a topic will be at least one year. According to this, the subject matter learnt in a class will be helpful to the subject matter to be learnt in the next higher class. With this pupil do not get bored with the instruction of the teacher.

From the above discussion it can be identified that dividing each topic into parts and introducing them according to their difficulty are required for better arrangement. This implies that this method is a child centred method.

Movement down a long road

One view of curriculum organization is that it is like movement down a long road, where learning arrangements or practices once considered adequate are left behind forever. All that is abandoned becomes the traditional. The new which is at hand is the right way or the modern. A shift from broad fields' curriculum to subject matter curriculum and then to activity curriculum adequately describes the movement down a long road pattern. In this view we move from one emphasis to another with no return for a second look (Miel, 1971). Another example of the type will be shift from special schools for the physically challenged (differentially abled) students to mainstreaming.

The Swing of a Pendulum

Another way of looking at Curriculum organization is to draw an analogy to the swing of a pendulum back and forth at the same groove. Opinion may shift from favouring homogeneous grouping to heterogeneous grouping and back again to the same original position with no variation and no learning from previous experience. This view of curriculum pattern appears to be near to the truth. The abandoned position in education is reconsidered and later accepted as valid. The new version in a careful observation will reveal that it is different in many ways (Miel, 1971). Opinions may shift from general science curriculum to specialized subjects such as chemistry and physics. Thus, the shift is from integration to specialization. The cycle is repeated with some modifications.

HISTORICAL APPROACH

Science has a history of its own and every invention or discovery has its historical background. The historical approach emphasizes the organizing of the science course in accordance with the evolution of science i.e. the stages through which science has passed in its actual course of development from the very beginning. Subjects such as chemistry and physics have a history of development. The current status of knowledge has evolved over time. Both concepts and theories are being subjected to modification in the light of further empirical observation. Science is really a grant expression of human spirit and it is essential that this aspect should be felt by every student. The romance of science will be felt only if it is treated historically. Pupils should be led into the spirit of the intellectual life of great men of science. The history of scientific advancement shows how in any particular field scientists had to work in order to reach the present state despite the difficulties that cross the path of those scientists. This approach puts an emphasis on process and not on the product. The students are given valuable insights into the process of science. When the historical method is adopted, the proceedings should be similar to the usual lessons in history. The lesson on any topic should be planned in accordance with the sequence of events which actually occurred in its development. E.g. Periodic Table. One of the first attempts to investigate the connection between chemical properties of elements and their atomic must was made by a German chemist, Johann Dobereiner (1780- 1844). He examined groups of 3 elements such as C1, Br, I (known as triads) and noted that bromine seems just half way in its properties, between Cl and I. His ideas were published on 1829. It was in 1864 that the English chemist, John Newlands (1838-1898) came up with another classification in which the 8th element starting from as given one is a kind of repetition of the 1st, like the 8th note on an octave of music. He called this rule, the law of Octaves. He arranged all the 50 elements in the order of atomic masses and demonstrated his law. It was in 1869 that a Russian Scientist, Dimitri Mendeleev published the periodic table on which all later version of periodic table has been based. Mendeleev stated that when the elements are arranged in the order of atomic mass, similar properties recur at intervals. One year later a German chemist Lothar Mayer published a graph showing wave like repeating patterns. He also discovered that periods differ in length. In this way, in there is sequencing in the historical approach in curriculum organization.

UNIT APPROACH

We can also adopt the unit approach for the proper organization of the curriculum. In doing so one has to first divide the selected contents and learning experiences meant for the study of a subject at a particular stage (elementary or secondary) into some appropriate and meaningful units and then putting them into the curriculum of any of the grades or classes according to their suitability to the age and mental level of the students. Quillen and Hanna says, "A unit refers to material organized around a common principle, process, culture or an area of living and directed toward the achievement of significant outcomes thus giving unity to learning experiences." In this way the selected subject material and learning experiences meant for teaching of any subject at a particular stage of school education are divided into a series of units, each unit developed around a major theme related to the students' social environment, their experiences, social problems, social relationships and individual and social needs. These units are then allotted to various grades or classes belonging to the stage according to the needs, interests, mental state and educational level of the students. E.g.: means of communication, our solar system, life on earth, pollution and our health, the food we eat, the air we breathe, national unity, our community, the climate we have our forest wealth, our national heritage, etc.

INTEGRATED APPROACH

Integrated approach towards curriculum organization works on the principle of integration and coordination. According to this principle knowledge exists as a whole. The curriculum developed by adopting an integrated approach is termed as integrated curriculum. Integration is in contrast to fragmentation of the curriculum which typifies the compartmentalization or specialization. It is for the simple reason that the origin, existence, concept and instructions in the subject are totally based upon and guided by the integrated approach. As a result, instead of teaching it in the form of separate subjects of the social science disciplines like history, geography, civics, economics, etc. we are teaching it as a full subject of the school curriculum up to the tenth class of our education system. Integrated curriculum adopts a student-centred approach where students are free to reach conclusions on their own and they are provided with many different perspectives, affording students the opportunity to question the conclusions of their teachers. The teachers of the integrated curriculum view their course as an opportunity for students to gain a deeper understanding of our society, the history and their ability to recognize and appreciate diversity is expanded. A major driving force behind integrated teaching and learning is the belief that when themes, subjects or projects are combined students begin to see meaningful connections between the subject matter.

CHARACTERISTIC OF GOOD CURRICULUM ORGANIZATION

A good organization is one that faithfully includes the materials which have been selected as socially desirable. Following are the characteristics of a good curriculum organization:

- The materials should be arranged in a learnable manner
- The organization should provide for smooth and continuous progress from topic to topic and from class to class.
- The materials in science should be arranged in such a way as to establish relationship and connection b/w various subjects in curriculum.
- Provisions should be given for actual learning experiences, activities, general knowledge and contemporary affairs and generalizations.
- It should be flexible and not rigid.
- A good organization provides for repetition i.e., the supplementary kind of repetition that includes additional facts, generalizations etc.

- Curriculum must be arranged so as to facilitate transfer of learning.
- The curriculum should provide materials that are suited to students with varied interests, abilities and talents.
- It should consider the individual differences of students.
- It should have philosophical, sociological and psychological dimensions.

ROLE OF TEACHER IN CURRICULUM ORGANIZATION

Teachers play the respective role for each step of curriculum development process. The most important person in the practice curriculum is the teacher. With their knowledge, experience and competencies teachers are central to any curriculum improvement effort, they are responsible for introducing the curriculum in the classroom and outside the classroom as well. Handal and Herrington (2003) also stress the central role of the teachers in implementing the curriculum and call on policy makers to take teachers attitudes and perceptions into account. A teacher does more than just implement curriculum. While curriculum specialists, administrators and education experts spend countless hours developing curriculum it is the teachers who know best what the curriculum should look like. After all, they work directly with the students who are meant to benefit from the curriculum. In order to create strong curriculum teachers must play an integral role in every step of the process.

- **Teacher's role in planning the curriculum:** Teachers know their students better than others involved in the curriculum process. While the state often dictates the skills covered by the curriculum, a teacher can provide insight into the types of materials, activities and specific skills that need to be included. Teachers from multiple grade levels may collaborate to identify skills students need at each level and ensure that the curriculum adequately prepares students to advance to the next grade-level.
- **Teacher's role in the design of the curriculum:** A teacher can gauge whether an activity will fit into a specified time frame and engage students. All teachers should be allowed to provide input during the creation stage. As teachers provide input, they will gain ownership in the product and feel more confident that the curriculum was created with their concerns, and the needs of their students in mind.
- **Teacher's role in the implementation of the curriculum:** Teachers must implement the curriculum in their own classroom sticking to the plan that has taken so much time and effort to create.

When a teacher fails to properly implement a strong curriculum, she risks not covering standards or failing to implement effective practices in the classroom. That does not mean a teacher can't make minor changes. In fact, a strong curriculum is designed to allow a teacher to be flexible to add a few personalized components, from a selection of activities.

- **Teacher's role in the evaluation of the curriculum:** Evaluation of the curriculum allows teachers and others involved in the process to find any weaknesses in the curriculum, and attempt to make it better. Teachers may reflect on curriculum in multiple ways such as keeping a journal as they implement the curriculum giving student reviews and surveys, analysing results and assessments, data about student's individual performance. Not only can reflection serve to improve a specific curriculum, it may guide the creation of a new curriculum.

CONCLUSION

There are several approaches to curriculum development. They vary in their major focus. After topics have been selected according to the relevant fundamental principles described above, they have to be systematically arranged so as to facilitate meaningful and effective transaction. The content should be arranged in a systematic manner. A good curriculum should be well organized based on the maxims of teaching. A curriculum should arouse interest in students and develop their scientific attitude. The topics in the curriculum should be continuous and well arranged. To make the teaching process effective curriculum should be changed according to the need of the society. All of the approaches mentioned above may play a substantial role in the organization of a curriculum.

Chapter - 7

Types of Curriculums

INTRODUCTION

There are different types of curriculum designs which were developed at different times in educational history in accordance with societal conceptions of the role of education, the nature of the learner and of the learning process as well as societal needs. In designing each of them, consideration was given to continuity, sequence and integration.

ACTIVITY / EXPERIENCE-CENTERED CURRICULUM

Activity is the natural urge of the child. Activity is used as a media or means for imparting knowledge and skills. It is a play way of learning things. Activity is the greatest motivation, provided to the child enjoys the freedom of expressing himself fully. This type of curriculum is learner-centred. Consideration in this type of curriculum is given to learners' interest, needs and motivation. It is also regarded as problem solving. Activity curriculum is an approach with very flexible ideas and adaptation of curriculum to the needs of children in the natural setting of human growth and development. One characteristic of the activity curriculum is that children's interests determine the content and structure of learning. It also helps learner psychologically as the can express their emotions through active participation in something useful. It inspires the students to apply their creative ideas, knowledge and mind in solving problems. The method also promotes better understanding of a lesson among students as they learn the lesson by practicing the task themselves. The most important feature of Activity based curriculum is learning by doing. So, this method can fulfil the natural urge of a growing child on one hand also can help them learn their lesson. Within the activity-centred curriculum tradition, the role of the teacher is that of an instructor and work supervisor while their students are learners as well as productive workers. Here, the teacher is mostly that of a facilitator rather than of authority in knowledge.

Advantages of Activity Based Instruction:

- The method promotes better understanding of a lesson among students as they learn the lesson by practicing the task themselves.
- It inspires the students to apply their creative ideas, knowledge and minds in solving problems as well as promoting competitive spirit among them.
- It also helps learner psychologically as they can express their emotions through active participation in something useful.
- The method also helps in developing their personalities, social traits and inter-personal management skills.

Disadvantages of Activity Based Instruction:

- The activity-based instruction method requires long-term planning with minute details of the whole process because before engaging the learners, the teacher has to make sure that all students have sufficient knowledge and skills regarding the task they are going to perform. So, this method cannot be used on a regular and daily basis as it involves a lengthy procedure.
- The objectives of the method can only be fulfilled if the planning of the lesson is flawless. If there is slightest flaw in the planning, this method would do more harm than good.
- Learners have varied levels of merit and understanding. So less meritorious students might not prepare for a task as other which might lead to failure of objectives of the whole process.
- Many renowned educationists also are of the opinion that the activity-based method is more suitable for branches of experimental sciences and less useful for subjects of social sciences.
- Activity curriculum is not applicable to all stages of education.
- Personal supervision is needed for every activity which is not possible in school.
- Activity curriculum attaches too much importance on activities. It neglects other activities needed for intellectual development of the child.

CHILD-CENTRED CURRICULUM

The philosophy underlying this curriculum design is that the child is the centre of the educational process. The curriculum should be built upon his interest, abilities, purposes and needs. This type of curriculum emerged from the extensive research carried on in the 20th century carried by John Dewey and his followers. Child-Centred Curriculum means children take command of their own learning. Teachers are there to provide support and facilitate the child's learning but children determine the direction of their own learning following their natural curiosities, interests and passions. When the claim of a curriculum approach is that a worthwhile curriculum is solely constructed by reference to needs, wants and interests of the child, it becomes a child centred curriculum. Curriculum developers in this type of curriculum should be very careful when exploring children's needs, wants and interests in curriculum matters to make children do what they want with qualification. When this is done, the curriculum could be regarded as a worthwhile school curriculum. Barrow (1976) observed that by concentrating on children's actual wants or interests, it is possible for the teacher to help them find aspects of value in those wants and interests.

Scope

- This is an "active learning" educational approach that seeks to meet a child's needs on all levels social, cognitive, physical, and emotional.
- With this approach children are mentally and physically active using their whole bodies and all their senses to explore and learn about their world.
- It views play as children's work – a time when children are planning, testing, questioning, and experimenting to construct their own knowledge about people, objects, events, and ideas

Merits

- Help children become independent, responsible and confident
- Give children and adults opportunity to invent and discover together as they explore materials and ideas and experience events
- Maintain children's interest by allowing them to do what is important to them
- Give children the opportunity to develop skills in which to take care of their own needs and solve problems
- Avoids Borden
- Help child develop executive skills (self-control)

- Help children gain knowledge and skills in content areas such as creative representation, language and literacy, initiative and social relations, movement and music, classification and serration, number, space and time

Demerits

- Teachers sometimes are not prepared to adapt to changing concepts of child development.
- In this effort to free the child, many critics charged that the basic purposes in the establishment of schools are ignored
- Selection of activities is difficult
- Focus is on activities rather than subject

SUBJECT – CENTRED CURRICULUM

The Subject-centred Curriculum is the traditional model that was laid out by Ralph Tyler in 1949 in his seminal book, Basic Principles of Curriculum and Instruction. Also called the Knowledge-centred Curriculum, it is the most widely-used method of instruction. This type of curriculum is concerned with the collection and arrangement of school subjects which are generally studied separately or sometimes in relation to each-other. For instance, in our secondary schools, subjects in the curriculum include: English, Mathematics, Biology, Chemistry, Physics, Economics, Geography, Home, Economics, Agricultural Science, Government, Social Studies and Integrated Science (in Junior Secondary School). In this system of organization, the science course is split up into compartments such as physics, chemistry, botany, zoology etc. Topics from all compartmental subjects are treated separately without any attempt for correlating and integrating the subject matter.

This type of curriculum lays greater emphasis on the subjects themselves rather than on the children. Students are expected to gain mastery of subject matters from academic disciplines that have been predetermined by a panel of experts. These are prescribed for the students without much regard to their actual interest or point of view. The curriculum is organized around content units and the sequence of what is taught follows the logic of the subject matter. Knowledge and skills are taught sequentially over time and students have to remember these for the purpose of examination or an interview for a white-collar job. The teacher in a subject-based curriculum is seen as a scholar who will be using a variety of teaching strategies to share their knowledge.

In this type of curriculum, mastery of the subject matter is usually the basis through which educational outcomes are achieved. Its scope, however, is determined by the quantity of subject matter existing within each subject as well as the range of subjects to be included in the school time-table. The characteristic feature of this type of curriculum is orderliness. If learners follow the bodies of subject matter, they build their store of knowledge. They can readily make use of such store of knowledge when needed. This type of curriculum is convenient to teachers since they were trained in subject areas. They can easily plan, organize and teach their areas of specialization. Examination which is the yardstick for admission and selection of candidates into schools, colleges and universities appear in subject areas. Employment in some cases is done on the basis of the subject candidate studied. A more tangible quality of the subject-centred curriculum is its tight organization. The content is rigidly sequenced. When using this design, teachers can, and almost always do, follow the sequence of the textbook. This makes the task of keeping track of where each lesson ends and where the next one begins easy. This tight organization helps the teacher avoid accidental duplication of content and makes the testing simple. The tightly organized subject-centred curriculum is easy to implement.

Features of Curriculum

- The scope of the curriculum is determined by the subjects that are included in the curriculum.
- The internal structure and organization of each of the subject will decide the sequence or continuity in curriculum.
- Curriculum is said to be determined because a lot of pre-planning is possible on the part of the teacher and school. The method of teaching used is mostly lecture method.
- Education is said to be subject -centred and the medium of instruction is the printed word.
- Evaluation of learning is done through written tests.
- It is considered to be the best pattern of curriculum organization for producing scholars and high-grade specialists.

Limitations

- Among the limitations of the subject-centred curriculum is its failure to consider the unique needs and interest of the students and its detachments from contemporary events in the world. It ignores the natural activities and interests of children.

- Separation: Subject-centred curriculum prevents students from understanding the wider context of what they're learning. In the traditional method of learning, students learn math in one period, English in another, science in another and social studies in yet another, separate class. Every subject is taught as though it exists in and of itself without regard for how one subject impacts another subject.
- Lack of Integration: A traditional subject-centred curriculum so focuses on each subject in an individual context, students don't understand how one subject impacts another subject or how each works together. Learning is fragmented into little boxes instead of flowing together toward deeper comprehension of subject matter as a whole. Students are not taught to use different aspects of their knowledge in an integrated fashion.
- Passivity: In the traditional or subject-centred curriculum, students are discouraged from entertaining a different point of view than what textbook or teacher presents. The subject matter has already been chosen by experts in the different subjects, by school boards and by teachers and deemed of value for students to learn. The subject-centred curriculum fosters not excitement about learning and knowledge, but passivity.
- Authority: The traditional subject-centred curriculum depends upon a system of authority. Students are not part of the authority hierarchy. Material is covered and does not change regardless of the needs of individual students or classes. The material must be taught and students are expected to absorb the material in the time allotted. Testing, then, is often based solely on reproducing the material and not on overall comprehension or the practical use of the material in everyday life to solve problems.
- It fails to develop effective habits of thinking and the arrangement of content is not psychological
- Emphasis is given to the product aspect of science alone, neglecting the process aspect.
- Despite this, the subject design is by far the most popular approach. It is easy to do and practical.

COMMUNITY-BASED CURRICULUM

Community-based curriculum allows students to combine service in the community with academic inquiry. Community-based learning is a type of experiential learning; it is not simply community service nor is it an internship. Community-based learning is curriculum based, meaning that the community work is profoundly connected to and enhanced by the classroom learning. As an educational philosophy, community-based learning fosters reciprocal earning and critical engagement and prepares students to be responsible participants in both their profession and their communities. Community based curriculum can play an important role in challenging students to use their acquired knowledge in new contexts. This offers a common-sense approach for linking living and learning. A growing number of schools and community partners are adapting courses that allow students to learn in their communities. This link between schools and community partners is a critical element of community-based curriculum, offering students ways to develop the skills and knowledge necessary for success in adulthood. The aim of these courses is to more fully engage young people, by harnessing their natural interest in where and how they live and by using their own community as a source of learning and action.

Community-based curriculum goes beyond cognitive capacities and encompasses the social and emotional aspects of learning. Community-based curriculum is centred on the student's ability to recognize and support the needs of the surrounding community. In this way, students become accountable for providing values which stem from their freedom to express, develop, and solve the inherent problems or concerns they have for their community. Students and teachers are the fuel that generates community-based education. Parents, community leaders, administrators, school board members, and citizens are an integral part in the development, production, implementation, and assessment of community-based education. This cohesive interplay is designed to foster trust and belief in fellow human beings. It also creates collaborative efforts between school and community to solve various problems

As an intentional dimension of the curriculum, community-based learning helps students acquire, practice, and apply subject matter knowledge and skills. At the same time, students develop the knowledge, skills, and attributes of effective citizenship by identifying and acting on issues and concerns that affect their own communities. Community-based learning helps students build a sense of connection to their communities. At the same time, it challenges them to develop a range of intellectual and academic skills in order to understand and take action on the issues they encounter in everyday life.

Initiatives for a more community-based curriculum

- Engaging students in learning through community-based learning:

community service, civics and citizenship, environmental education, student action teams, and work-based learning. These Activities aim at community development and include community projects, first aid, social service, etc. these activities also help in the socialization of the child.

- Involving students, parents and other partners in curriculum-making. When reviewing the curriculum, some schools organize forums to engage students, community members and parents whose voices may be less frequently heard in curriculum conversations.
- Building links with organizations to develop the curriculum. These include other schools such as a small cluster of primary and secondary schools, community and health services, business and industry, cultural organizations and local government.
- The purpose of community learning and development is to develop the capacity of individuals and capacity of communities, to improve their quality of life. Central to this is their ability to participate in democratic processes.

CORE-CURRICULUM

Core curriculum came up as a result of a reaction again the piece-meal learning (fragmentally) from isolated conventional subjects. According to the exponents of the core curriculum, knowledge is synthetic and would remain as a unit and as a whole. It cannot be imparted in isolated sections; head, heart and hands are to be trained simultaneously. Knowledge to be real and factual must come in its natural setting and should be related to real life. Education is to aim at a balanced and a well-integrated society comprising of harmoniously developed individuals. As a result of this kind of thinking the core curriculum was emerged.

The terminology core is applied to that curriculum which is concerned with those types of experiences necessary for all learners, irrespective of what occupation, they may expect to follow or where they may happen to live. Core is the minimum that an individual needs for leading a satisfactory life in one's own society. It prepares him for living. It teaches subject matter which may help in the solution of problems that he may face as an adult. i.e. Core is used to describe a portion of the curriculum, usually those courses prescribed for all. In this type of curriculum, there exist a set of common learning i.e. there exists a set of common learning (knowledge, skills and values) that should be provided to all learners in order to function effectively in a society. Essentially, core curriculum is meant to develop unified studies based upon common needs of the learners and organized without restriction by subject-matter. This is a curriculum in which all or some of the subjects or courses are based on a central theme in order to correlate the subjects and the theme. This type of curriculum organization was designed as a synthesis of all and to specifically integrate all subject areas, serve the needs of the students, promote actual learning and enhance the relationship between life and learning.

Core curriculum is not intended to provide education in vocational skills and knowledge in any discipline. Core curriculum helps students in the following areas:

- Proficiency in the use of languages
- Civic understanding and competence
- Intelligent action as consumers
- Family relationships
- Appreciation of beauty
- Ability to use time efficiently and to budget it wisely
- Respect for other persons and ability to work cooperatively with others.

The work experience emphasized by the Kothari Commission and Gandhi's basic education are extended forms of the core curriculum. Here the whole pedagogical work is wound around a social activity of a basic craft. This system is severely criticized as it doesn't give a sound and systematic knowledge of subject matter. It can result in huge gaps in the pupils' knowledge of various branches of science. Also, there may be discontinuity of experience from class to class and overemphasis to activity at the cost of subject matter. Core curriculum is used variously to designate Basic Studies, General Studies, General Education and indeed all subjects and courses (or part of the curriculum) which educational authorities consider necessary for all students.

Characteristic features of core-curriculum

- Relates learning experiences to life problems and student's interest. Here, it was thought that all people have similar problems confronting them at all times.
- In realizing this, Core curriculum focuses on real life problems that are meaningful to the students. The method of teaching is essentially problem-solving techniques and critical thinking.
- Flexibility in arrangement of time and content

- Teachers can consider more seriously the development sequence of growth and the behavioural objectives.
- Brings to the fore the social role of the school through the emphasis on life problems.

Merits

- Common learning provides to all learners
- Common learning is expected essential for the learners to function effectively in the society
- These common learning vary according to different experts
- It emphasizes that all students would experience a set of common and essential learning that were necessary for learners to function effectively in society.

Demerits

- Selection of content may difficult
- It does not offer significant and systematic knowledge. The organization of all learning experiences around new centres have not been successful because the people involved themselves are not versed enough in this area of integration.
- The curriculum then reflects on combination of subject disciplines rather than integration. Owing to this, a particular subject often dominates the other "cooperating" subjects.
- It is difficult to discover a problem that will have significant validity and scope for curriculum purpose.
- There is inadequacy of teachers with broad competence to cope with such curriculum.
- Teachers themselves were trained in specialized subject areas. Implementing the core curriculum thus becomes an encumbrance.

THE HIDDEN CURRICULUM

Hidden curriculum refers to the unofficial, unwritten curriculum of the school or that which is not ordinarily addressed through regular curriculum planning but which nevertheless influences what and how students learn. The hidden curriculum encompasses what students learn outside the formal curriculum. It is pervasive and complex and can be deeply instilled in institutional cultures. The hidden curriculum has been regarded as a powerful detrimental force that undermines the professed commitment of the school to foster intellectual development.

The school as an agent of socialization of the young, has its rules and regulations governing social conduct of students within the context of the educational programmers, and a system of procedures that make it an acceptable institution in the larger society. What is, however, learnt from the hidden or subtle curriculum is frequently more powerful and lasting than that which is learnt from the more obvious planned curriculum. The hidden curriculum is the unintended curriculum-what students learn from the school's culture and climate. It includes such elements as the use of time, allocation of space, funding for programs and activities, and disciplinary policies and practices. For example, if an elementary school allocates 450 minutes each week to reading and 45 minutes to art, the unintended message to students is that "art doesn't matter."

For instance, a teacher decided to teach a topic not using the traditional lecture method but the group investigation model where learners are grouped to work on the topic. Apart from the content of the topic which they will work at in group, the leader will learn to lead, coordinate the affairs of the group while carrying out the task; learn to respect the views of others by being receptive to them while other members of the group will learn to follow for the success of the group. The nurturing values here can be regarded as the hidden curriculum. The method nurtured was not planned by the teacher. Since the hidden curriculum is just as much as part of the school programme as any course or subject or unit that is offered, it should be considered as a powerful and pervasive source of learning. In schools, learners offered opportunities to learn about themselves and their relationship with others. These learning are not always planned or intended in curriculum plans. They instead grow out of the day-to-day life of the school and its organization. Because such learning are embedded in features of the school rather than in curriculum, they are often referred to as the hidden curriculum.

DIFFERENTIATED CURRICULUM

Students are individuals who learn at different rates and in different ways. These individual differences may influence how students respond to instruction and how they demonstrate what they know, understand and can do. Individual differences may include:

- cognitive abilities, including students' current level of understanding and ability in relation to a particular topic or skill
- prior learning experiences
- learning styles and preferences

- motivation and engagement with learning
- interests and talents.

Through differentiated planning and programming, teachers can consider students' varying abilities, learning styles, interests and needs. Differentiation relates to understanding individual differences and devising strategies to cater for students' needs. A differentiated curriculum is a programme of activities that offers a variety of experiences for students who differ in abilities, knowledge and skills. In a differentiated curriculum, teachers offer different approaches to what students learn (content), how students learn (process) and how students demonstrate what they have learned (product). Differentiated curriculum is one that is individualized to meet the diverse needs of all of the students in one class. Curriculum differentiation is a broad term referring to the need to tailor teaching environments and practices to create appropriately different learning experiences for different students

Purpose of Differentiated Curriculum

- Provides teaching, learning and assessment for learning experiences that cater for the diversity of learners so that all students can learn effectively
- Provides alternative methods and choices for students to demonstrate their knowledge, understanding and skills
- Considers what resources and stimulus materials will assist students
- Includes a range of activities and resources appropriate for students with different learning needs and levels of achievement
- Promotes flexible learning experiences and encourages students to work at their own pace to develop their knowledge, understanding and skills
- Monitors student learning over time using evidence of student achievement to guide future teaching and learning opportunities
- Considers how individualized feedback to students can help identify student strengths and areas for improvement.

Differentiated programming provides students with opportunities to:

- Demonstrate, in different ways, what they know, understand and can do at different points of the learning cycle

- Discuss with their teachers their preferred learning style and new ways of learning
- Explore, experiment and engage with the concepts and principles underpinning what they learn
- Develop higher-order thinking and creative and critical thinking skills.

Areas of Differentiation

Maker's model of differentiated curriculum (Maker, 1986) suggests that curriculum needs to be differentiated in terms of:

Learning environment: The aim is to create a learning environment which encourages students to engage their abilities to the greatest extent possible, including taking risks and building knowledge and skills in what they perceive as a safe, flexible environment. It should be:

- Student-centred - focusing on the student's interests, input and ideas rather than those of the teacher,
- Encouraging independence - tolerating and encouraging student initiative,
- Open - permitting new people, materials, ideas and things to enter and non-academic and interdisciplinary connections to be made,
- Accepting - encouraging acceptance of others' ideas and opinions before evaluating them,
- Complex - including a rich variety of resources, media, ideas, methods and tasks, and
- Highly mobile - encouraging movement in and out of groups, desk settings, classrooms, and schools.

Content modification: The aim is to remove the ceiling on what is learned, and use the student's abilities to build a richer, more diverse and efficiently organized knowledge base. This building can be facilitated by encouraging:

- Abstractness - with content shifting from facts, definitions and descriptions to concepts, relationships to key concepts, and generalizations,
- Complexity - with content shifting to inter-relationships rather than considering factors separately,
- Variety - with content expanding beyond material presented in the normal program,

- Study of people - including the study of individuals or peoples, and how they have reacted to various opportunities and problems, and
- Study of methods of inquiry - including procedures used by experts working in their fields.

Process Modification: The aim is to promote creativity and higher-level cognitive skills, and to encourage productive use and management of the knowledge the students have mastered. This can be facilitated by encouraging:

- Higher levels of thinking - involving cognitive challenge using Bloom's Taxonomy of Cognitive Processes, logical problems, critical thinking and problem solving,
- Creative thinking - involving imagination, intuitive approaches and brainstorming techniques,
- Open-endedness - encouraging risk-taking and the response that is right for the student by stressing there is no one right answer,
- Group interaction - with highly able and motivated students sparking each other in the task, with this sometimes being on a competitive and sometimes on a cooperative basis (depending on the task and its objectives),
- Variable pacing - allowing students to move through lower order thinking more rapidly but allowing more time for students to respond fully on higher order thinking tasks,
- Variety of learning processes - accommodating different students' learning styles,
- Debriefing - encouraging students to be aware of and able to articulate their reasoning or conclusion to a problem or question, and
- Freedom of choice - involving students in evaluation of choices of topics, methods, products and environments.

Product modification: The aim is to facilitate opportunities for talented students to produce a product that reflects their potential. This can be encouraged by incorporating:

- Real problems - real and relevant to the student and the activity,
- Real audiences - utilizing an "audience" that is appropriate for the product, which could include another student or group of students, a teacher (not necessarily the class teacher), an assembly, a mentor, a community or specific interest group,

- Real deadlines - encouraging time management skills and realistic planning,
- Transformations - involving original manipulation of information rather than regurgitation, and
- Appropriate evaluation - with the product and the process of its development being both self-evaluated and evaluated by the product's audience using previously established "real world" criteria that are appropriate for such products.
- A number of management strategies that are often useful in implementing curriculum differentiation strategies include:
- The use of contracts - allowing individualized and student negotiated programs and promoting the student's time-management skills and autonomy,
- Conferencing - allowing dedicated student negotiation and review, and
- Grouping strategies - facilitating children to work with "like minds" and encouraging group interaction

Gifted Students

Giftedness refers to the cognitive superiority, creative skills and high motivational level of sufficient magnitude that sets the child apart from the vast majority of learners of the same age level. The purpose of differentiating the curriculum is to provide appropriate learning opportunities for gifted and talented students. Three important characteristics of gifted students that underscore the rationale for curriculum differentiation (Van Tassel Baska, 1988) are the capacity to, (a) learn at faster rates, (b) find, solve and act on problems more readily, (c) manipulate abstract ideas and make connections.

Keirouz (1993) suggests typical procedures in the case of gifted and talented students include: (a) deleting already mastered material from existing curriculum, (b) adding new content, process, or product expectations to existing curriculum, (c) extending existing curriculum to provide enrichment activities, (d) providing course work for able students at an earlier age than usual, and (e) writing new units or courses that meet the needs of gifted students. Differentiated curriculum for gifted students include the following:

- Individual enrichment
- Group-oriented work
- Encouraging individual research

- Flexibility in teaching units
- Assigning projects
- Opportunity to probe into the depth of the content matter.
- Assigning challenging questions
- Provision for library, laboratory, field work.
- Assigning special groups within the general class.

Creative Learners

Creative students refer to those who have high creative abilities and are able to think and act with originality and naturalness. Creativity is the process of becoming sensitive to problems, deficiencies and gaps of knowledge; and are able to identify difficulties and search for solutions. Curriculum for creative learners:

- Independent study/ Project work
- Synectics Model for creativity
- Brain-storming
- Activities to develop spontaneity and opportunity for expression.

Slow Learners

Slow learners include those who are unable to cope with the normally expected of children belonging to their age group. They have weakness of memory. Often referred to as dull, retarded or educationally sub-normal. Curriculum for slow children:

- Curriculum based on logical, physical and social aspects.
- Specially designed curriculum to assist the total growth as well as to develop the basic skills and knowledge.
- Curriculum includes central core language and learning of numbers, periphery subjects of environment, creative and aesthetic activities, and practical interests.
- Provision for extra remedial work.
- Flexible curriculum which would be related to the requirements and needs of individual students.
- Concentration on concrete aspects of work.
- Crafts conducive to them include leatherwork, cane work, knitting, tailoring etc.

Underachievers

Underachievement occurs at any level of intellectual ability. Some underachievers have superior intellectual ability and special talents. Others have mild to severe learning problems or inability to take effort. Causes of underachievement include individual, familial, school or other environmental factors. Curriculum for underachievers consists:

- Providing motivating environment.
- Flexibility in curriculum
- Remedial instruction
- Importance to practical work like woodwork, leatherwork, knitting etc.
- Physical education to develop physical abilities.
- Audio-video instruction.

Learning Disabled

Learning disability refers to a retardation disorder or delayed development in one or more of the processes of speech, language, reading, spelling, writing or arithmetic, resulting from a possible cerebral dysfunction or emotional or behavioural disturbance, and not from mental retardation, sensory deprivation, cultural or instructional factors. Types of learning disabilities include: dyslexia, dyscalculia and dysgraphia. Curriculum for learning disabled includes:

- Medical-neurological approach– Considers the learning-disabled child as a patient affected with minimal brain dysfunction.
- Psycho-educational approach – Considers the child not as a patient, but a learner waiting to be taught.
- Multi-sensory approach
- Specialized schooling with special teachers in a regular school.
- Can be given inclusive education.

Developing curriculum that is sufficiently rigorous, challenging, and coherent for students is a challenging task. The result, however, is well worth the effort. Appropriately differentiated curriculum produces well-educated, knowledgeable students who have had to work very hard, have mastered a substantial body of knowledge, and can think clearly and critically about that knowledge. Curriculum differentiation, while it may be a more difficult challenge for the instructor, can be very beneficial for students at all levels, giving them the opportunity to grow and learn at their own pace. If implemented appropriately, differentiation does not have to mean more work for the teacher. In fact, it will allow a teacher to spend his or her time more efficiently with a greater number of students.

MAJOR HIGHLIGHTS OF PHYSICAL SCIENCE EDUCATION IN NCF/KCF

National Curriculum Framework (NCF 2005)

National Council for Educational Research and Training (NCERT) during the last many years of its existence has come up with three different National Curriculum Frame work during the year 1986, 2000 and 2005. This document provides the frame work for making syllabus, text books and teaching practice within the school education programmes in India. The main features of the National Curriculum Framework for School Education 2000 pertaining to science education has been:

- Teaching of environmental studies as a single subject of study at the primary stage instead of science and social science.
- Teaching of 'Science and Technology' in place of 'science' at the upper primary and secondary stages, so as to familiarize the learner with various dimensions of scientific and technological literacy and
- To continue the practice of teaching science at the higher stages as separate disciplines: physics, chemistry and biology
- Compulsory teaching of science and environmental orientation to science teaching up to secondary stages.

The NCF 2005 document draws its policy from earlier Government reports on education as "Learning Without Burden "and National Policy as Education 1986 & 1992 and the focus group discussion. The main features of NCF 2005 given as under. The document is divided in to 5 areas; viz. Perspective, Learning and Knowledge, Curriculum Areas, School stages and Assessment, School and Classroom Environment, and Systemic Reforms. This document is a very useful one which has kept children in mind. It brings in a fresh outlook on curriculum making: there has been a lot of advocacies on including more and more subjects into education like environment, peace etc. The document tries to break the information overload on the children. Focus is on creativity and overall development of the child.

The Guiding Principles of NCF 2005

- Connecting Knowledge life to outside school.
- Learning away from rote.
- Enriching curriculum.
- Overall development of children.

- Not text book centric.
- Reduces examination stress.
- Curriculum from the context of Elementary Education.
- Taking care of the interests of the social diversity.

As per NCF 2005, the Science education should enable the learner to:

- Know the facts and principles of science and its application, consistent with the stages of cognitive development,
- Acquire the skills understand the methods and processes that lead to generation and validation of scientific knowledge,
- Develop a historical and developmental perspective of science and to enable her to view science a social enterprise,
- Acquire the requisite theoretical knowledge and practical technological skills to enter the world of work,
- Cultivate 'scientific temper'- objectivity, critical thinking and freedom fear and prejudice.

Curriculum at Different Stages

- **Primary Stage:** At the primary stage, the child should be engaged in joyfully exploring the world around and harmonizing with it. The main objective at this stage is to arouse curiosity about the world and to engage the child in explanatory and hands on activities. At the upper primary stage science education should provide a gradual transition from environmental studies of the primary stage to elements of science and technology. At this stage the child should be engaged in learning the principles of science through familiar experiences, working with hands to simple technological models.
- **Secondary Stages (Class IX and X):** At the secondary experience may come to occupy a stage, the beginning made at the earlier stage introduces science as a discipline is to be further strengthened without emphasis on formal rigor. Hence concepts that are beyond direct experience may come to occupy an important place in the science curriculum. Since not all phenomena are directly observable, science also relies on inference and interpretation. Experimentation, often involving quantitative measurement, as a tool to discover/verify theoretical principles should be important part of the curriculum stage. The technological modules introduced at this stage should be more advanced than at the upper primary

stage. Experiments (and, as far as feasible, the technological modules) should be part of the content of the secondary stage textbook, to avoid their marginalization or neglect. Participation in co-curricular activities must be regarded as equally important at this stage.

- **Higher Secondary Stage (Class XI and XII):** This curriculum at this stage should be disciplinary in its approach, with appropriate rigor and depth. Care should be taken not to make the syllabus heavy. The theoretical component of higher secondary science should strongly emphasize problem solving, awareness of conceptual pitfalls, and critical interrogations of different topics. Emphasis should be on environment friendly materials; this is the stage to introduce microchemistry as a means of experimentation for the chemistry laboratory, and possibly also for some biology laboratory work.

The co-curricular activities at this stage could be of several types; adopting a problem-solving approach on local issues involving science and technology; participation through creative/investigate projects in national science fairs and participation in mathematics and science Olympiads. Students should be encouraged to participate in debates and discussions on issues at the interface of science, technology and society. The enormous potential of ICT in science pedagogy should be exploited the classroom atmosphere should be such that it provokes questioning, discussions and debates and enhances students' Metacognitive skills.

Other Features of Science Curriculum in NCF 2005

- Activity based teaching.
- Emphasize of creative expression of students.
- Avoid content dominated curriculum.
- Encourage practical/technological components of the curriculum through conformed channels.
- ICT in science Education.
- Hands- on, inquiry-based science curriculum
- Flexible examination system and time schedule
- Integration of theory and practical work in teaching learning of science
- Emphasized the need for child centred education
- Science should be related to every day experiences of students

Guidelines for Curriculum Transaction as per NCF (2005)

The NCF (2005) aims to guide the development and transaction of curriculum in schools and to address the problems of transmission of information and rote learning. It includes guidelines for curriculum transaction to make learning active, social and meaningful. Schools are supposed to adopt these guidelines and the current five-year plan of the Indian government reiterates this. The guidelines are as follows:

- Connecting knowledge to life outside the school: The first guideline aims to contextualize learning and ensure that the content gets a broader perspective as it is linked to the life of the learners during the instructional process.
- Ensuring that learning shifts away from rote methods: The second guideline intends that learners are enabled to link new and old learning so that they develop conceptual clarity and are encouraged to think critically and apply learning.
- Enriching the curriculum so that it goes beyond textbooks: The third guideline aims to address the problem of considering textbooks as the sole and final source of knowledge. It is in fact an extension of the first guideline and requires that learners be introduced to various sources of knowledge. This will introduce learners to various views, sometimes even contradictory ones and help them to build a perspective that may accommodate diverse opinions.
- Making examinations more flexible and integrating them with classroom life: The fourth guideline seeks to make assessment a formative process so that teaching and assessment determine each other and the meaningfulness of learning can be ascertained on a continuous basis.
- Nurturing an overriding identity informed by caring concerns within the democratic polity of the country: The fifth guideline underscores the need to raise awareness, nurture a sense of identity and the ability for critical thinking on socio-political realities. It also intends that learners are helped in internalizing India's constitutional values of equality, justice, liberty and fraternity so that democracy does not remain only as a form of governance but becomes a way of life for them. Thus, while making learning an active process to be carried out through group activities, it seeks to impart training in citizenship for India.

Kerala Curriculum Framework (KCF 2007)

The state's curriculum reform effort gained further impetus with the formulation of NCF 2005. NCF 2005 and the position papers provided ground for introspection and formulation of the Kerala curriculum frame work 2007.

- The education system that is envisaged should be capable of promoting a social order based on the equality and justice.
- To develop a sense in preserving all available resources in nature and to utilize them judiciously.
- To develop each child as a responsible citizen of the society.
- Creating a generation upholding nationalism and capturing the meaning of unity in diversity.
- To create an awareness on once on right and right of others in children

Aim of Science Education as in KCF 2007

By the time the learner of today gets involved in the process of production in the society, the nature and the needs of the society would have changed considerably. Besides, the changes occur at a rapid pace and Science and Technology would continue to occupy a central position in becoming the inspiration behind such changes. Thus, the aims of science education include:

- Development of scientific temperament and its application in daily life
- Engagement in scientific methods like observation, experimentation, data collection, interpretation of data, analysis, theorizing, examining for construction of knowledge
- Nurturing the ability to examine scientifically the problems of daily life as well as social issues and seeking logical solutions
- Recognizing and developing one's own interests and abilities in technical and vocational fields
- Encouraging the development of logical thinking
- Imbibing a humanistic outlook and developing a world view based on it
- Recognizing the importance of understanding historical development of ideas.
- Nurturing lateral thinking ability for enabling the learners to look at things from different perspectives and to seek new solutions

- Developing scientific literacy that provides for building awareness of scientific process

Changing Approaches

The approach of science education has to be changed to achieve the aims stated above. Prominence is given to the view that there are other areas to be considered apart from process and content. They are; Knowledge Domain, Science Process Domain, Creativity Domain, Attitudinal Domain, and Application Domain.

The importance of scientific enquiry as given in KCF 2007

The pivot of science education should be the development of the spirit of scientific enquiry. With the help of science education, all learners should acquire. Skills like investigating, planning and execution of experimental study and identification of the tools and equipment to be used and data collection. There should be a spirit of enquiry in the learners to understand the research methodology of scientists and construct new forms of knowledge.

Learning Methodology as given in KCF 2007

When there is a change in the attitude towards the skills that are to be inculcated in science education, there will be a change in the learning methodology as well. Science learning is something that students do, not something that is done to them. Science education should be an active learning process.

- Activity-Based
- Individual learning: Every student fixes a specific aim and works towards the achievement of it.
- Competitive learning: Students compete with each other and learn.
- Co-operative learning: Students co-operate and work towards the achievement of a common goal.

The nature of science and science education as given in KCF 2007

By interacting with the society, a child develops a variety of notions about the nature of science. The supremacy of science and the perfection of scientific theories form a part of this. The personal experience of the learner through suitable learning activities provides him/her proper awareness on this. A mere learning of scientific ideas and theories will not enable the learner to understand the nature of science. Acquisition of scientific ideas will not, by themselves, develop a scientific perspective. Experiences that facilitate this should be provided to the learner right from the beginning of his/her schooling. At the beginning stage, the student should go through concrete experiences that help him/her get acquainted with various aspects of nature. This does not mean that the curriculum should avoid abstract ideas. A learner who goes through a proper learning experience would gradually gain processing skills and the ability to internalize abstract ideas. A learner who possesses the spirit of enquiry should be encouraged to discuss and share his/her findings with the peer group. This will enable the learner to internalize the concrete experiences and to assimilate the abstract ideas.

The relevance of the history of science

It is not suggested that the learner should find out everything for himself/herself or that he/she should find answers to all questions. Depending on the learner's age, nature, the specific subject taught, other methods may have to be used. At some points, a historical method may have to be used. This is also essential to inculcate a scientific temperament. This is one field that is not sufficiently considered in present-day textbooks. This is necessary for the student to understand how science works, and for the recognition that the present advanced state of science and technology is the accumulated result of the work of many scientists over the centuries. However, we must be conscious of the fact that when studying about the revolutionary contributions of some of the extraordinarily brilliant scientists (the contributions might have arisen from their intellectual brilliance, from the opportunities they came across, or even accidentally) the learner may come to the conclusion that science is a field of endeavour meant only for the extraordinarily brilliant. Learners must be made to understand that there are several others who are actively engaged in scientific enquiry around the world. They should believe that activity in science is meant for everyone.

Relevance of laboratory as given in KCF 2007

A well-equipped laboratory is not an indispensable factor at the lower level to make science education effective. For the effective use of laboratories teachers need to think of.

- Keeping the laboratory clean.
- Classifying and labelling every piece of equipment.
- Ensuring freedom and opportunity to all teachers to handle the equipment in the laboratory.
- Providing opportunities for all the learners to handle all the equipment and articles in the laboratory.

- Ensuring safety measures in handling the equipment.
- Providing the learner the opportunity to do the experiments instead of the teacher doing all experiments for the learners.

Evaluation: A comprehensive and continuous evaluation is the practice of evaluation we put forward for the entire subject. The traditional method of class test is not sufficient to evaluate a child. All the abilities of the child should be subjected to evaluation.

CONCLUSION

Curriculum is the crux of whole educational process. Without curriculum, we cannot conceive any educational endeavour. School curriculum of a country, its constitution reflects the ethos of that country. Curriculum is intimately related with all aspects of education. While education is a developmental process, geared towards a coveted goal, curriculum is the input as well as the medium that provides with the goal-oriented direction to that process.

Chapter - 8

Learning Resources in Physical Sciences

INTRODUCTION

In the pursuit of understanding the intricate workings of the physical world, access to a variety of learning resources is paramount. Chapter 8 delves into the essential learning resources available to students and researchers within the realm of physical science. From traditional repositories of knowledge like the Science Library and Science Laboratory to the vast expanse of online resources, this chapter explores the functions and utility of each resource in facilitating a deeper comprehension of physical phenomena. The Science Library stands as a bastion of printed knowledge, housing a diverse collection of books, journals, and reference materials. Within its walls, students and scholars alike can immerse themselves in the rich tapestry of scientific literature, gaining insights and perspectives from generations of researchers. Complementing the traditional library setting is the Science Laboratory, a space dedicated to hands-on experimentation and discovery. Equipped with specialized equipment and apparatus, the laboratory provides a dynamic environment for conducting experiments, testing hypotheses, and honing practical skills essential to the scientific process. As technology continues to advance, the landscape of learning resources expands into the digital realm. Online libraries offer unprecedented access to vast repositories of scientific literature, breaking down geographical barriers and enabling researchers to explore a wealth of information from the comfort of their own devices. Similarly, the emergence of online laboratories has revolutionized experimental science, providing virtual environments where simulations and interactive experiments can be conducted remotely. These platforms offer flexibility and accessibility, allowing students to engage in practical learning experiences regardless of their physical location. Moreover, the chapter discusses the significance of online journals and science journals in disseminating cutting-edge research and fostering scholarly discourse. From peer-reviewed publications to specialized journals focusing on specific disciplines, these resources play a crucial role in advancing scientific knowledge and fostering collaboration within the scientific community. By elucidating the functions and benefits of these diverse learning resources, Chapter 8 serves as a guide for students and researchers navigating the ever-expanding landscape of physical science education and research. Whether within the confines of a traditional library or amidst the boundless expanse of cyberspace, the quest for understanding the mysteries of the physical world is enriched by the wealth of resources at our disposal.

SCIENCE LIBRARY AND ITS FUNCTIONS

A well-equipped science library should be the primary requisite of every school. Secondary education commission has suggested that every teacher should be well occupied with the collection of books for their growth and expansion of knowledge. The quality of books finally determines the quality of teachers and the strength of knowledge that is transferred to the students. Science library is an essential part in science learning process. Science library should be kept separate from the general library under the charge of science teachers. Science being one of the most important areas of the school curriculum, the content which rapidly goes on changing, both teachers and pupils should have to concentrate more on updating their knowledge. This can be done by reading books only. The library books should supplement what has been taught in the class. The books must provoke thinking and discussion, to develop interest in matters of science, to stimulate further reading, to help to articulate and elucidate scientific concepts and problems, to suggest further problems and to give insight into social implications and contributions of science. Science library should have books on various branches of science, on invention and discoveries, on hobbies and leisure, reference materials, advanced text books, popular and standard journals and on many other areas that directly and indirectly relate to science.

Objectives of Organizing a Science Library

- To help teachers and pupils to update scientific knowledge
- To facilitate self-studies and learning to learn
- To enrich curricular experiences
- To enable pupils to participate in discussion and project work meaningfully

- To make co-curricular activities such as participation in science club activities more meaningful and dynamic
- To create interest in science as a subject of study
- To develop the habit of concentrated reading of knowledgeable books with a purpose
- To develop in the student's critical attitude and capacity for independent judgment
- To develop the habit of reading as a useful leisure time activity.

Organization of Science Library

A well-equipped science library should be the primary requisite of every school. It is a matter of controversy whether the science library should be kept separate from the general school library under the charge of science teacher or should form a part of the general library. The different aspects of organization of science library are:

- A separate science library under the charge of science teacher should be an integral part of the science department. The library should be organized adjacent to the science class rooms for the immediate reference of teachers and students.
- Science teacher should concentrate on the fund for the organization of the library. The science grants available to the school can be utilized for this. The money can be generated from donations and other available sources.
- Science library should have almirahs, shelves, and table and if possible, there should be place for reading also with desks and benches.
- Colourful bulletin boards should be placed to attract pupil to library.
- Membership should be provided to members and teacher should inculcate the love for reading and ability to use reference books. Pupil should be asked to write the review of the books they read.
- Science books and articles should be constantly reviewed by both the teacher and the pupil and good reviews should be published in the science magazines or school magazine.
- A cross-reference index may be maintained in which teachers and pupils should briefly indicate the information furnished in the books read by them under suitable headings.

Library should be divided in various sections as suggested below:

- Text Books: This section should have text books of various classes; practical books can also be provided.
- Background Books - The Story of Moon, The Story of Earth, The Human Machine, The Story of Penicillin, The Story of Steam engine etc.
- Inspirational Books - Wonders of Pond Life, The Harvest of Sea, The Romance of Chemistry etc.
- Biographies
- Reference Books - Common Birds, Common Plants, A dictionary of Science, An encyclopaedia of Science, History of Science etc.
- Science Magazines - Vigyan Shikshak, Delhi (Quarterly, English), Science Reporter, Delhi (Monthly, English), Science Today, Mumbai (Monthly, English), School Science NCERT Delhi (Quarterly, English), Junior Scientist, Chennai (Quarterly, English), Science Reporter, Resonance, Yojana, VijnanaKairali etc
- Experimental Books - Experimental Chemistry, A book of Experiments Teacher's Guide
- Teaching of Science - The Scientific Method, Science and Life, UNESCO Source Book for Science Teaching etc

Functions of a Science Library

- To encourage students the habit of learning.
- To develop ability to learn from books when left to themselves.
- To remove inflexible time-table which isolates the subjects
- To supplement the knowledge of the classroom
- To provide opportunity for social training.
- To help the students to use their spare time in a right manner.
- To help the teachers for developing their up-to-date knowledge.
- To reduce the chance of discipline in the school.
- To develop the habit of supplementary reading among the students.
- It is economical as the texts may be used for a number of years.

Importance of Science Library

- Make the students know everything about the surrounding world.
- Develop the students to be anxious to know more and more about science.

- Facilitate self-study and self-education.
- Help in putting progressive method of teaching science.
- Develop the teachers to extend their scientific knowledge.
- Develop scientific attitudes among students.

Advantages of science Library

- The science library is helpful for the pupil to become aware of the latest developments in science.
- It helps the gifted students to explore new fields according to their capacity
- It helps the slow learners to get a clear idea about the concepts which were not clear for them
- Science library always promotes interest towards science subject and this keeps people away from superstitions.
- Reading is indeed a pleasurable and worthwhile experience, promotes reading habits of Children
- It provides suitable base to the knowledge acquired in the classroom teaching.
- It gives experience and training in science
- Improves linguistic abilities of students

SCIENCE LABORATORY AND ITS FUNCTIONS

D. S. Kothari said that, "To learn science is to do science. There is no other way of doing science". Experiments play a crucial role in the progress of science. A large number of paths breaking discoveries and inventions have been possible through investigations done usually in laboratories. The experimental work is, therefore, an essential component of any course in science. A course on practical work in science curricula in schools at the secondary stage is essentially designed to acquaint the learners with the basic tools and techniques used in a science laboratory. It also envisages developing problem-solving skills. These skills help the learner to acquire ability to identify a problem, to design and to set up the experiment, to collect and analyse data through experiment, and to interpret data to arrive at plausible solution in due course of time. These are, in fact, the long-term objectives of laboratory work and become the nucleus of the philosophy of construction of knowledge by the learner.

A school science laboratory is a place where basic experimental skills are learnt by systematically performing a set of prescribed and suitably designed experiments. Performing experiments by one's own hands is not only a thrilling experience but is also important because it entails learning by doing. It also facilitates understanding the concepts of science. The experiments and project work suggested at the secondary stage intend to develop basic skills of measurement; handling of some common measuring instruments, equipment and chemicals; setting simple apparatus; handling microscope and preparing slides; making observations; collecting data and presenting it in appropriate format; interpreting and drawing conclusions; and preparation of report. So, to make science teaching effective and efficient science laboratory is very essential. The important function of science laboratory is that deepening of the students' understanding that science concepts and theories are originated from the natural environment.

Functions of Science Laboratory

Science is different from any other subject. In order to understand its concepts, one has to look beyond the books and conventional classroom teaching. Effective teaching and learning of science involve seeing, handling, and manipulating real objects and materials. A Science lab is a workplace for the conduct of scientific research.

- To help students to understanding and remember scientific concepts better
- To transfer the experience to other learning situations
- To provide controlled conditions in which scientific research, experiments and measurement may be performed.
- To cultivate interest in science and science learning
- To develop Scientific practical skills and problem-solving abilities
- To develop Scientific habits of mind
- To understand the nature of science
- To promote application of scientific knowledge to everyday life.
- To engage students with different abilities, learning styles, motivational patterns, and cultural contexts
- To develop scientific reasoning abilities
- To increase understanding of the complexity and ambiguity of empirical work
- Encouraging social skills development and improving teamwork abilities.

Laboratory experiences will be more likely to achieve these goals if they (1) are designed with clear learning outcomes in mind (2) are thoughtfully sequenced into the flow of classroom science instruction

(3) integrate learning of science content and process and (4) incorporate ongoing student reflection and discussion.

Planning of Science Laboratory

Laboratory should be an integral part of instruction in science. While constructing a science laboratory the schools, science teachers and science educators should collaborate to build a standardized plan to draw out best educational purposes. The factors that should be kept in mind before setting up the laboratory are:

- The position of the laboratory in the school premises. If it is a multi storied school the laboratory should be kept at the ground floor. The place of the laboratory should be such that the gas and vapors do not affect the rest of the building
- How many pupils will be working in the laboratory at the same time and the minimum space required for each pupil for comfortable working.
- Space should be kept for the store room for Chemicals and apparatus, Gas chamber etc.
- Electrical and plumbing facilities should be provided
- Fittings and furniture should be planned to be convenient for use and economical in the long run.

Design of the Science Laboratory

The design of the science laboratory as given by UNESCO States that there should be a study room (36 sq. m for 36 students) which may be used for varied types of activities by the pupil such as writing, listening, drawing sketches and carrying out practical work. The laboratory room should be preferably lighted and ventilated so that light should preferably enter from the left. The total wall space taken up by doors and windows should be above $1/4^{th}$ of the floor space. The ventilators should be below one foot of the ceiling. Rooms should have high walls, large windows opposite to each other. Floor should be smooth without the possibility of dirt lodging.

Furniture and Fittings

Working tables where students have to work should be placed in parallel to the demonstration table preferably between the windows. The tables should have shelves. The top of the table should be made smooth with tiles or can be given paraffin glazing. The height of each table may be around 3 ft. Demonstration Table: Demonstration table should be kept (2500 X 300 X 850 mm) on a platform made on the front of the room. The demonstration table should be in such a position that all pupils can view the demonstrations performed on the table. There should be electrical points near the demonstration table. A blackboard should be kept behind the table so that teacher can write equations draw figures, connections etc. while performing demonstrations.

- Sink to be fitted on the side walls of the laboratory
- There should be enough bottle shelves
- Fume cupboard should be placed in one corner
- Enough waste boxes should be kept in the lab
- There should be separate store room for keeping chemicals and apparatus
- There should be light, water and drainage facilities

Selection and Purchase of Apparatus

Science teacher should prepare a list of experiments to be performed by the pupils and demonstrated by the teacher. The list of apparatus and materials to be purchased must be prepared according to the details of the above experiments. There should be many sets of apparatus for the experiments to be done by pupils and one set of apparatus for the experiments to be demonstrated. The number of units of costly apparatus must be reduced by allowing the pupils to work in combination. If the lab is almost saturated with apparatus, teacher must give priority in buying costly equipment like camera, LCD, Some original working models etc. The teacher must give due consideration to different parts of a subject in preparing the list. When the list is prepared full specification regarding the type and nature of the material, quality, capacity, number of items etc. should be given in detail. After finalizing the list teacher can invite quotations from science firms dealing with the supply of apparatus and chemicals. It is always better to select reliable firm which has a fine reputation. When the items are delivered in the lab the teacher must carefully verify each and every item in terms of quality, breakage, manufacturer, number etc. and finally it can be received to the laboratory and entered into the stock register and placed in suitable positions.

Laboratory Management

All the apparatus should be arranged in subject wise almirahs. The glass wares should be kept separate from the other items. The chemicals should be arranged in alphabetic order with the letter of the alphabet displayed on the shelf. The concentrated acids in bulk should be kept away from the reach of the pupils and if separate chamber is there it can be placed on that. There shall be two open shelves fixed on the walls on either side of the recess for balances. In one shelf glass stopper bottles containing solutions of ammonia, sodium hydroxide, potassium hydroxide, silver nitrate, ferrous sulphate, barium chloride, barium nitrate, copper sulphate, litmus etc. there may be another shelf for keeping common acids both dilute and concentrated. Other chemicals should be provided in bottles with labels. Apparatus kept in the lab should be regularly inspected, cleaned and always should be kept away from moisture. Lubricants should be applied in the joining, screws etc. to keep the apparatus always proper in working condition. The apparatus which is not in use should be kept in boxes. The overall view of the laboratory should be systematic and appealing.

Maintenance of Laboratory Workshop

There should be small work shop with proper fittings for wood work and metal work in the laboratory. This equipment enables the laboratory work to be done without interruption and can suggest improvements in the selection of apparatus. In laboratory workshop there should be small carpenters' bench and tools for wood work. There should be metal working tools like hammers, players, spanner, drill press, nails, screws, nut and bolt etc.

Planning for the laboratory work

Science teaching should correlate with laboratory work. Pupil should be made well aware about the nature and scope of the work. It is not that students should come mechanically in the laboratory and imitate what the others do or try. They should be aware about the concepts that they are working with. If there is large number of students then the students should be admitted in batches in the laboratory. The laboratory should be decorated with the photos of scientist and their biographies. Pupil should use laboratory for solving problems by observing things and relationships around their problems. The problems to be worked in the laboratory are discussed in classrooms and students can hypothesize their problems and real investigations can be done in the laboratory. Students can choose problems from their daily experiences and from nature other than the classroom problems. All things that the pupil does in the laboratory should be like a scientist working on problems to establish facts and relations.

Laboratory Rules

Laboratory is a place of potential dangers so the science teacher must be the supreme authority in the laboratory and she should see that her orders are strictly obeyed. The sign of good discipline is an atmosphere of healthy work. The discipline should be maintained by making pupil familiar about what should be done in the laboratory and what not. Some suggestions for making discipline in the laboratory are

- No pupil should be allowed to enter in the laboratory in the absence of the teacher
- Every student has a place assigned to him, where he will perform his experiment
- The arrangement of laboratory should be such that there is no need for pupil to move away from his seat
- The practice of raising hands should be followed in the laboratory for calling the teacher
- When pupils are working in groups the discussions should be in low tone without affecting the class
- All unnecessary talks should be strictly prohibited
- Students should not be allowed to play with the apparatus
- Reagent bottles should be returned to the shelf immediately after use and should not be misplaced
- Waste filter papers, burnt up match sticks etc. should not be thrown into sink. Waste boxes should be kept for this purpose
- Scribbling figures on furniture should never be permitted
- All work should be finished five minutes before the end of the period so that apparatus should be disconnected, washed and placed in proper place before leaving the seat
- The teacher can take the help of the students to distribute apparatus and materials, to clean them after use and to replace them at the end
- Bottles must be labelled carefully
- Any breakage in the apparatus must be noted down in the breakage register
- Wall of the laboratory must be decorated with the pictures of scientist and diagrams of apparatus
- A bucket full of water or sand must kept always in the laboratory for safety purpose

Accidents in the Laboratory

Accidents are common in the laboratory and science teacher has legal and moral responsibility to see that pupils are as far as possible free from dangers of laboratory. The teacher should maintain proper discipline in the laboratory. Teacher should give a brief idea about the dangers caused by specific equipment. Dangerous chemicals should be kept on open shelves. The experiments should not be started with the permission of the teacher. Some of the substances should be handled with proper care are: Concentrated acids, Strong alkalis, Gases such as H_2S, SO_2, Cl_2 and CO, Inflammable materials like petrol, alcohol, CS_2, Salt of Lead, Mercury and Zinc.

First Aid: Accidents usually occur in the laboratory. It is essential that first aid kit should be kept in every laboratory in a separate cup board. It must contain bandages, cotton, plaster, tincture iodine, boric acid, sodium bicarbonate, carbolic acid, Dettol, Vaseline etc. some common cases of first aid treatment are

Burns in the Laboratory: Burns can be caused due to steam, hot water, acids or alkali. The first aid treatment required for burns caused due to each one of them is different. The first treatment to be provided for some of them is as follows:

- **For burns caused by steam or hot water**, wash the affected part with cold running water. Do not use ice. Once the affected part is cool, dry it gently with clean cloth and then apply an antiseptic ointment.
- **For an acid burn**, wash the wounded part with water and apply a dilute solution of sodium hydrogen carbonate. Wash again with water. Dry gently with a clean cloth and apply an antiseptic ointment.
- **For an alkali burn**, wash with ample of water to remove all the alkali and then wash with dilute acetic acid. Dry the affected part with a clean cloth and apply an antiseptic ointment
- **For Phosphorous Burns,** wash with plenty water and cover with cotton wool soaked in silver nitrate solution

Glass Cuts and Wounds: Carefully remove all the visible pieces of glass from the wound. Protect the wound from dirt and dust. Wash with cold water to remove smaller pieces of glass sticking to the wound, if any. Control the bleeding by pressing a clean piece of cotton or cloth on the wound. Apply on antiseptic solution antiseptic cream. Take the victim to the doctor, if required.

Eye Injuries: In case of injury to eyes, wash the eyes with cold water. Do not rub the eyes. Consult the doctor immediately. In specific cases like acid in the eye it should be washed well in water and then with dilute sodium bicarbonate solution. If it is alkali in the eye, wash well in water and then with a solution of 1% boric acid.

Electrical Shock: Switch off the electric supply, beat with wooden stick and admit in the hospital

Fires: One should not run around if clothes catch fire. Immediately lie down on the floor and roll. If a Container with inflammable liquid catches fire while heating, turn off the gas burner immediately, and take the container away from all reagents and chemicals. Cover the mouth of the container with a damp cloth. Fire extinguishers should be used if the fire goes out of control. In case the fire is because of the short-circuiting of electrical circuits, switch off the main switch of the electric supply and through soil in the affected area. Do not use water in such a case.

Inhalation of Gases: If gases such as sulphur dioxide, chlorine or bromine are inhaled by any student, take the student at once to the open air and let the victim breathe deeply and then ammonia vapours. If the gas inhaled is ammonia, drink any fruit juice or lemon juice. Inhale dilute ammonium hydroxide if acid vapours are inhaled. Report the accident to your teacher immediately to get the medical attention at the earliest.

Registers to be kept in the Laboratory

- Permanent Stock Register: It contains details of articles which are not liable to be consumed or broken. Some articles like ammeter, stop watches, thermometer, and voltmeter are also entered in this register as they are considered non consumable. Working and non-working models, charts, telescope and microscope can be entered in this register.
- Breakable Stock Register: It includes articles of glassware, flasks, test tube, beakers, pipettes, burettes, funnels, conical flask etc.
- Consumable Stock Register: It includes chemicals and other fluids liable to be consumed such as acids, alcohol, distilled water, potassium permanganate and the like.
- Order Register: It includes the record of orders sent for the purchase of new apparatus
- Requirement Register: Requirement register highlights the future requirement of the lab by taking suggestions from teachers, science personnel and the requirements should be given with priorities.

ONLINE LEARNING RESOURCES- ONLINE LIBRARY, ONLINE LABORATORY, ONLINE JOURNALS

Learning resources refers to any resource available on the Internet in an online educational environment. It might be HTML documents such as course or chapter, lecture notes, assignments, audio or video lessons, interactive exercises or exams, or documents providing links to other Web sites. Khan Academy, EdX, SchoolTube, Coursera, HubSpot Academy, Instructables, Hack Design, E - Pathshala, Swayam learning portal, NPTEL (National Programme on Technology Enhanced Learning), Virtual Labs, e-ShodhSindhu etc.

ONLINE LIBRARY

Library and information centres are providing numerous types of information resources and services. All conventional libraries basic functions focus on collection, organization and dissemination of information resources. Traditionally a "library is a place in which books, manuscripts or other literary and artistic materials are kept for use but not for sale". The internet has brought forth new dimension to libraries of modern digital world. In this new library, digital networking and communication infrastructure provides a global platform over which the people and organization devise strategies, interact, communicate, collaborate and search for information. This platform includes a vast array of digitalized products which are delivered over the digital infrastructure anytime, anywhere in the world. Most of the Libraries today, offer a wide range of online services to their users. Hence, it is the time for a Library to be virtual and develop its online presence in order to further facilitate and enrich the educational processes. In this direction, Virtual Libraries provide a new way of serving the new generation users of the libraries

Terms such as digital library, electronic library, virtual library and online library are often used synonymously. While these terms are used interchangeably, they are in fact not the same thing. A digital or electronic library consists of a networked collection of multimedia information in digital or electronic format typically available in one location, while a virtual library or online library comprises a set of links to various resources on the Internet, such as documents or databases. The links in a virtual library are transparent to users and it provides them with one interface to information (Kawatra, 2000). Virtual libraries rely on interactivity that allows benefactors to explore sites and to use resources.

Virtual Library is another kind of Digital Library which provides portal to information that is available electronically elsewhere. A Virtual Library has been defined by Gapen (1993) as, "the concept of remote access to the contents and services of libraries and other information resources, combining an onsite collection of current and heavily used materials in both print and electronic form, with an electronic network which provides access to, and delivery from, external worldwide library and commercial information and knowledge sources". The speedy and wide access to current information contents makes virtual libraries a global symbol of the information access paradigm. The function of a Virtual Library is to ensure the systematic development of the means to collect, store, and organize information and knowledge in digital form and to provide easy and affordable access to it around the clock from various locations. A Virtual Library provides remote access to a variety of national and international content (e.g. curricula, learning materials, books, journals, magazines, newspapers), services traditionally offered by libraries and other information sources. Virtual Libraries thus combine materials in electronic format with an electronic network which ensures access to and delivery of those materials. To become an effective educational tool in the public service, it must respond to the needs of and provide affordable access for prospective users - students, teachers, researchers and academics. Emphasis should be given to building up collections that are in the public domain and that are accessible through, e.g., applications of free software on the basis of affordable Internet tariffs.

Features of an online or Virtual Library

- Provides speedy and wide access to updated information in a global manner.
- It has changed the traditional library system of cataloguing only book materials. Cataloguing of Non-Book Materials includes not only databases but also websites.
- Greater emphasis is on access and not on collection.
- Time saving

Purpose of the Virtual Library

- to underpin learning and acquisition of knowledge to provide a more solid basis for education and
- to enhance quality of life by drawing on digitally available (preferably on-line) books, materials and journals via ICT-based tools.

Functions of a Virtual Library

- Collection, storage and processing of vast information and knowledge into a systemic project through digitalization and the internet, while providing convenient and highly efficient retrieval and inquiry services

- Provide ICT-based access to a range of digitally available publications for educational purposes available in the public domain and from other sources
- Contribute to the efficient delivery of information to students, researchers and teachers of all universities and other educational institutions
- Strengthen communication and collaboration between and among the research, library and educational communities, nationally, regionally and internationally
- Offer lifelong learning opportunities
- To provide friendly interface to users
- To enhance advanced search, access and retrieval of information
- To enable one to perform searches that is not practical manually

Advantages

- Virtual libraries provide immediate access to a range of resources not available in physical collections. Virtual libraries allow unprecedented access to information and ideas. "A paradigm shift takes place from libraries as collectors of items to libraries as facilitators of access to all kinds of information, provided by anybody, located anywhere in the world, accessible at any time".
- Physical libraries operate with designated hours, virtual libraries are available anytime and anywhere where there is an Internet connection.
- Virtual libraries offer opportunities for learning that are not possible in their physical counterparts. Virtual libraries complement other virtual learning environments, such as those provided in distance education and courses offered online, and like virtual learning environments, providing flexibility of time and place.
- The user is able to use any search term (word, phrase, title, name, and subject) to search the entire collection. Digital libraries can provide very user-friendly interfaces, giving click able access to its resources.
- Virtual libraries often contain more up-to-date information than physical collections. Their sources can be searched more

efficiently than those in physical libraries, and the information they contain can be updated more frequently.

- Well-designed virtual library collections are organized and managed to increase productivity and efficiency of the user.
- Virtual libraries empower the user and promote informal learning.
- Virtual libraries can be customized for particular schools, grades, and subjects. This variety of formats in presentation and navigation is quite different from that of a physical library. Thus, virtual libraries support specific communities of interest, thereby, creating global communities of learners.
- Virtual libraries break down the physical barriers between users and information sources. Through the use of audio and video, virtual libraries can also make resources available to users that are visually and hearing impaired, and they make these resources available in their homes.
- No physical boundary. The user needs not to go to the library physically; people from all over the world can gain access to the same information, as long as an Internet connection is available.
- Round the clock availability. People can gain access to the information at any time
- Multiple accesses. The same resources can be used at the same time by a number of users.
- Networking can provide a link to any other resources of other digital libraries very easily; thus, a seamlessly integrated resource sharing can be achieved.
- Preserve the valuable documents, rare and special collections of libraries, archives and museums
- Provide faster access to the holding of libraries worldwide through automated better catalogues

Virtual Library - Examples

- World Digital Library. A source for manuscripts, rare books, films, maps and more in multilingual format.
- Universal Digital Library. A collection of one million books.
- Project Gutenberg. More than 33,000 e-books to read and download.
- Bartleby. An immense collection of books for consultation, including fiction, essay and poetry.

- ibiblio. E-books, magazines, academic essays, software, music and radio.
- Google Books. More than 100,000 books for consultation, download or on-line purchase.
- Internet Archive: The largest digital library for downloading e-books and audio-books for free.
- Open Library
- National Digital library of India

ONLINE LABORATORY / VIRTUAL LABORATORY (VL)

Laboratories are the important environment for students learning where students get hands on training. A deeper understanding of technical concept may be achieved through laboratory work that encourages active involvement and hand out to extend critical thinking. Today to setup a physical laboratory is challenging work for institutions due to budget, limited technical expertise, high setup and maintenance costs. In this response virtual laboratories have been developed to attend to these challenges. The rapid growth in Information and Communication Technologies (ICT) has made it possible for virtual laboratories to be used as a substitute or supplement to the traditional laboratories. Virtual laboratories can work as an alternative or complement to the physical or real laboratories.

Virtual laboratories allow users to perform practical work or experiments on real systems via interactive web-based tool. Virtual laboratory is an online learning system where students can access and perform their laboratory work on software applications which are virtually installed. Virtual laboratories are web based interactive multimedia objects to enhance teaching and learning experience. Interactive multimedia objects used in virtual laboratory consists of web-resources, video-lectures, graphics, text, hypertext, sound, images, and animations. It is a web-based platform designed to improve learning approaches by introducing a safe and interactive lab environment for students.

Virtual laboratory has been defined as "a laboratory experiment programmed, using the computer for simulating the operations in the real laboratory, which helps students to link easily between the theoretical and practical aspects" (Keller and Keller, 2005). It has also been defined as "software-tools; that allow users to design repeated experiments to test the effects of variables" (Toth 2016).

The importance of using Virtual laboratories in science education lies in the fact that they offer the best solution for conducting laboratory activities as the students can perform lab activities using computer software, which is cheaper and more efficient. Furthermore, VLs allow students to repeat an experiment many times without any risk of danger. Also, VLs help students examine anomalous data that do not concur with prior knowledge, theories, and expectations. Such data are hard to investigate in traditional laboratories (Widodo et al. 2017). Indeed, students who are taught using VLs often perform better than those who learn in traditional laboratories (Falode and Onasanya, 2015). The VL could improve the learning environment and deliver information to the students more clearly. The students who used the VL were able to understand the concept of experiments, their objectives, and the results. Moreover, the system is considered as a smart environment where it provides the students with adequate feedback during the learning process and enables the teacher to follow and assess the student's performance.

Major objectives of Online Laboratory / Virtual Laboratory (VL)

- To motivate students for conducting experiments on their own interest
- To reduce maintenance cost
- To learn basic and advanced concepts of experiments
- To help students conduct laboratory experiments in a safe and interactive manner
- To allow science teachers to set laboratory tests and evaluate their students' performance
- To build up knowledge easily and improve fundamental concepts with practical work
- To enhance the learning environment and make it more constructive

Characteristics of Virtual Lab

- Creating new intellectual model in education better than the real
- Knowledge-building and inculcate information
- Develop an exploration based on scientific assumptions and processes
- Encouraging and guiding students
- Registering students' information and evaluating them automatically
- Performing experiments, which are difficult to be performed in the traditional lab due to its danger and high cost
- Reducing the learning time spent in the traditional lab
- Permanently updated

Benefits/Advantages of Virtual Lab

- Flexible access: The experiments are done on the student's own time, at the student's convenience and when he or she learns best.
- Instant feedback: Students can analyse what went wrong immediately and can redo experiments on the spot. All the results are recorded, making communication between teachers and students more efficient.
- Top-notch equipment: Schools and students that use virtual labs have access to cutting-edge technology when it comes to experimentation. With a virtual lab, students do not have to settle on outdated, yet expensive, equipment because a school cannot afford to replace it consistently.
- Lower costs: There is a fee associated with using virtual labs but the capital and maintenance costs are drastically reduced. This allows school to provide a better learning experience for students at a fraction of the cost.
- Increases the students' interest in science and improve their understanding of the subject
- Absent students can make them up at home. It is web-based tool access from home and performs their practical.
- To improve effectiveness and better understanding, Students can repeat experiments many times.
- Real looking components to give the user a feel of the real laboratory.
- The students can understand more detailed experiments through changing different variables or parameters.
- To easily solve a large set of complex problems through the design and construction of new approaches using virtual laboratory.
- Available 24x7, students can do laboratory work as per their own schedule.
- The importance of using VLs in science education lies in the fact that they offer the best solution for conducting laboratory activities as the students can perform lab activities using computer software, which is cheaper and more efficient.
- Furthermore, VLs allow students to repeat an experiment many times without any risk of danger.
- Virtual labs can be very useful in the teaching of science, particularly in cases were; the experimental activities are to

be done quickly and do not easily allow observation and safe measurement, the experimental process is very slow and / or complex and not compatible with the teaching time available, the experiments involve risks to the health and physical integrity of learners

- Virtual labs support IBSL in learning science in cases where; Laws in science arise from a detailed observation process, with clearly more chances of clarification, understanding and acceptance if regarded in detail
- It encourages collaboration and communication between teachers and students. Teachers participate actively in the learning process by asking questions, trying to find answers, organizing procedures and commenting on them, helping in formulating conclusions, understanding mistakes and highlighting any misconceptions.
- With virtual labs, students acquire a tool with which to experiment without limitations of space or time. They are available all year, as opposed to school laboratories, limited to a specific place and for a limited time.
- The use of virtual environments makes students acquire better computer skills, which can be considered skills for lifelong learning.

Examples of Virtual Lab

- PHET http://phet.colorado.edu
- Library of Labs https://www.library-of-labs.org/
- Labshare http://www.labshare.edu.au/
- Open Sources Physics http://www.compadre.org/osp
- Smart Science http://www.smartscience.net/
- Molecular Work-bench http://mw.concord.org/

- Explore Learning http://www.explorelearning.com
- Chem-Collective http://www.chemcollective.org/
- Skoool http://skoool.com
- iLab-Central http://ilabcentral.org
- Lab2Go http://www.lab2go.net

Limitations of Virtual Lab

- The scarcity of the virtual labs, which rely on regional language.

- The lack of real interaction between hardware, tools, teachers & peers
- The need for computers and tools with special standards.
- The need for specialized working staff, instructors and curriculum experts for designing and production.
- The lack of lab social skills gained in the virtual lab compared to the real lab.

ONLINE JOURNALS

Journals have always played an important role in information management i.e., information creation and dissemination. A journal helps to understand the actual status of a subject. In recent times, the evolving demand of the information society for easier, cost effective and reliable mechanisms of information management complemented by the advances in Information and Communication Technology (ICT), has resulted in the development of modern means of information management. Developments in information technology have brought e-journals as basic information sources to research community and these are emerging as major sources of scholarly communication. Journals that are published exclusively in electronic format present an innovation in a way that scientific information is communicated easily to the community.

E-Journals are also called online journals, Virtual journals, Digital journals, e-zines etc. Electronic journals are scholarly publications that are published online. An electronic journal is a periodical publication which is published in electronic format, usually on the Internet. McMillan defined e journal "as any serial produced, published, and distributed nationally or internationally via internet". It is a digital periodical dedicated to publishing articles, essays, and analyses on the internet that have been read and commented upon initially by a select group of editors and reviewers, to meet a certain arbitrary standard of excellence (as determined by the editors) for a given discipline addressed by the journal itself. The medium distinguishes an electronic scholarly journal from its print counterparts but the process of developing content for both print and electronic peer-review scholarly journals is generally the same. The digital medium allows the editorial process to occur at a faster pace than in print by providing authors with information quickly to revise and otherwise modify their work to meet editorial standards. There are different types of access to e-journals like free access, exclusive subscription, selective access, fee-based access and consortium access. The advantages of saving storage space and the availability of multimedia information also seem to be non-negligible factors in the usage of e-journals. Individual e-journals or package of journals are called a database. Individual e-journals can be purchased from a subscription service/agent or directly via the publisher.

Benefits of E-Journals

- Up-to-date information
- Convenient: information at your fingertips
- Value-added features: search facilities, other links, video, graphics, audio, dictionary, etc.
- Export, email, cite, print, save, make notes

Examples of Databases or packages of e-journals: ProQuest, SCOPUS, Science Direct, Sage Publications, Taylor& Francis etc.

Functions of e- journals

- To make the results of original research available to the widest possible audience.
- To provide a permanent record or archive of research which has been carried out
- To enable an individual scientist or technologist to establish the fact that, he was the first person to make a particular discovery, the process being formally known as the assignment of priority
- To ensure a guaranteed standard of quality in the papers accepted for publication, this being achieved through the refereeing system

Advantages

E-journals as defined to be publications available in electronic form and has numerous advantages as they are space saving, provide powerful searching tools, hypertext links and multimedia that the printed journals cannot offer. The electronic formal offers many advantages to both users and publishers which paper publications cannot match; they are:

- Customization: Only the articles of interest are, "delivered" and the user has some control over the appearance of the article both printed and on the screen.
- Full text searching or navigation: Navigation and search are two of the most attractive features that an online journal can offer. The retrieval capabilities of journals in electronic form are far better than those in paper. Every word in the article is potential retrieval point so that even a caption of figure can be used find a half-remembered article.

- Speed of access: It takes some minutes or even seconds rather than hours or days to access. Much less time is required to browse through electronic journals than print journals.
- Speed and cost of publication: Avoiding the printing and mailing process can easily drop 2 or 3 weeks off the current publication cycle. Machine readable text from author is gradually lowering cost and reducing time as authoring and publishing system become better integrated and as electronic transmission is used more in the review process. Hence, additional time will be saved.
- Integration with other work: As the capabilities of computers grow, a situation is rapidly developing in which many people do most of their work at personal computers. The ability to refer to articles at the same time on the same machine as other tasks are performed will become invaluable.
- Economical: E-journal could be distributed more economically than print journals, because the main cost of preparing the text, the review process and other such procedures are not as capital intensive as the costs of printing and mailing print copies.
- Hypertext links: Existing journal articles contain a large number of links both within the articles and to other articles. They will gradually become useful links in the electronic version where a simple click on a reference will either lead on to where it was cited, to an abstract of it, or to the article itself.
- Can be saved digitally: Saving the article as text, html, or PDF files is extremely easy and can be accessed any number of times.
- No physical processing: Activities like accessioning, classification and cataloguing pertaining to print journal subscription is completely avoided, and the time of the library staff can be saved.
- Multimedia facility: E-journals can include text, audio and video images as well which help to easy understand the text.
- Save physical storage: Generally, an electronic journal has no space restrictions, i.e. an e-journal can publish a greater number of articles and lengthy articles compared with a print journal. No shelve space is require to store them.
- Search capabilities are tremendous: Search based on titles, keywords, author, subjects, abstract, article, full text, can be executed to identify the journals and articles of interest by the user. Viewing an article's abstracts from an e-journal allows you to judge whether the article is worth using or not.

- Multiple simultaneous access: E-journals can be can be simultaneously use by more than one user, which is possible with print journals.
- Less paper: Paper has many excellent qualities, but electronic version of documents consumes fewer resources and is easier to manage.
- Availability: E-journals provides 24/7 accessibility and remote access to the user. They are available at the same time for readers all around the world, round the clock across geographical barriers, makes them Omni present.

Disadvantages of E-Journals

- Difficulty in reading computer screens: The main disadvantage of electronic journals is the limitations of the computer monitor. Long reading from screen can cause eyestrain.
- Reliance on equipment: Unlike print journals, an electronic journal needs the availability of electricity, telephone system, computers, internet, appropriate software and hardware etc.
- Less permanent: Electronic version of online journal is easy to lose and their reliance on software and hardware makes them impermanent. This is a problem both for institutions such as libraries that might want to preserve them and for individual as well who wish to maintain their own collection.
- Higher cost: The system needed to display and network needed to retrieve electronic articles are added cost to the end user. Access to electronic article is easier to monitor than to paper collections. Hence, there is more possibility of publishers for collecting free for use.
- Complexities for acquisition: Acquiring electronic journals is in some way entirely difficult that acquiring print journals. There are license agreements to negotiate and librarians end up dealing with vendors whose subscription rates and cost models aren't always crystal clear.
- Lower quality: Computer screens have lower resolution than paper and are usually smaller than two pages of journals. Sometimes photographs too scanned incorrectly.
- Frustrating interfaces: Anyone who has used computers at all has encountered the frustration being incapable of accomplishing a simple task. The same sort of thing can happen to conventional library users, but it is often less obvious and frustrating, and

very often there is someone available to ask what to do manual solutions are often more obvious and easier to remember as well.

- Requirement to log on: This is at least an annoyance and can lead to higher or at least more immediate costs. Requiring a password also raises a barrier to use since it requires remembering it.
- There are also privacy issues; electronic access is only private when designed to be so and publishers are obviously interested in what and how much material is being used and to some extent and by whom.
- Maintenance: E-journals provide many facilities but it takes more and expertise staff to maintain e-journal finders, records in OPAC etc.

SCIENTIFIC JOURNALS

A scientific journal is a periodical publication intended to further the progress of science and mankind, usually by reporting new research. Scientific journals represent the most vital means for disseminating research findings and are usually specialized for different academic disciplines or sub-disciplines. They are multidimensional gateways for the exploration of scientific discoveries and new researches in various fields. Science organizations and science associations usually bring out journals in science. These journals publish research-based, experience based and popular science articles. A number of magazines also publish articles on scientific issues. These materials can be helpful for the enrichment of teaching-learning of science. Scientific journals represent the most vital means for disseminating research findings and are usually specialized for different academic disciplines or sub disciplines. Often, the research challenges common assumptions and/or the research data presented in the published scientific literature in order to gain a clearer understanding of the facts and findings. Depending upon the policies of a given journal, articles may include reports of original research, re-analyses of others' research, reviews of the literature in a specific area, proposals of new but untested theories, or opinion pieces.

CONCLUSION

In conclusion, Chapter 8 has provided an insightful exploration of the diverse learning resources available in the field of physical science. From the foundational institutions of the Science Library and Science Laboratory to the dynamic capabilities of online platforms, this chapter has underscored the crucial role that access to information and experimentation plays in advancing scientific knowledge. The Science Library stands as a repository of printed knowledge, offering a wealth of resources for researchers to delve into historical discoveries, contemporary theories, and emerging trends in physical science. Meanwhile, the Science Laboratory serves as a crucible for hands-on exploration, where students can engage in practical experimentation to reinforce theoretical concepts and develop essential scientific skills. In the digital age, the landscape of learning resources has expanded to encompass online libraries, laboratories, and journals. These online platforms transcend geographical boundaries, democratizing access to information and fostering collaboration among researchers worldwide. Whether through virtual simulations in online laboratories or access to a vast array of scientific literature in online libraries and journals, students and scholars have unprecedented opportunities to engage with the forefront of physical science research. By harnessing the collective power of these learning resources, students and researchers are empowered to navigate the complexities of the physical world, uncovering new insights, and pushing the boundaries of scientific understanding. As technology continues to evolve and knowledge continues to expand, the importance of accessible and diverse learning resources in physical science education cannot be overstated. In essence, Chapter 8 serves as a testament to the enduring pursuit of knowledge in physical science and the pivotal role that learning resources play in shaping the scientists of tomorrow. Through a multifaceted approach that integrates traditional and online resources, this chapter equips readers with the tools and resources necessary to embark on a journey of discovery and innovation in the fascinating realm of physical science.

Chapter - 9

Instructional Supports - Traditional and Modern

INTRODUCTION

In the present technological age, the full potential of resource materials needs to be explored by the teachers and learners of science. Printed materials are essential part of science curricula play a vital role in teaching and learning, at the same time over-dependence upon the text book for instance, limits the advantages of other materials in teaching and learning. Nowadays there is wide variety of learning materials in science and these include the traditional textbooks, workbooks, supplementary readers etc. and the highly sophisticated online learning materials, digital libraries and other software solutions in science learning.

SCIENCE TEXTBOOK

Textbook is one of the important aids in teaching learning process and has occupied a pivotal role in educating the school children. They are the most widely used of all instructional materials. A text book is an economical device for teachers and students as it gives direction and saves time and energy. A text book should be really designed for the pupil rather than the teacher. They can help the pupils learn how to learn. The science textbook should aim at aiding the pupil in the development of personality, in developing open-mindedness, critical attitude in order to enable him to discover new knowledge.

Functions of a Text Book

- A good science text book should help to form correct understanding of basic concepts and principles of science

- It should inculcate scientific attitude in the pupils and develop an understanding of the scientific method
- It should supplement and enrich classroom learning
- It should give information about the past discoveries, and some thrilling experiences made by scientists
- It should help pupil in doing home assignments
- It should help the pupil for systematic and speedy revision of the lesson they have finished

Characteristics of a Text Book

- Text-books that are intended to be used should be useful for the students as well as teachers.
- The size of the book should be handy. It should be possible for the students to carry them properly. They should not be bulky.
- Printing and get-up of the books should be interesting and attractive. They should be printed in the letters that they do not require strain on the eyes of the students. On the other hand, they should be correctly and neatly printed.
- The exterior of the picture should be attractive. If the exterior is attractive, students would like to carry them and keep them.
- They should serve the purpose of the subject- matter as well as the aims and objectives of teaching. They should be written with a view on the aims and objectives of teaching.
- The text-books should be accurately written. They should present the subject-matter in such a manner that there is no fault in them. The subject-matter, presented therein should be up to date.
- The style of the books should also serve the psychological requirements of the students of different stages.
- In the text-books meant for higher classes the author may use the regional method or some other method that is useful for the students of the stage.
- The text-books should continue to keep the interests of the students alive in the subject-matter. The subject-matter should be presented in a simple and lucid style and clear form.
- The text-books should contain all the necessary and relative material required for a particular stage of education.
- The text-books of different stages should be complimentary to each other. Text-books that are used in primary classes should

have some bearing and connection with the text-books that shall be used by the students in the Junior High School classes.

- Text-books should be free from prejudice. The presentation of the subject-matter should be unbiased. There should be no material which can injure the susceptibility of any class or category of people. They should contain objective description of the people and conditions of different countries.
- The text-books should contain charts, maps, diagrams etc. as and where required.
- At the end of every chapter of the text-book there should be certain questions that may be used for the revision of the subject-matter. Without these questions the text-books shall not be useful.
- If required the text-books may give a summary of the chapter at the end of each lesson. Such a provision will help the students to grasp the subject-matter properly.

Criteria for the selection of text book

Louise F. Vogel developed an evaluation scale called Vogel's score card that may be a guide for selecting a science text book. The major criteria suggested are grouped under ten major headings. The several characteristic features that we have to concentrate while selecting text-book are:

- The author - his qualifications and experience: The qualification and experience of the author is very important in the case of text-book writing. Only the author who has certain amount of experience of teaching the subject should be allowed to publish a book because he can understand the actual learning situations and difficulties of the students. Moreover, he is conversant with the changing concepts and techniques of teaching. Certain minimum academic qualifications may also be prescribed for the author.
- Mechanical features of the textbook: The paper, the binding, the print and type of letters should be attractive. The size of the print, spacing and the length of the lines should correspond to the visual capacity of the pupils so as to facilitate easy reading. The quantity and quality of illustrations need consideration. Science text-book should be well illustrated with diagrams, sketches, photographs etc. diagrams should be carefully drawn accurate and attractive. Photographs should be clearly reproduced; illustrations should amplify the materials printed on the same page.
- Subject Matter - Its nature and Organization: The subject matter should be addressed by taking care of the following criteria (a)

The subject matter should be developed as far as possible in psychological sequence. Care must be taken for the mental growth and interest of the pupils, (b) There should be consistency of the subject matter and the text-book should stand for the objectives of science teaching. It should lead to inculcation of scientific attitudes, disciplinary and cultural values and should suggest project or activities for the pupils, which may help to give a better understanding of the principles and concepts, and Each chapter should begin with a brief introduction and end with a summary.

- Each chapter should contain assignments at the end conforming to the following: Application to life situations; New types of self-assessment tests; Suggestions and experimental work of projects; Suggestions for further study; and Numerical examples, where is desirable; Headings and sub headings should be in bold type. The matter should be suitably presented in varied and distinctive form.
- Each text-book should contain a detailed table of contents and an index. The book should be written in lucid, simple and precise scientific language. A standard terminology of scientific and technical terms should be used. English equivalents should also be given within brackets. It should also contain glossary of technical terms used in the book. It should be free from any type of ambiguity in language, terminology and information.
- It should suggest some good methods of learning. It should contain helpful and practical suggestions for preparing and improving the science apparatus.
- It is better if the text-book contain examples from environments. Weightage should be given to those methods and materials which draw upon the social community resources and school society interaction.
- Adequate provision should be made to correlate general science with craft, social environment and physical environment.
- Each text-book should be accompanied by a laboratory handbook or manual.

REFERENCE BOOKS

Reference books are very important in science. Science is a subject which is dynamic and goes on changing with the laws of nature. What we see and perceive today as right becomes false on tomorrow. In such case reference books play an important role in acquiring conceptualization in science for teachers. In school science library there should be large number of reference materials in science pertaining to all branches of study. Good reference books act as the immediate source of solution of teacher's problems and in higher classrooms reference books can act as substitute for teachers. Reference books are effective aids to learning and students must be given training to use reference books. Reference works include dictionaries, thesauruses, encyclopaedias, year book, annual reports, History of science, almanacs, bibliographies etc. Many reference works are available in electronic form and can be obtained as application software, CD-ROMs, DVDs, or online through the Internet.

Advantages of Reference Books

- Reference books are effective aids to learning
- Students must be given training in the use of reference books
- The teacher should bear in mind that the reference material should be easily comprehensible and readily available for the pupils
- It supplements classroom instruction
- It instils the pupil's self-study habits and the spirit of self-work
- It helps the pupils to workout assignments
- It stimulates scientific thinking and inculcates the elements of scientific attitude

Disadvantages of Reference Books

- Some of the reference books are very difficult to understand for students
- The language used in reference books can be accessible only to advance learners
- They can only supplement knowledge and not act as a substitute for learning in all cases
- Cost of the reference books are very high

WORK BOOK

Work book vary greatly in content and organization. Some of the workbooks are replication of the text book, where some illustrations are given for content and space for marking and writing etc., whereas some other types make provision for many different types of activities, forms for reporting data, diagrams to be labelled, blank spaces for sketches and clippings, suggestions for supplementary work, study guides for reading assignments and self-testing devices. Workbooks of the latter type serve as a combined course of study, a study guide and record book.

Advantages of Work books

- Heavily burdened teachers find the better workbooks useful in saving time and energy
- Help pupil who are working under self-direction to study more effectively
- Works can be carried out after school hours so as to help premature learners
- Work books provide a direction for the learning activities for an inexperienced teacher

Workbook fosters scientific thinking

- Disadvantages of Work books
- Workbooks are relatively inflexible
- The content is highly organized and cannot be altered easily
- There is little supervision for the inclusion of new materials
- Workbooks are directed towards uniform outcomes, if they dominate the programme, pupils have equal opportunities to develop special interests and talents
- Work book deny pupils any participation in the planning process, any incentive to do independent work, any practice in formulating their own problems and any encouragement to do their own thinking.

TEACHERS TEXT BOOK (HANDBOOK)

Teacher's handbook is an excellent reference material for teachers for effective science teaching. Teacher's handbook is a valuable teaching device suitable for a wide range of interest and abilities. It contains list of teaching aids, summarization of learning, an exercise in organization, a medium for self-expression, an indication of progress and assignments of various kinds. It gives sufficient additional points that teachers can use in classrooms, which are more socially relevant to the immediate surroundings of the students and more acceptable to their cognitive sense.

Advantages of Teacher's handbook

- It is a device for review work
- It suggests the teacher to adopt appropriate strategies to teach every topic
- Finding the learning experiences for each topic is easy

- Tangible evidence for the progress of the students
- Work of the teacher is fostered
- Not easily available to all teachers

Disadvantages of Teacher's handbook: Teacher becomes lazy and does not try to learn more in the topic. Teacher always takes help from this material other than applying reasoning.

IMPROVISED AIDS

The plea of most of the science teachers against effective demonstration and experimentation is the lack of adequate apparatus. This occurs as a result of the inability of schools to meet the cost of these materials due to insufficient funds to purchase all the necessary equipment and apparatus needed for science teaching. If we want to train school students in scientific method, we need large amount of money in setting up of laboratories, the only solution to this economic problem is the improvisation of apparatus. Improvisation of materials for science teaching and learning or substituting Science materials are clearly an effort towards cost reduction in science teaching. Improvisation means the preparation of ordinary laboratory apparatus from simple or locally available materials. The science teacher with a certain amount of skill and enthusiasm can replace many pieces of apparatus by adequate improvised substitutes. Low cost or No cost teaching aids have an advantage of offering learning by doing approach to the teaching learning process. When teachers and students plan, produce or create their own educational materials, they invariably manifest pride and pleasure in utilizing them to the maximum. Locally produced low-cost equipment, teaching aids or models can serve the needs of the teacher, the student and the curriculum more effectively and is easier to maintain. Teacher with the help of students may carry out the process. To design the effective low-cost teaching aid, teacher should have thorough knowledge of the objectives and science concepts. The teachers should have adequate knowledge to provide learning experiences, locally available resources and environmental conditions.

Characteristics of Improvised Apparatus

The following are the some of the characteristics of improvised apparatus:

- The raw materials are easily available either free or at low cost in the locality
- The materials do not involve specialized skills and can be made by pupils, teachers or members of the community

- The materials can be easily and effectively used by the teachers and pupils in clarifying the set of objectives
- The process involved in the production of the materials is simple and inexpensive
- The material is simple, accurate and appropriate to the age level of the users
- The material stimulates thinking, reacting, discussing, experimenting or further study
- The material is free from distractions, conflicts or bias
- The production of the material is not time consuming

Process of Developing Improvised apparatus

The different steps involved in the process of developing improvised apparatus are:

- Definition of Objectives
- Preparation of a design
- Development of materials
- Pilot testing of the materials
- Finalization of materials
- Production and distribution

Advantages

- Well-designed simple or improvised apparatus of good quality will help the pupils to understand the idea behind the experiment more easily
- Overcome the problem of lack of apparatus
- Save money by using local materials
- Help pupils develop positive attitudes towards science
- Acquire manual skill
- Learn to apply principles of science
- Supply school laboratory with equipment
- No fear of breaking or damaging as with expensive apparatus
- It helps to have more knowledge and understanding
- Improvisation makes science doing instead of talking
- It promotes pupils' maximum participation in the learning process
- Improvisation ensures longer retention of the information gained
- It provides firsthand experience in a variety of ways

- Cultivates research mindedness in children
- Promotes interaction between teachers and students and among students
- Improvisation generally adds an interest and involvement in the lesson
- Encourage co-operative attitude in children
- Develops self-confidence of pupils
- Helps the students to make use of their leisure time and to understand the dignity of labour
- Helps the school to become self sufficient
- With the help of the improvised aids the presentation of the content will also be attractive and stimulating
- It accelerates the rate of learning and increases the span of retention
- Learning experiences appending to the senses are far more effective than abstract learning experiences.

ROLE OF VIRTUAL CLASSROOMS IN PHYSICAL SCIENCE LEARNING

Virtual Classroom is a simulated classroom via Internet, which provides a convenient communication environment for distance learners just like traditional face-to-face classroom. They will not be present physically in the classroom but connected to the classroom via Internet. A virtual classroom is an online learning environment (Wang & Newlin 2012). The delivery format goes by a number of names: e-learning, Internet learning, distributed learning, networked learning, tele-learning, virtual learning, or web-based learning (WCET, 2004). Virtual classroom aims to simulate the experience of attending a class over the web. So everyone is able to see other participant virtually. A virtual classroom allows learners to attend a class from anywhere in the world and aims to provides a learning experience that is similar to a real classroom. A Virtual Classroom is a scheduled, online, teacher-led training session where teachers and learners interact together using computers linked to a network such as the Internet.

A virtual classroom enables to bring learners from around the world together online in highly interactive virtual classes while greatly reducing the travel, time, and expense of on-site teaching/training programs. It can be used as a solution for live delivery and interaction that addresses the entire process of creating and managing our teaching-learning process. It facilitates instructor and student in teaching-learning events, such as a seminar, online discussion or a live training for employees in company.

As in traditional classroom, there are professor and fellow learners present with the student; we have many participants present in virtual classroom. They can talk with each other as in the traditional classroom via chat. Similarly, presenter uses whiteboard, gives notes/resources, and gives presentation as given in traditional one. Thus, virtual classroom can be visualized as a classroom where a lecture or session is conducted using Internet. Virtual science classes typically offer opportunities for learning to take place through individual review of online lectures, virtual and at-home laboratory activities, and student-to-student as well as student-to-teacher interaction. Virtual schools are considered flexible because students can access course content 24 hours a day, 7 days a week, and nearly all year round. Students can proceed at a pace comfortable for their learning needs and can choose to engage with online lectures or do laboratories or assignments as they wish. Virtual science courses often integrate e- resources into the course design that have been found to be effective with science learners. Any website can be brought into a course as a resource for learners.

Teaching science online requires a new set of teaching skills, although underlying principles of classroom-based science teaching such as a constructivist philosophy equally apply to facilitating science learning online. For example, both classroom based and virtual science teachers need to scaffold students' scientific inquiry, set and communicate high expectations, and facilitate tasks that encourage active learning. Yet, new instructional strategies and approaches to teaching also are needed. In virtual science classrooms, the teacher can structure learning tasks, open discussions with provocative questions, invite student participation, facilitate group collaboration, provide electronic mentoring, point to additional online resources, and structure transitions between learning activities. Online synchronous learning is, in many ways, similar to a physical classroom. For example, both physical and virtual classrooms allow for immediate feedback, interactions with instructor and peers, and guided exercises to motivate and increase student learning. With asynchronous communications, students engage with the learning materials at their own pace and interact with peers and instructors via e-mail and discussion boards at a time convenient for their schedules. The online virtual classroom has another advantage as interactions which are learner-content, learner-instructor, and learner-learner in the online environment.

Designing a Virtual Classroom

- **Step 1** - Assess the needs and the necessary conditions: The main purpose of this step is to assure the existence of a need for the proposed virtual classroom and the basic infrastructure to develop it

- **Step 2** - Estimate the development cost, effort, and implications: The main purpose of this step is to reach a clear, accurate, quantitative estimate of the overall cost of developing the virtual classroom.
- **Step 3** - Plan the virtual classroom: After having estimated the overall cost of developing the virtual classroom, assessed its impact on existing structures, and established some of its minimum requirements, it is time to look more closely at the project from an educational perspective. (Deciding the educational goals, accomplishment of those goals, approaches used to achieve a given goal etc.)
- **Step 4** - Design the virtual classroom: Decides the layout for a typical course page and related hardware/software
- **Step 5** - Prepare and distribute contents
- **Step 6** - Enable communication: There are basically two possible ways of implementing communication between instructor and students in a virtual classroom: synchronous and asynchronous. A successful virtual classroom implementation should use both synchronous and asynchronous techniques to enable one-to-one (normally instructor-to-student), one-to-many (typically instructor-to-class) or many-to-many interactions.
- **Step 7** - Implement online student assessment methods
- **Step 8** - Implement class management procedures
- **Step 9** - Set up the system
- **Step 10** - Maintain and update the virtual classroom

Advantages of Virtual Classroom

- Removal of geographical barriers (Anywhere learning): A virtual classroom allows learners and teachers to attend a single live training session from any place in the world, provided they have a computer and Internet connection.
- Sessions can be recorded: If learners miss a traditional classroom-based training session, they have very little opportunity to engage in the learning experience that took place. A virtual classroom has a facility to record the session so learners or teachers can replay it afterwards. Teachers to get an opportunity to review their own or their colleagues' performance.

- Quicker to organize: Training can be organized more quickly than traditional classroom-based training. Classrooms and projectors do not need to be reserved; materials do not need to be distributed. The sessions are easier to schedule or reschedule since attendees will not be traveling to the venue of the session.
- One to one communication: In a virtual classroom environment, learners can talk to the teacher and to each other, and although this communication is not as rich in a traditional classroom, it still can help learners, since it is one to one.
- Due to these advantages, concept of virtual classroom is getting very popular. Since it allows learners to attend sessions from anywhere in world, it is very useful for distant learners and for peoples who cannot meet face to face because of lack of time. Though it gives lots of advantages, it has some pitfalls also.

Limitations of Virtual Classroom

- Teachers and students need to become familiar with the tools. Teachers and students are familiar with the workings of a traditional classroom, that is, they understand the concepts of hand raising, the whiteboard, assignments, and so forth. With a virtual classroom, all attendees must become familiar with the way the virtual classroom works before virtual classroom-based training starts.
- Time dependency for Live Sessions: Attending virtual classroom training is restricted to a certain scheduled time.
- Infrastructure for the participants: PC needs to be prepared, Virtual classroom sessions need to be scheduled, teachers need to be invited, and participants' PCs need to be prepared.
- Technical Limitations: Technical issues such as bandwidth, speed of the connection or power failure may create problem while presentation is going on.

SMART BOARD

A Smart Board is a type of interactive whiteboard used in education to enhance teaching and learning. The Smart Board looks like a regular whiteboard but has many more features that make it a useful tool for teachers and students. There are three main parts to using a Smart Board - the whiteboard, a projector and a computer. The whiteboard is mounted on the wall and the projector is angled to display data onto the board. A computer is connected, either wirelessly or through a USB cable. Since the surface of the Smart Board is interactive, teachers and students can use it as a touch screen to manipulate, move and record information. A SMART Board is an interactive whiteboard, that, when used with a computer and a projector, enables students to interact with the material presented in ways that would otherwise be impossible. The SMART Board is a touch-sensitive whiteboard that is connected to a computer and a projector. Lessons or presentations are made on computer programs and then the projector displays the image onto the whiteboard. The computer is then controlled by either using your finger to open or close programs and move objects, or by electronic pens to write words. SMART Boards are powerful learning tools as they enable teachers to instruct using the latest technology, with access to the internet, videos, and educational software (Fernandez & Luftglass, 2003). This empowers students to learn and explore new concepts with technology to create a more dynamic learning experience. SMART Board is an interactive whiteboard that allows projecting a presentation, writing over the projection, save the changes, and creating new presentations, show videos, DVDs and link to the internet. It is an easy tool to use requiring no special expertise.

SMART Board "fosters an environment that allows students to go beyond the surface and dig deeper into a concept" (SMART Technologies, 2007). Students in classrooms, have varying ability levels. However, e SMART Board "not only fosters critical thinking in these students, but also cultivates differentiated learning" (SMART Technologies, 2007). With a SMART Board interactive whiteboard, instructors can interact with dynamic multimedia content and write notes in digital ink, then save them instantly and distribute this material to students with ease. SMART Board interactive whiteboards make learning a visual, engaging experience for students, which helps deepen understanding and promote retention of course material.

Advantages of Smart Board

- Smart Classrooms make a remarkable difference in how teachers teach and learners learn
- Students are active inventors rather than passive recipients.
- Smart Classrooms can enhance content and presentation
- Teacher can stand at the front of the classroom interacting with the screen and students
- Can control any computer applications through the board
- Can take and save notes for future reference

- Can convert handwriting into text
- Motivates students to use the smart board and to participate in lessons and discussions
- Bring in experts through videoconferencing
- Can write in digital ink over web pages, applications and videos
- Harness the Power of the WWW
- Improves classroom management
- Provides academic & digital learning
- Limited opportunities for distraction by focusing students' attention on lessons
- Visual and tactile lessons lead to multisensory engagement in the learning process
- Enhance instruction and learning in distance education
- Make the communication more interactive between tutor and learners
- The SMART Board interactive whiteboard has the flexibility to engage all learning styles.
- Visual learners can easily see colourful, movable images and diagrams that the interactive whiteboard displays, even from the back of the classroom
- Kinaesthetic learners can interact and explore by moving letters, numbers, words and pictures with the touch of a finger
- Auditory learners can be immersed in a complete multimedia experience using optional USB speakers or SMART Audio

Limitations of Smart Board

- Could be hard to write on as light source from the projector falls directly on the body and cast shadows on the screen where writing is done.
- May be hard to write neatly
- Difficult to move
- Expensive

CONCLUSION

In conclusion, Chapter 9 has explored a spectrum of instructional supports, blending traditional and modern approaches to enhance the learning experience in physical science. From the cornerstone of the science textbook to the supplementary resources like reference books and workbooks, this chapter has underscored the importance of comprehensive instructional materials in fostering a deeper understanding of scientific concepts. The chapter has also highlighted the crucial role of teachers' textbooks, providing educators with valuable insights, lesson plans, and pedagogical strategies to effectively deliver curriculum content. Moreover, the inclusion of improvised aids demonstrates the ingenuity and creativity employed by teachers to bring abstract scientific concepts to life, fostering active engagement and comprehension among students. Embracing modern technology, the chapter has explored the evolving landscape of instructional supports, with a particular focus on the role of virtual classrooms and smart boards in physical science learning. Virtual classrooms offer dynamic platforms for interactive learning, facilitating real-time collaboration, experimentation, and discussion among students and teachers across geographical boundaries. Meanwhile, smart boards leverage multimedia capabilities to deliver engaging and interactive lessons, catering to diverse learning styles and enhancing retention of complex scientific concepts. By integrating these modern tools into the instructional framework, educators can create immersive learning environments that inspire curiosity, critical thinking, and problem-solving skills in students. In essence, Chapter 9 has underscored the importance of embracing a diverse array of instructional supports, leveraging both traditional and modern approaches to cater to the evolving needs of physical science education. By harnessing the power of innovative technologies alongside time-tested pedagogical methods, educators can empower students to navigate the complexities of the physical world with confidence and enthusiasm.

Bibliography

1. Abdi, A., Laei, S., & Ahmadyan, H. (2013). The effect of teaching strategy based on multiple intelligences on students' academic achievement in science course. *Universal Journal of Educational Research, 1*(4), 281-284. https://doi.org/10.13189/ujer.2013.010401
2. Adelman, H.S., & Taylor, L. (2005). Classroom Climate. In S.W. Lee (Ed.), *Encyclopaedia of School Psychology* (pp. 88-90). Thousand Oaks, CA: Sage Publications.
3. Aljohani, M. (2017). Principles of "constructivism" in foreign language teaching. *Journal of Literature and Art Studies, 7*(1), 97–107.
4. Apple, M. (2008). Curriculum planning: Content, form and the politics of accountability. In F. M. Connelly, M. F. He, & J. Phillion (Eds.), *Sage Handbook of Curriculum and Instruction*. Thousand Oaks, CA: Sage.
5. Backhoff, E., Larrazolo, N., & Rosas, M. (2000). The Level of Difficulty and Discrimination Power of the Basic Knowledge and Skills Examination (EXHCOBA). *Revista Electrónica de Investigación Educativa, 2*(1), 1-16.
6. Bailey, K. M. (1986). The best laid plans: Teachers in class decisions to depart from their lesson plans. In K. M. Bailey & D. Nunan (Eds.), *Voices from the Language Classroom: Qualitative Research in Second Language Classrooms* (pp. 15-40). New York: Cambridge University Press.
7. Baker, E., et al. (2010). *Problems with the Use of Student Test Scores to Evaluate Teachers*. EPI Briefing Paper, 278. Economic Policy Institute.
8. Baker, S., & Taylor, L. (1972). The relationship of visualization skill to achievement in freshman chemistry. *Journal of Chemical Education, 49*, 775–777.
9. Balan, R.M., Manko, T.P., & Phillips, K.F. (2011). Instructional improvement through professional development. *Transformative Dialogues: Teaching & Learning Journal, 5*(2), 1-18.
10. Ball, D., & Cohen, D. K. (1996). Reform by the book: What is – or might be – the role of curriculum materials in teacher learning and instructional reform? *Educational Researcher, 25*, 6–8.
11. Baum, W.M. (2005). *Understanding Behaviourism: Behaviour, Culture, and Evolution* (2nd ed.). Malden, MA: Blackwell.
12. Bean, J. A. (1995). Curriculum integration and the discipline of knowledge. *Phi Delta Kappan, 76*(8), 616-622.

13. Beane, J., Toepfer, C. F., & Alessi, S. J. (1986). *Curriculum Planning and Development*. Boston, MA: Allyn and Bacon.
14. Ben-Naim, D., Marcus, N., & Bain, M. (2007). *Virtual Apparatus Framework Approach to Constructing Adaptive Tutorials*. Paper presented at the International Conference on E-Learning, E-Business, Enterprise Information Systems, and E-Government.
15. Bereiter, C. (1994). Implications of postmodernism for science, or, science as progressive discourse. *Educational Psychologist, 29*(1), 3–12.
16. Blood, D. F., & Budd, W. C. (1972). *Educational Measurement and Evaluation*. New York: Harper and Row.
17. Boopathiraj, C., & Chellamani, K. (2013). Analysis of test items on Difficulty level and Discrimination Index in the test for Research in Education. *International Journal of Social Science and Interdisciplinary Research, 2*(2), 189-193.
18. Bower, M., & Richards, D. (2005). *The Impact of Virtual Classroom Laboratories in Computer Science Education*. In Thirty-Sixth SIGCSE Technical Symposium of Computer Science Education (pp. 292-296). ACM Press.
19. Brady, L., & Kennedy, K. (2012). *Curriculum construction*. Sidney: Pearson.
20. Brindley, G. (2001). *Assessment*. Cambridge: Cambridge University Press.
21. Brophy, J. E. (1982). How Teachers Influence What is Taught and Learned in Classrooms. *Primary School Journal, 83*, 1–13.
22. Brown, F. (1983). *Principles of Educational and Psychological Testing* (3rd ed.). New York: Holt, Rinehart & Winston.
23. Brown, F., & Frederick, G. (1971). *Measuring Classroom Achievement*. Halt Richard and Winston, U.S.A, pp. 101-110.
24. Brown, J. S., & Burton, R. B. (1978). Diagnostic models for procedural bugs in basic mathematical skills. *Cognitive Science, 2*, 155-194.
25. Bullough, R. (1987). Planning and the First Year of Teaching. *Journal of Education for Teaching, 12*, 231–250.
26. Calfee, R., & Peri, P. (1993). Student portfolios: opportunities for a revolution in assessment. *Journal of Reading, 36*, 532-537.
27. Cashdan, A., & Pumfrey, P. D. (1969). Some Effects of Remedial Teaching of Reading. *Educational Research, 11*(2), 138-142.
28. Cohen, P. A. (1980). Effectiveness of student-rating feedback for improving college instruction: A meta-analysis of findings. *Research in Higher Education, 13*, 321–341.
29. Cooper, J. (1990). *Classroom teaching skills*. Canada: D.C. Health and Company.
30. Daehler, K. R., & Shinohara, M. (2001). A complete circuit is a complete circle: Exploring the potential of case materials and methods to develop teachers' content knowledge and pedagogical content knowledge of science. *Research in Science Education, 31*(2), 267–288.
31. Daniel, I.Y. (2001). *Improvisation and use of instructional materials in science teaching*. Paper presented at NCCE/UNESCO Workshop for Train the Korancora Nigeria.

32. Danielson, C., & McGreal, T. (2000). *Teacher evaluation: To enhance professional practice*. Alexandria, VA: ASCD.

33. Das, R. C. (1985). *Science teaching in schools*. New Delhi: Sterling Publishers.

34. Davydov, V. V. (1995). The influence of LS Vygotsky on education theory, research, and practice. *Educational Researcher, 24*(3), 12–21.

35. de Jong, O., van Driel, J. H., & Verloop, N. (2005). Preservice teachers' pedagogical content knowledge of using particle models in teaching chemistry. *Journal of Research in Science Teaching, 42*(8), 947–964.

36. Derry, G. N. (1999). *What science is and how it works*. Princeton, NJ: Princeton University Press.

37. Doyle, W. (1992a). Curriculum and pedagogy. In P. W. Jackson (Ed.), *Handbook of Research on Curriculum* (pp. 486–516). New York: Macmillan.

38. Doyle, W. (1992b). Constructing curriculum in the classroom. In F. K. Oser, A. Dick, & J. Patry (Eds.), *Effective and Responsible Teaching: The New Syntheses* (pp. 66–79). San Francisco, CA: Jossey-Bass.

39. Ebel, R. L. (1972). *Essentials of Educational Measurement* (1st ed.). New Jersey: Prentice Hall.

40. Egeler, D. J. (1993). Factors that Influence the Instructional Planning of Teachers. *Educational Planning, 9*(3), 19–37.

41. Ertmer, P. A., & Newby, T. J. (1993). Behaviourism, cognitivism, constructivism: Comparing critical features from an instructional design perspective. *Performance Improvement Quarterly, 6*(4), 50–72.

42. Escalada, L., & Zollman, D. (1977). An investigation on the effects of using interactive digital video in a physics classroom on student learning and attitudes. *Journal of Research in Science Teaching, 34*, 467–489.

43. Farrell, T. S. C. (2002). Lesson Planning. In *Methodology in Language Teaching: An Anthology of Current Practice* (Eds. J. C. Richards & W. A. Renandya). New York: Cambridge University Press.

44. Fischman, G. E., & Mclaren, P. (2005). Rethinking critical pedagogy and the Gramscian and Freirean legacies: From organic to committed intellectuals or critical pedagogy, commitment, and praxis. *Cultural Studies-Critical Methodologies, 5*(4), 425-447.

45. Fullan, M. (2008). Curriculum implementation and sustainability. In F. M. Connelly, M. F. He, & J. Phillion (Eds.), *Sage Handbook of Curriculum and Instruction*. Thousand Oaks, CA: Sage.

46. Gagne, R., Wager, W., Golas, K., & Keller, J. (1992). *Principles of instructional design*. Orlando: Harcourt Brace Jovanovich College Publishers.

47. Gardner, H., & Hatch, T. (1989). Educational implications of the theory of multiple intelligences. *Educational Researcher, 18*(8), 4–10.

48. Gay, G. (1991). Curriculum development. In A. Lewy (Ed.), *The International Encyclopaedia of Curriculum* (pp. 293–302). Oxford: Pergamon.

49. Glatthorn, A. A. (1993). Helping Teachers to Better Instructional Planning. *Education Digest, 59*(2), 16–19.

50. Goldhaber, D., & Anthony, E. (2007). Can teacher quality be effectively assessed? National Board Certification as a signal of effective teaching. *Review of Economics and Statistics, 89*, 134–150.
51. Goodlad, J. I., et al. (1979). *Curriculum Inquiry: The Study of Curriculum Practice*. New York: McGraw-Hill.
52. Gowdhaman, K., & Nachimuthu, K. (2013). Item Analysis of History Achievement test on Difference Index (DI) in the Criterion Referenced Measurement. *Research Journal of Educational Sciences, 1*(5), 1-8.
53. Grossman, P. L. (1989). A study in contrast: Sources of pedagogical content knowledge for secondary English. *Journal of Teacher Education, 40*(5), 24–31.
54. Grossman, P. L. (1990). *The making of a teacher: Teacher knowledge and teacher education*. New York: Teachers College Press.
55. Gutek, G. L. (2009). *New Perspectives on Philosophy and Education*. New York: Pearson College Division.
56. Haslam, F., & Treagust, D. F. (1987). Diagnosing secondary students' misconceptions of photosynthesis and respiration in plants using a two-tier multiple-choice instrument. *Journal of Biological Education, 21*, 203-211.
57. http://www.thetechedvocate.org/tech-edvocates-2017-list-116-best-teaching-learning-apps/
58. https://www.educatorstechnology.com/2017/05/18-good-educational-android-apps-for.html
59. https://gradeup.co/the-role-of-curriculum-in-science-teaching-i
60. International Society for Technology in Education. (2000). *National educational technology standards for teachers*. Eugene: International Society for Technology in Education (ISTE) NETS Project.
61. Jalongo, M., Rieg, S., & Heltebran, V. (2007). *Planning for learning: Collaborative approaches to lesson design and review*. New York: Teachers College Press.
62. Joseph, T. T. (1982). *Modern Trends in Science Education* (2nd ed.). Kottayam, Kerala.
63. Kesik, F., & Bayram, A. (2015). The Evaluation of Education System from the Perspective of Critical Pedagogy. *Mersin University Journal of the Faculty of Education, 11*(3), 900-921.
64. Kevin, D. Crehan. (1974). Item analysis for Teacher-made Mastery Tests. *Journal of Educational Measurement, 11*(4), 255–262.
65. Klenowski, V. (1995). Student self-evaluation processes in student-centred teaching and learning contexts of Australia and England. *Assessment in Education: Principles, Theory & Practice, 2*(3), 145-163.
66. Kneller, F. G. (1964). *Introduction to the Philosophy of Education*. Milton, Queensland, Australia: John Willey & Sons, Inc.
67. Kohli, V. K. (1986). *How to Teach Science*. Ambala City, Haryana: Vivek Publishers.
68. Laurillard, D. (2002). *Rethinking University Teaching: A Conversational Framework for the Effective Use of Learning Technologies*. Routledge.

69. Laurillard, D. (2008). The teacher as action researcher: using technology to capture pedagogic form. *Studies in Higher Education, 33*, 139-154.

70. Lee, S. W. (Ed.). (2005). *Encyclopaedia of School Psychology*. London: Sage Publications.

71. Levin, B. (2007). Curriculum policy and the politics of what should be learned in schools. In F. M. Connelly, M. F. He, & J. Phillion (Eds.), *Sage Handbook of Curriculum and Instruction* (pp. 7–24). Thousand Oaks, CA: Sage.

72. Loughran, J., Milroy, P., Berry, A., Gunstone, R., & Mulhall, P. (2001). Documenting Science Teachers' Pedagogical Content Knowledge through PaP-eRs. *Research in Science Education, 31*(2), 290–307.

73. Magnusson, S., Krajcik, J., & Borko, H. (1999). Nature, sources, and development of pedagogical content knowledge for science teaching. In J. Gess-Newsome & N. Lederman (Eds.), *Examining pedagogical content knowledge: The construct and its implications for science education* (pp. 95–132). The Netherlands: Kluwer Academic Publishers.

74. Maitra, K. (1991). *Teaching of Physics*. New Delhi: Discovery Publishing House.

75. Marcus, N., Cooper, M., & Sweller, J. (1996). Understanding instructions. *Journal of Educational Psychology, 88*, 49-63.

76. Mathew, T. K., & Mollvkuttv, T. M. (2011). *Science Education: Theoretical Bases of Teaching and Pedagogic Analysis*. Chenaanoor: Rainbow Book Publishers.

77. McArdle, G. (2010). *Instructional design for action learning*. New York: Amacom.

78. McCutcheon, G. (1980). How Do Primary School Teachers Plan? The Nature of Planning and Influences on It. *Primary School Journal, 81*, 4–23.

79. McLeod, S. (2020). *Behaviourist approach*, Retrieved from https://www.simplypsychology.org/behaviorism.html#ev

80. Michael, D. B. (1974). Achievement test Reliability as a function of pupil Response Procedures. *Journal of Educational Measurement, 11*(2), 109–114.

81. Mohan, R. (1995). *Innovative Science Teaching for Physical Science*. New Delhi: Prentice Hall.

82. Niess, M. L. (2005). Preparing teachers to teach science and mathematics with technology: Developing a technology pedagogical content knowledge. *Teaching and Teacher Education, 21*, 509–523.

83. Nunan, D. (1989). *Learner-centred Curriculum Design*. Cambridge: Cambridge University Press.

84. O'loughlin, M. (1992). Rethinking science education: Beyond piagetian constructivism toward a sociocultural model of teaching and learning. *Journal of Research in Science Teaching, 29*(8), 791–820.

85. Özmen, H. (2003). Chemistry Student Teachers' Levels of Linking Their Knowledge with Daily Life about Acid and Base Concepts. *Kastamonu Education Journal, 11*(2), 317-324.

86. Peterson, R. (1986). *The development, validation and application of a diagnostic test instrument measuring year 11 and year 12 students' understanding of covalent bonding and structure*. Unpublished master's thesis, Curtin University of Technology, Perth, Australia.

87. Phillips, D. C. (2000). Constructivism in education: Opinions and second opinions on controversial issues. In *Ninety-ninth yearbook of the national society for the study of education*. Chicago: University of Chicago Press.

88. Posner, G. J. (1998). Models of curriculum planning. In L. E. Beyer & M. W. Apple (Eds.), *The Curriculum: Problems, Politics, and Possibilities* (2nd ed., pp. 79–100). New York: State University of New York Press.

89. Rajan, K. M. (1992). *Psychology in Education*. New Delhi: Sterling Publishers.

90. Ravitch, D. (2010). *The Death and Life of the Great American School System: How Testing and Choice are Undermining Education*. New York: Basic Books.

91. Reys, B. J., & Reys, R. E. (1999). Curriculum trends in mathematics education. In F. K. Lester Jr. (Ed.), *The Handbook of Research in Mathematics Education* (pp. 37–54). Reston, VA: National Council of Teachers of Mathematics.

92. Richards, J. C., & Rodgers, T. S. (2001). *Approaches and Methods in Language Teaching*. Cambridge: Cambridge University Press.

93. Ricks, T. E., & Vila, R. (1994). *Diagnostic teaching of reading: Techniques for instruction and assessment*. New York: Guilford Press.

94. Roberts, J. K. (2002). *The Unfinished Journey: Curriculum Theory in Historical Perspective.* New York: SUNY Press.

95. Roehler, L., & Cantlon, D. (1997). Scaffolding: A powerful tool in social constructivist classrooms. In K. Hogan & M. Pressley (Eds.), *Scaffolding Student Learning: Instructional Approaches and Issues* (pp. 50–72). Cambridge, MA: Brookline Books.

96. Rogers, C. R. (1983). *Freedom to Learn for the 80's*. Columbus, OH: Charles E. Merrill.

97. Saettler, P. (1990). *The evolution of American educational technology*. Englewood, CO: Libraries Unlimited.

98. Saunders, S. A. (2011). *Curriculum planning: A contemporary approach* (9th ed.). Hoboken, NJ: John Wiley & Sons.

99. Savin-Baden, M., & Wilkie, K. (2004). *Challenging Research in Problem-based Learning*. Maidenhead: Open University Press.

100. Schneider, S. (2009). *A History of Western Thought*. Upper Saddle River, NJ: Pearson Prentice Hall.

101. Schwab, J. (1973). The practical 4: Something for curriculum professors to do. *Curriculum Inquiry, 4*(3), 207–225.

102. Schwab, J. (1978). The practical: A language for curriculum. *School Review, 86*(1), 9–20.

103. Scott, P. (1998). Teacher Talk and Meaning Making in Science Classrooms: A Vygotskian Analysis and Review. *Studies in Science Education, 32*, 45-80.

104. Shepard, L. A. (2000). The role of assessment in a learning culture. *Educational Researcher, 29*(7), 4-14.

105. Shulman, L. S. (1986). Those who understand: Knowledge growth in teaching. *Educational Researcher, 15*(2), 4–14.

106. Skinner, B. F. (1954). The Science of Learning and the Art of Teaching. *Harvard Educational Review, 24*(2), 86-97.

107. Skinner, B. F. (1968). *The Technology of Teaching*. New York: Appleton-Century-Crofts.

108. Sowell, E. J. (1989). Effects of selected teaching strategy variables on the student's achievement and attitude in the university chemistry laboratory. *Journal of Research in Science Teaching, 26*(1), 47–57.

109. Stiggins, R. J. (1991). Assessment literacy. *Phi Delta Kappan, 72*, 534-539.

110. Sweller, J. (1994). Cognitive load theory, learning difficulty, and instructional design. *Learning and Instruction, 4*(4), 295-312.

111. Sweller, J. (2005). Implications of Cognitive Load Theory for Multimedia Learning. In R. E. Mayer (Ed.), *The Cambridge Handbook of Multimedia Learning* (pp. 19-30). Cambridge University Press.

112. Taba, H. (1962). *Curriculum development: Theory and practice*. New York: Harcourt, Brace & World.

113. Tanner, D., & Tanner, L. (1980). *Curriculum development: Theory into practice*. New York: Macmillan.

114. Taylor, L. (2008). Learning environment. In N. J. Salkind (Ed.), *Encyclopaedia of Educational Psychology* (pp. 605-610). Thousand Oaks, CA: Sage.

115. Tobin, K., & Tippins, D. (1993). Constructivism as a Referent for Teaching and Learning. In K. Tobin (Ed.), *The Practice of Constructivism in Science Education* (pp. 3–21). Hillsdale, NJ: Lawrence Erlbaum.

116. Van Driel, J. H., Verloop, N., & De Vos, W. (1998). Developing science teachers' pedagogical content knowledge. *Journal of Research in Science Teaching, 35*(6), 673–695.

117. Vasta, R., & Sarmiento, J. (2002). *Educational Psychology: A Bilingual Approach*. New York: McGraw-Hill.

118. Vygotsky, L. S. (1978). *Mind in Society: The Development of Higher Psychological Processes*. Cambridge, MA: Harvard University Press.

119. Ward, T. B., Patterson, M. J., & Sifonis, C. M. (2004). The role of specificity and abstraction in creative idea generation. *Creativity Research Journal, 16*(1), 1–9.

120. Weimer, M. (2013). *Learner-Centred Teaching: Five Key Changes to Practice*. John Wiley & Sons.

121. Westwood, P. (2003). *Commonsense methods for children with special educational needs* (4th ed.). London: RoutledgeFalmer.

122. Wiggins, G. (1998). *Educative Assessment: Designing Assessments to Inform and Improve Student Performance*. San Francisco: Jossey-Bass.

123. Wong, D., & Wong, H. (2009). *The First Days of School: How to Be an Effective Teacher*. Mountain View, CA: Harry K. Wong Publications.

124. Wood, D., Bruner, J., & Ross, G. (1976). The role of tutoring in problem solving. *Journal of Child Psychology and Psychiatry, 17*, 89-100.

125. Woolf, B. P. (2009). *Building Intelligent Interactive Tutors: Student-Centred Strategies for Revolutionizing eLearning*. Morgan-Kaufmann.

126. Wright, A. (2009). *Planning lessons and courses: Designing sequences of work for the language classroom*. Cambridge University Press.

127. Yero, J. L. (2002). Constructivism and its implications for the classroom. *Educational Horizons, 80*(3), 112-113.

128. Zeichner, K. M., & Tabachnick, B. R. (1981). Are the effects of university teacher education "washed out" by school experience? *Journal of Teacher Education, 32*(3), 7–11.

Appendices

APPENDIX - 1: UNIT PLAN

General Information

Name of Teacher:

Standard: VIII

Name of School:

Strength:

Subject: Chemistry

Unit: Metals

Content Overview: Metals, properties of metals (malleability, ductility, hardness, sonority, thermal conductivity, electrical conductivity) reaction of metals, corrosion

Content Analysis

Terms: Metals, malleability ductility, hardness, metallic lustre, sonority, thermal conductivity, electrical conductivity, alloy, melting point, boiling point, corrosion

Facts

- Gold is lustrous, they are resistant to corrosion
- Metals are beaten to thin sheets
- Metals can be beaten into thin sheets
- There is a shining appearance when the metal is cut
- Metal are pure substances
- Metallic vessels are used for cooking
- Metals can conduct beat
- Silver is a good conductor of heat
- When metals are tapped on a hard surface, metal makes sounds

- Silver is a conductor of electricity
- Metal differs in physical and chemical properties
- Iron articles kept outside our house get destroyed through rusting over a period of time
- When sodium is introduced in water it forms sodium hydroxide and hydrogen gas
- Magnesium reacts with hot water to form magnesium hydroxide and hydrogen gas
- Brass is an alloy
- Brass is an alloy of copper and zinc
- Aluminium, Iron and magnesium react with acid
- Iron is a metal used extensively in our daily life
- Iron gets rested when it reacts with oxygen and moisture
- Metal reacts with different components of air

Concepts

- Metals can be beaten into thin sheets by hammering this property is known as malleability
- Metal can be drawn into thin wires. This property is known as ductility
- Metals are hard
- The newly formed surfaces, when the metals are cut has a shiny appearance, this property is called metallic Lustre.
- Metals are thermal conductors
- Metals are conductors of electricity
- The ability of metal to produce sound when tapped with a hard material is known as sonority
- When metal come into contact with atmosphere, they undergo chemical reaction with different components of air
- Under favourable conditions, certain metal react with water to form hydrogen gas. e.g.: $2Na+2H_2O$ □$2NaOH+H_2$
- An alloy is a solid solution which is a homogenous mixture of 2 or more metals. E.g.: Brass
- Metals like Aluminium, Zinc, Magnesium and Iron react with acids, hydrogen gas is formed along with salt of metal.
- Iron gets rusted when it enters into a chemical reaction with oxygen and moisture present in atmosphere

- Iron and number of metals react with different components of air and form new products it is called corrosion

Definitions

- Malleability: metals can be beaten into thin sheet by hammering this property is called malleability.
- Ductility: metal can be drawn into thin wires; this property is called ductility.
- Metallic lustre: when metals are cut the newly formed surface has a shining appearance it is called metallic lustre.
- Thermal conductivity: The ability to conduct heat is called thermal conductivity.
- Electrical Conductivity: The ability to conduct electricity is termed as electrical conductivity.
- Sonority: The ability of metals to produce sound when tapped with a hard material is known as sonority.
- Melting point: Temperature at which a solid change into liquid is called melting point.
- Boiling point: Temperature at which a liquid boils and changes into gas is its boiling point.
- Alloy: An alloy is a solid solution which is a homogenous mixture of two or more metal.
- Corrosion: Iron and number of metals react with different components of air and form new product this process is called corrosion of metal

Symbols

- Cu- copper
- Au- gold
- Ag- Silver
- Mg- Magnesium
- Ca- Calcium
- Na- Sodium
- Fe- Iron
- Al- Aluminium
- Cl- Chlorine
- H- Hydrogen

Equations

- $2Na+2H_2O \rightarrow 2NaOH+H_2$
- $Zn+2HCl \rightarrow Zncl_{2+}H_2$
- $Mg+2HCl \rightarrow Mgcl_2+H_2$
- $Fe+2HCl \rightarrow 2Alcl_3+3H_2$

LEARNING OBJECTIVES

Knowledge domain: The pupil develop knowledge and understanding about the above-mentioned terms, facts etc.

Specific Objectives

The pupil

- Develops an understanding of definition of metal
- Recognises between metal and non-metal
- Develops an idea about property of metal
- Recalls property of metal that are familiar
- Explain properties of each metal
- Understand the reason behind wage of metal in different fields
- Describes metals on basis of their physical properties
- Describes metals on basis of their chemical properties
- Recognises every metal has its own unique properties
- Realises of metal react with air, water and acid
- Understand rusting of iron is a chemical process
- Realises that metal are subjected to corrosion

Process domain: The pupil acquires process skills required to develop knowledge and understanding of above-mentioned topics.

Specific Objectives

The Pupil

- Observes the surroundings and find different metals
- Communicates ideas related to different types of metals
- Collect data on properties of metal
- Define metals and its properties
- Identifying which are metals and which are no-metals
- Observes and classifies metal on basis of their property
- Identifies chemical properties of metals
- Raises question about various reactions of metals

- Raises question on various uses of metals
- Communicates idea related to the reaction of metals with air, acid and water
- Defines corrosion
- observes and find examples of corrosion

Application domain: The pupil applies acquired knowledge and skills in new and unfamiliar situation

Specific Objectives

The pupil

- Finds different examples of metals from daily life
- Correlates science with life
- Applies acquired knowledge to real life situation
- Integrates science with another subject
- Find instance from daily life related to metals
- Evaluates which of the reaction of metals are useful
- Links with real life situation and sites out examples for metallic reactions
- Applies learned knowledge about metal and its properties to real life situation

Creativity domain: The pupil develops creative abilities related to the topic

Specific Objectives

The pupil

- Advances unique ideas related to the topic
- Learns in real life relation to make learning more effective
- Develops creative thinking ability
- Visualises properties of metals
- Give multiple reasons to an open-ended question related to metals
- Elaborate the idea of metals
- Thinks about different reactions and find the chemical equations

Attitudinal domain: The pupil develops scientific attitude and values by learning topic

Specific objects

The pupil

- Develops self confidence

- Develop positive attitudes towards oneself
- Interact in a healthy atmosphere
- Develops sense of dedication
- Develops knowledge about metals and its properties
- Shows co-operation while doing activities, discussions etc.
- Develops positive attitude towards science, scientist and science teachers

Learning strategies: Group discussion, lecture method, demonstration, experimentation, ICT, group activity

Learning Materials: Metal, test tubes, activity card, chart, beaker, acids, water, ICT videos related to metals, experiments and metal properties.

Preconception and first aid: The experiments should be conducted with care

Subjective Reality

Preconception:

- Pupil know some of the physical properties of metals
- Pupil know that metal is hard
- Pupil know that metal when tapped in hard surface can make sounds
- Pupil know different examples of metals
- Pupil know to differentiate between metals and non-metals

BODY OF UNIT PLAN

Sl No	Curricular objective	Content outline	Learning strategy	Learning activity	Learning resource	Duration	Evaluation
1.	To develop knowledge and understanding about physical property of metal	Malleability Ductility hardness of metal	Group discussion	Discussion 1. About common property of metal 2. Malleability, ductility, hardness	• Pictures of metals • Iron rail • Aluminium foil paper • Copper wire	40'	Classification of metals based on its properties-chart preparation
		Lustre, thermal conductivity, electrical conductivity	Video presentation	• Video presentation of metallic lustre of sodium • Group discussion on thermal and electrical conductivity	• ICT video • Copper wire	40'	Chart presentation prepare a chart showing metals which conducts thermally and electrically
		Sonority	Group discussion	• Discussion on melting point and density of different metals	Flash card activity card	40'	Test paper on physical properties of metals
		Physical characteristics	Group activity	Group activity on different uses of metal and filling activity card			
2.	To develop knowledge, understanding, and process skill on chemical property of metals	Reaction of metal with air	Demonstration group activity	Demonstration • Reaction of sodium with air Group activity • Activity using Al wire and sand paper	Sodium Aluminium wire sand paper	40'	List out other metals that react with air
		Reaction of metal with water	Video presentation	Showing video of reaction of copper and sodium with water	ICT, video	40'	Write down the chemical equation of the reaction that took place in the experiment

		Reaction of metal with acid	Demonstration and group discussion	1. Demonstration of reaction of Zn, Al, Fe, Cu, with HCl 2. Demonstration of common product formed in above reaction	HCl, Zn, Fe, Cu, Al etc	40’	• Find the reason why butter milk is not stored in Aluminium vessel • Find the reason for wing steel knife to cut lemon instead of Iron knife
3	To develop an understanding about corrosion and develop ability to suggest precautions to avoid corrosion of metals	Corrosion of metal and its prevention	Project and discussion	Project • To prove the factors that influences the corrosion of Iron	• Test tubes • Iron rail • CaO • Nacl Solution	40’	Prepare an assignment on different measures that can be adopted to prevent corrosion

Follow up Activities

Written Assignment

- List out different physical properties of metals?
- What is an alloy?
- Write down examples of alloys?
- Explain reaction of metal with air with an example?

APPENDIX 2: PHYSICS LESSON PLAN

General Information

Name of teacher:

Date:

Name of School:

Std: VIII

Subject: Physics

Strength:

Unit: Reflection of light in Spherical Mirror

Duration: 40 minutes

Topic: Focal length, focal plane, image formed by Spherical mirror

Content Overview: Focal length and focal plane of spherical mirror, images formed by spherical mirror.

Content Analysis

Terms

- Spherical mirror, convex mirror, concave mirror, focal plane, reflection facts
- Images appear on mirror
- There are different types of mirrors
- Some mirror has plane surfaces and some curved surface
- We can see reflection in still water
- Images appear on both surface of spoon
- Subjects appears in small size in rear view mirror of cars.
- Image appears enlarge in shaving mirror

Concept

- Distance from the pole of a mirror to its principal focus is the focal length
- Focal length of a spherical mirror is half the radius of curvature of the mirror
- Focal plane is a vertical plane passing through the principal focus and which is perpendicular to principal axis

Equations

R- Radius of curvature

f- Focal length

$f=R/_2$

General Objectives

- To develop mental reasoning power in students
- To develop scientific attitude in students
- To make students understand scientific facts
- To develop scientific temper in students

Learning Domain: The pupil develops knowledge and understanding about the above-mentioned terms, facts, concepts etc.

Specific Objectives:

The pupil

- Understand meaning of focal length
- Understands method to calculate focal length
- Recognises position of focal plane is spherical mirror
- Understands image formation in spherical mirrors
- Understands features of images is spherical mirrors

Process Domain: Pupil acquires process skill required to develop knowledge and understanding of above-mentioned concepts, definition etc.

Specific objectives:

The pupil

- Objectives formation of images in spherical mirror
- Calculates focal length
- Draws focal plane on diagram of spherical mirror
- Analyses ray diagram
- Raising questions on image formation
- Communicating and understanding communication of others

Application domain: Pupil applies acquired skill in new and unfamiliar situations

Specific objectives:

The pupil

- Uses the concept to solve real life problem
- Correlates science with life
- Observes the image formed in spherical mirror in daily life
- Finds out practical use of spherical mirror

Attitudinal Domain: The develop scientific attitude and values by learning topic

Specific objectives: The pupil

- Generate faith in one's ability
- Thinking rationally about individual values and taking decision accordingly
- Develops positive attitude toward others

Creativity Domain: Pupil develops creative abilities while learning the topic.

Specific objectives:

The pupil

- Visualizing image formation in spherical mirrors
- Visualizing position of focal plane
- Thinks about relation between position of the object and image
- Thinks about practical uses of spherical mirrors

Learning Strategies: Group discussion, Group activity

Subjective Reality

Pre-conception: Pupil knows that images formed in concave and convex mirror are different

Learning Resources: Chart, ICT video

Classroom Transaction

Activity	Assessment
Sensitization Teachers Starts Class by raising a question. We often use proper convex mirror as real view mirror why? can a concave mirror be used as rear-view mirror? No. of Groups-6 **Session–I:** Teacher Shows a Diagram of Spherical Mirror to Students **Discussion Hints:** 1. What Is F And P? 2. What Is CP? **Answer:** 1. Principal Focus, Pole 2. Principal Axis **Idea to be consolidated** Distance from the pole of a mirror to its principal focus is the focal length (f). PF indicates focal length. $F= R/_{2,}$ R= radius of curvature **Session–II:** Teacher Gives a Problem to Students to Solve using the Equation $F= R/_2$. • The Radius of curvature of a spherical mirror is 20 cm calculate the focal length? **Answer** $F= R/_2\, F= 20/_2 = 10$ cm R= 20 **Discussion Hints** 1. What is R? 2. What is relation between Rand F? **Answer** 1. Radius of curvature 2. $F= R/_2$ **Idea to be consolidated:** Focal length of spherical mirror is half the radius of curvature if mirror **Session–III:** Teacher shows an animation video of rays of light coming from infinity to a spherical mirror. **Discussion Hints** 1. Are the reflected rays focus at one point? 2. The plane formed by the points were the rays focused is __________ to the principal axis	**Participation and Activities:** Pupil were divided into different groups as to engage in all activities. Pupil actively participated in all activities, doing problems, group discussion etc. **Concept Formation:** Teachers starts class along with a question which enables creative thinking among the child-pupil then realises what is focal length and formula for calculating it. They pupil recognises relation between focal length and radius of curvature. **Presentation:** The class conducted of 4 sessions, through first session pupil understood ray diagram its terms like focal length, the 2nd session consisted of a mathematical problem so pupil understood calculation of focal length. Through session 3 as ICT video is shown rays to understand the focal plane. The last session was an experiment through its pupil understood when object is placed in different position. Image forms at different position and has different characteristics. **Acquisition of Skill:** Pupil understood how to calculate focal length, pupil understood position and characteristics of image when placed in different position. **Evaluation:** Through the class pupil became more aware of the terns about mirror, calculating methods, characteristics of images formed etc.

Answer 1. No 2. Perpendicular **Idea to be consolidated:** Focal plane is a vertical plane passing through the principal focus and which is perpendicular to the principal axis **Session–IV:** Teacher shows an experiment to understand the position, nature and size of an image formed by objects kept at different positions in front of a concave mirror **Discussion Hints** 1. What is the position of image when object is at c? 2. What is the position of image when object is at f? **Answer** 1. At c 2. Infinity	

Idea to be consolidated

Sl. No	Position of object	Position of image	Features of image
1.	At infinity	at f	real, inverted, diminished
2.	Beyond c	Between C and F	real, inverted, diminished
3.	At c	at c	real, inverted, diminished
4.	Between c and f	Beyond c	real, inverted, diminished
5.	At f	Infinity	real, inverted, diminished
6.	Between f and p	Behind the mirror	Virtual, erect, magnified

Application: A convex mirror always forms c diminished, virtual and erect image. Also, it allows lighter to fall because of the nature of its curvature hence it has more field of view.

Follow up Activity: Written Assignment: Write a note on image formation in spherical mirror.

Activity Assignment: The focal length of a convex mirror in a bus is 0.6m find the radius of curvature?

APPENDIX 3: CHEMISTRY LESSON PLAN

General Information

Name of Teacher:

Name of School:

Subject: Chemistry

Unit: Water

Topic: Surface Tension

Date:

Std: VIII

Strength:

Duration: 40 minutes

Content Overview: Surface tension

Content Analysis

Terms: Surface tension, water, Molecule

Facts

- Water strider can randomly move on surface of water
- Frogs can't move on surface of water
- Small water drops can be seen in spherical shape
- Water surface behaves like starched membrane
- Molecules of the surface attract only from lower directions
- Molecules inside water attract to all directions
- Carefully placed blade on surface of water floats on water

Concepts

- The number of molecules in vapour form just above surface of water is less than those on the surface
- The liquid surface behaves likes a stretched membrane. This behaviour cause surface tension
- Surface tension act in such way so as to reduce the surface area of liquid for a definite mass of a substance, surface area is minimum for spherical shape. That is why liquid droplets assumes spherical shape

General Objectives

- To develop mental reasoning power in students
- To develop scientific attitude

- To make students understand scientific facts
- To develop scientific temper in students

Learning objectives

Knowledge domain: Pupil develop knowledge and understanding about the above-mentioned terms, facts, concept

Specific objectives

The pupil

- Realises denser objects can't move on water
- Recognises why liquid droplets assumes spherical shape
- Understand that number of molecules in vapour form just above surface of water is less than that on surface
- Realises surface tension is responsible for the property of why insets and blade float on water

Process Domain: Pupil acquires process skill required to develop the knowledge and understanding of above-mentioned facts, concepts.

Specific Objectives

The pupil,

- Does the experiment relate to surface tension
- Observes real instances of surface tension
- Communicating and understanding communication of others
- Raising questions about surface tension

Application Domain: Pupil applies acquired knowledge and skill in new and unfamiliar situation

Specific Objectives:

The pupil

- Identifies more situations were denser objects sink
- Cites out situations exhibiting the relation between surface tension and surface area
- Identifies the situation where property of surface tension exist in day to day life

Attitudinal Domain: Pupil develop scientific attitude and values by learning the topic

Specific Objectives:

The pupil

- Develop positive attitude towards, science
- Generates faith in oneself
- Shows curiosity on the idea of surface tension of water

Creativity Domain: Pupil develop creative ability related to the topic

Specific Objectives:

The pupil

- Visualizing the process of surface tension
- Relating concept in new ways
- Visualises the flouting of objects on surface of water
- Thinks about spherical shape of water droplets

Learning strategies: Group discussion, group activity

Subjective Reality: Preconception, Pupil have knowledge about attraction of molecules, Misconception, Pupil may think that small object can float on water only because of density.

Learning Resource: ICT

CLASSROOM TRANSACTION

Activity	Assessment
Sensitization Have you ever seen small insects moving on surface of water? Why they can move like that? Can all insects move like this? No. of Session - 3 No. of. Groups-7	**Participation and Activity** All the pupil were divided into different groups. The pupil actively participated all activities also session etc.
Session–I: Shows an experiment using blade and water in a glass and asks pupil to place a blade randomly in water and then place it carefully on the surface? 1. In which situation does the blade sink? 2. Does the blade sink in 2nd situation?	**Concept Formation** The pupil understood in new property of water, pupil understood that surface tension is a property of water and why water existing in spherical shape
Answer 1. When placed randomly 2. No **Idea to be consolidated:** Carefully placed blade can float on water. Its due to a characteristic property of water **Session–II:** Pupil Observes the picture showing the interaction of molecules inside and out on the surface of water	**Presentation** The class consisted of three sessions, two of them are presented with the help of ICT and one with demonstration method, pupil understood concept easily with help of aid.

Discussion Hints 1. Does molecule of water attract each other? 2. What is the nature of attraction of molecules inside the water? 3. What about molecules on surface of water? **Answer** 1. Yes 2. Attraction is in all directions 3. Attracts only downwards **Idea to be Consolidated:** The number of molecules in vapour form just above the water surface is less than those on the surface. Hence the attraction towards the sides and the interior will be greater. Consequently, the liquid surface behaves like a stretched membrane. This behaviour cause surface tension. **Session–III:** Pupil does an experiment using a bangle. Tie a thread to a bangle then immerse it in a soap water and creates a soap film. Pick a portion of film using a pin. **Discussion Hints** 1. What is the shape of the remaining portion of the film? 2. Then what happens to surface area of soap film? 3. How can you relate surface tension in terms in terms of surface area? **Idea to be consolidated:** Surface tension acts in such a way so as to reduce the surface area of liquid for a definite mass of a substance surface area is minimum for spherical shape **Application:** Surface tension is the characteristic properly of water. The liquid surface behaves like stretched membrane because of this property water strider or small insets can move on surface of water. **Follow up activity** Written Assignment: Why water drops assumes spherical shape? Activity assignment: Cite out examples for surface tension from day-to-day life?	**Acquisition of skills** Pupil realized new property of water, surface tension and reason behind spherical shape of liquid **Evaluation** Pupil became aware about water and its properties through the class.